SOUL

TO

SOUL

Yelena Khanga *with* Susan Jacoby

Soul

TO

Soul

A Black Russian American Family 1865–1992

W · W · Norton & Company New York · London

The text of this book is composed in Bembo,
with the display set in Bodoni.
Composition and manufacturing by the Haddon Craftsmen, Inc.
Book design by Guenet Abraham.

Library of Congress Cataloging-in-Publication Data
Khanga, Yelena.
Soul to Soul: a Black Russian American family, 1865–1992 /
Yelena Khanga with Susan Jacoby.
p. cm.
1. Khanga, Yelena. 2. Afro-Americans—Soviet
Union—Biography. 3. Blacks—Soviet Union—Biography. I.
Jacoby, Susan. II. Title.
DK34.B53K48 1992
947'.0049607302—dc20
[B] 92-7043
ISBN 0-393-03404-6

W. W. Norton & Company, Inc.
500 Fifth Avenue, New York, N.Y. 10110

W. W. Norton & Company Ltd.
10 Coptic Steet, London WC1A 1PU

1 2 3 4 5 6 7 8 9 0

To Lily Golden, my mother

In memory of
Oliver Golden and Bertha Bialek Golden,
my grandparents

Contents

*Illustrations appear following
pages 128 and 224.*

Acknowledgments

My mother, Lily Golden, helped me at every stage of this work. Her private memories and her perspective as a historian were equally indispensable.

I am indebted to the Rockefeller Foundation and its president, Peter Goldmark, for the Warren Weaver fellowship that enabled me to complete most of the research on my family. Frank Karel, the foundation's vice-president for communications, steered me in the right direction more times than I can count.

Lee and Maureen Young gave me their love, faith, and wise counsel.

This book could not have been written without the late Mamie Golden, my grandfather's niece, and Pearl Steinhardt, the only person living who knew my grandmother as a young woman. Both gave generously of their time and prodigious memories.

Other relatives who provided invaluable assistance include: Albert, Eugene, Mark, Irving, Minnie, and Sheila S. Bialek, Delores Harris, Ollie Morris, Gerald and Jacqui Robinson.

For information about my father, I wish to thank Oscar Kambona, former minister of foreign affairs and defense of Tanganyika; Ibrahim nur Sharif, Bimkubwa Hanga, and Anthony M. Astrachan.

In Mississippi, I could not have traced the Golden family without the help of Linda Crawford, head librarian of the B. S. Ricks Memorial Library in Yazoo City, and Darlene Johnson, assistant librarian, as well as JoAnn Prichard, Willie Morris, and George Penick, president of the Mid-South Foundation.

Joseph Roane and Percy Sutton filled in important details about the lives of black Americans in Uzbekistan.

Gennadi Gerasimov gave me my professional start when he hired me to work at *Moscow News;* Yegor Yakovlev, who succeded Gerasimov as the newspaper's editor, taught me how to be a real reporter.

In America, Kay Fanning became my "role model" of a professional woman.

David Crosson was the first person who believed in this book—and who made me believe I could finish it.

I also wish to thank my collaborator, Susan Jacoby, for helping me find a voice in the English language—and for the exchange of ideas from several cultures needed to tell my family's story.

Finally, I'm indebted to my editor, Ed Barber.

—Yelena Khanga

To acknowledge our ancestors means we are aware that we did not make ourselves, that the line stretches all the way back, perhaps, to God; or to Gods. We remember them because it is an easy thing to forget: that we are not the first to suffer, rebel, fight, love and die. The grace with which we embrace life, in spite of the pain, the sorrows, is always a measure of what has gone before.

—Alice Walker

Russia . . . where I had learned to love and weep
And where my heart lies buried deep.

—Alexander Pushkin
Evgeny Onegin

SOUL
TO
SOUL

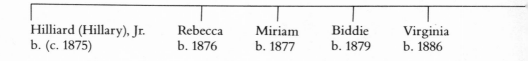

Hilliard (Hillary), Jr.	Rebecca	Miriam	Biddie	Virginia
b. (c. 1875)	b. 1876	b. 1877	b. 1879	b. 1886

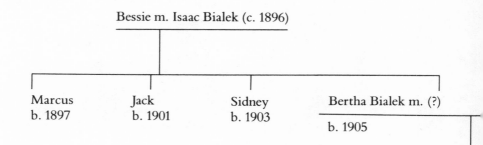

Bessie m. Isaac Bialek (c. 1896)

Marcus	Jack	Sidney	Bertha Bialek m. (?)
b. 1897	b. 1901	b. 1903	b. 1905

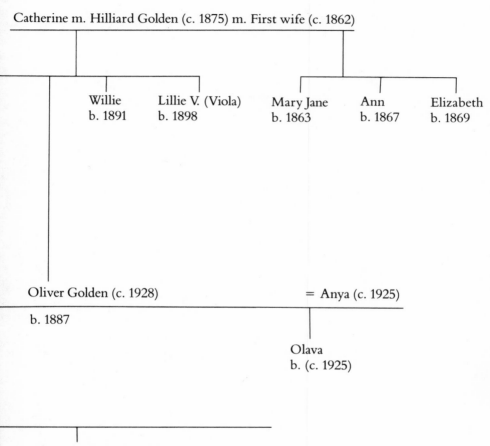

Catherine m. Hilliard Golden (c. 1875) m. First wife (c. 1862)

Willie
b. 1891

Lillie V. (Viola)
b. 1898

Mary Jane
b. 1863

Ann
b. 1867

Elizabeth
b. 1869

Oliver Golden (c. 1928)

b. 1887

= Anya (c. 1925)

Olava
b. (c. 1925)

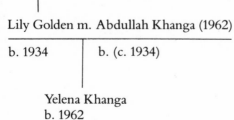

Lily Golden m. Abdullah Khanga (1962)

b. 1934

b. (c. 1934)

Yelena Khanga
b. 1962

CHAPTER ONE

DISTANT WORLDS

"Ba-a-aby," sings my mama, drawing out the syllable in a low voice that combines the smoky intonations of a black American blues singer with her classical Russian accent. "Baby, won't you please come home." Her fingers move over the piano keys in our Moscow apartment as she imitates the sounds she has heard on recordings by Billie Holiday and Ella Fitzgerald. I sing along happily—"I have tried in vain, never no more to call your name. . . ."

I'm only eight, but I already know and love these songs from the faraway America of our ancestors—just as I love the classical Russian melodies Mama plays, with verses by Pushkin. One thing every Russian schoolchild knows is that our country's greatest poet was descended from blacks—just like Mama and me. I'm proud to know that Pushkin's great-grandfather, Hannibal, was born in Abyssinia and grew up, through a strange destiny, to become a general in the army of Tsar Peter the Great. *"O krasavitsa"* (Oh, beautiful girl), I sing in my true, childish soprano as Mama plays one of Pushkin's romantic songs.

Even as a small girl, I understood that all of this music, all of this culture, somehow belonged to me. Today, as a woman of thirty, I know my heart will always be in thrall both to the blues and to the great Russian composers.

When I was growing up in Moscow, I never heard the American expression "melting pot." This description might have been invented for me—even if the pot now looks more like a stew with distinct chunks.

I am a black Russian, born and raised in the Soviet Union (at least, that's what we used to call it) and shaped by an extraordinary mixture of races and cultures.

I am descended from American idealists, black and white, who came to the new Soviet state in the 1930s with high hopes of building a more just society through communism. Although time proved them tragically wrong about the revolutionary experiment, there was nothing wrong with their heartfelt dream of racial and economic justice. Thanks to the unforeseen, unprecedented political changes in my native land, it has now become possible for me to explore the dreams and realities that shaped my ancestors—those who remained in America as well as those who journeyed back across the ocean in search of yet another New World. In seeking out those old dreams, I am trying to reclaim lost parts of myself.

One of my great-grandfathers was born an American slave, while another was a Polish Jew who left Warsaw for the United States just before World War I. Hilliard Golden became one of the largest black landowners in Yazoo County, Mississippi, after the Civil War, while Isaac Bialek taught Hebrew school and worked in a New York garment factory. My great-grandfathers had one important thing in common, though they probably wouldn't have recognized any common ground at the time: They were both religious men. Hilliard was a Methodist preacher, and Isaac was a rabbi in Warsaw before immigration transformed his settled existence.

I believe it's fair to say that 'only in America' would the children of two such different families and backgrounds have been drawn together in the 1920s. Those children—my black grandfather and white grandmother—joined the newly established American Communist Party and met in a New York jail after a union demonstration in 1928. Oliver Golden and Bertha Bialek soon fell deeply in love, defying both my grandmother's family (most of whose members never spoke to her again) and the larger American taboo against interracial marriage.

In 1931, Oliver and Bertha left the United States to pursue their common dream of building a new, more equitable society in the Soviet Union. They could not have known then what we know now, that the dream would turn into a nightmare as countless millions perished under the tyranny of Joseph Stalin.

My grandfather, an agronomist who studied under George Washington Carver at Tuskegee Institute, was sent to the Soviet republic of Uzbekistan, in central Asia, to help develop a cotton industry in what was then a primitive agricultural society. This move was never meant to be permanent. My grandparents intended to return to the United States—they had signed ordinary work contracts with the Soviet government—but changed their minds after my mother was born in 1934.

Oliver and Bertha named their daughter Lily. It has always seemed to me that Tiger-lily might have been more appropriate for this forceful child of an interracial love match spanning three continents. My mother is a tall, striking woman with a café-au-lait complexion and hazel eyes. In America half a century ago, her black ancestry—and her ambiguous status as the child of an interracial couple—would have severely limited her opportunities, in very different ways, in both black and white communities.

My grandparents saw no place for a family like theirs in segregated, pre–World War II America. Of course, there were havens where interracial couples were tolerated—in the bohemia of Greenwich Village and in certain open-minded segments of Harlem society. But how would my grandfather have supported his family? He was an agricultural specialist, not an artist or poet who might have carved an economic niche for himself in a cosmopolitan environment. The places where he could have worked—in farming areas of the South and Midwest, for instance—would not have tolerated a black man married to a white woman. This was a time when an African-American man could by lynched simply for looking the wrong way at a white woman. In these places, local blacks could hardly have extended a warm welcome to my grandparents or their child.

So my grandparents stayed in the Soviet Union, and my family took its place in a complicated, painful national history extending from the fear-filled depths of Stalinism, through the rebuilding that began when Mikhail Gorbachev inaugurated the *glasnost* era in 1985, and, finally, to the collapse of the system under which I grew up. Gorbachev's reforms signaled the beginning of the end for the fear that dominated Soviet society and cut off my family's contacts with America for fifty years.

In the Russia of my childhood, not to mention the terror-ridden country of my mother's girlhood, it was unimaginable that we would live to see young men and women impose their bodies in front of tanks and successfully defend the concept of government by the consent of the governed.

At the time of my birth, my mother's main goal was to bring up her child with integrity and individuality in a society that demanded conformity. This wasn't easy for any Russian parent, but Mama's task was especially hard because the color of our skin told everyone we were different. Our foreign connections were literally written on our faces.

My father was Abdullah Khanga, an African independence leader who spent years studying in Moscow before returning to his native Zanzibar (where he was murdered by political opponents in the mid-sixties). My mother met my father in Moscow as a result of her own African connections; she is a historian specializing in African music and culture.

Long before I was old enough to remember him, Abdullah Khanga left the Soviet Union for the last time. I was born on May Day, 1962. Mama was excited that day, because my father, whom the Soviets treated as a future government leader, had been invited to view the traditional May Day parade from atop Lenin's tomb. Mama intended to accompany him to the celebration, where thousands of Young

Pioneers and adult Party stalwarts, in the years before *glasonost,* always carried gigantic portraits of Lenin and Marx through Red Square. Instead, my mother went into labor and had to dodge unruly drunks, celebrating in their own fashion, as she made her way to the maternity hospital.

After my mother managed to detach herself from the crowds, I came into the world without untoward incident. I am the first native *Moskovichka* in my far-flung family (Mama having been born in the Uzbek capital of Tashkent).

In spite of the many strands in my heritage, I am also Russian to the core. Russian was my first language, though my mother and grandmother often spoke English at home. My schooling was Soviet, beginning with the kindergarten where I was taught to love *Dedushka* (Grandpa) Lenin. My mind and soul have been shaped by the compassionate irony of Chekhov, the poetry of Pushkin, the romantic music of Tchaikovsky.

Yet there was always a shade of difference; I had only to look in the mirror to see it. I was black—to be more precise, deep burnished copper—in a world where nearly everyone was white. My favorite song was "We Shall Overcome," which I learned in English as a small child. Those black American voices, resonant with a world of sorrow and joy, came to us on records, gifts from a steady stream of black American visitors who passed through our home. I was raised on tales of my grandparents' friendships with such great black Americans as the singer Paul Robeson, the poet Langston Hughes, and the father of pan-Africanism, W. E. B. Du Bois. In fact, Dr. Du Bois was responsible for the creation of the African Institute of the Soviet Academy of Sciences, where my mother worked. Dr. Du Bois was a friend of my grandfather, and he was talking with twenty-two-year-old Lily about her future on the day before he was scheduled to drop by the Kremlin for a chat with Premier Nikita Khrushchev. The year was 1958—a time when a dictator could still get something done in Russia!—and all Dr. Du Bois had to do was mention the need for an African studies institute to the impetuous Khrushchev. In as little time as it takes to say "It always pays to deal with the man at the top," my mother was ensconced as the institute's first scholar.

When Americans ask whether there is racism and discrimination in Russia, my answer can never be a simple one. The story of Pushkin isn't beside the point. His great-grandfather came to the court of Peter the Great in the early eighteenth century after being held hostage by the Turks. Peter immediately recognized the boy's intellectual gifts, sent him to France to study, and eventually made him a general after he returned to Russia as a mathematician and engineer. In portraits of Pushkin, it's easy to discern traces of his black ancestry—in spite of his very light skin—after three generations of intermarriage. He occupies the same position in Russian culture as Shakespeare does in the English-speaking world. As a black girl growing up in Moscow, it mattered to me that Russians considered Pushkin a purely Russian poet. In America, I suspect his ancestry would have led whites to consider him a marginal black rather than a purely "American" writer.

In Russian culture, I never felt like a stranger in my black skin. Unlike many African-Americans, I was never made to feel less intelligent, less capable, less likely to achieve than my white schoolmates.

Was my family, by virtue of its descent from one of the few American blacks who came to the Soviet Union in the thirties, a special case? Yes and no. In many ways, I was insulated from the kind of prejudice experienced not only by African students but also by mixed-race children of unions between Russians and Africans. Anti-black prejudices are not institutionalized in Russia; racism feeds on visible targets, and there are too few of us to attract the kind of bigotry directed toward larger minorities. (According to Western sources, there are only 5,000 to 10,000 native black citizens in the former Soviet Union, plus some 40,000 African students. But this estimate of native blacks is probably too low, not only because the law allows children to choose the nationality of either parent but because many blacks are officially registered under a "white" nationality on their internal passports.)

When I was growing up, I thought of my color not as a target for discrimination but simply—and not so simply—as a mark of separateness. No racist taunts were aimed at me, but I did attract persistent, usually polite curiosity. When I was very small, playmates would ask why my skin didn't turn white, since my family no longer lived in

Africa but in cold, snowy Russia. This kind of curiosity does not draw blood, but it does leave microscopic pinpricks. No one else could see the tiny jabs, but I always felt them. They didn't really hurt but left a prickly sensation, a reminder that I wasn't like everyone, or anyone, else.

And there was another difference, much less obvious to me and to the outside world. One of my earliest memories is the voice of my beloved grandmother, singing me to sleep with a Yiddish lullabye: *Lommir, Lommir, 'le zing'n a liddeleh vus dus maydel vil*—"Let's sing a little song, whatever the little girl wants."

Until last year, when my mother and I found our second- and third-generation Jewish cousins in the United States, I never knew that my grandmother spoke Yiddish or that it had, in fact, been her first language. I did know she immigrated to the United States from Warsaw in 1920 and her father was some sort of scholar, but she never discussed her Jewish heritage with me.

That part of her identity may have seemed less and less meaningful to her as time passed, but my grandmother also lived through a period in Soviet history when it was dangerous to be a Jew, especially one with indisputable foreign connections. In the late forties, when Stalin launched his campaign against "rootless cosmopolitans" (code for Jews and foreigners), my grandmother lost her job as a professor of English at the Institute of Foreign Languages in Tashkent. She must have thought it wouldn't do her daughter and granddaughter any good to emphasize what in Soviet terms was yet another liability.

But there was one time—and I have never forgotten it—when she made herself crystal-clear on the subject of Jewishness. I was just five years old when I came home from kindergarten talking about something "this *zhid*" had done. The Russian *zhid* is the equivalent of the American "kike" or "yid," but I didn't understand that at the time. To me, *zhid* was just a word used by schoolchildren, a bit of ordinary playground slang—and that, of course, says a good deal about the prevalence of anti-Semitism in ordinary Soviet life.

I was stunned when my grandmother slapped my face—the only time she ever hit me in my life—and said, "Every time you call a Jewish person a bad word, you're calling me and your mother and yourself bad. To hate them is to hate yourself. Because I am Jewish, and that means your mother is Jewish, and that means you are also Jewish."

My grandmother never explained further about Jews or Judaism. It was many years before I understood what she meant, that in traditional religious law, Judaism is inherited through the mother. But I clearly understood her real point. What she intended to impress upon me was that it's morally wrong to classify or stigmatize groups of people according to their race, nationality, or religion. Since that time, I have experienced an almost physical pain whenever Russians make derogatory remarks about Jews, Armenians, Gypsies, or any other group. For the most part, I don't hear slurs about blacks—not because no one makes them, but because no one I know would make them to my face. But I have heard anti-Semitic remarks from Russians, most of whom have no idea my grandmother was Jewish. Whenever I hear such comments—based, of course, on the assumption that I too will enjoy a good laugh at the expense of a dirty *zhid*—real friendship with the speaker becomes impossible for me.

I cherish the memory of my grandmother's voice today, especially as I try to come to grips with different forms of prejudice in the United States. It hurts when I hear certain white Americans talk about "lazy blacks," as if my being a Soviet citizen somehow renders me less black or less likely to feel pain and humiliation, and it hurts just as much to hear some black Americans describe all Jews as greedy or all whites as bigots. *To hate them is to hate yourself.*

In 1985, I would have laughed in disbelief if anyone had told me I would ever have the chance to discover America and to explore the American part of my family history on my own. A year after graduating from Moscow State University, I was an editorial assistant for *Moscow News*—then a stupefying dull publication noted mainly for putting readers to sleep in Russian, English, and several other languages. Although Gorbachev had just taken over leadership of the government, it was impossible for most Soviets to foresee the changes—involving everything from censorship to foreign travel—

that would sweep away the rules we had all taken for granted. Like most Russians, I had known about these restrictions since I was old enough to understand the meaning of *nyelzya* (it's impossible, no way).

One rule—even more powerful because it was unwritten—decreed that no one with a foreign background would be allowed to travel outside the "fraternal socialist" countries of eastern Europe. If that seems crazy, think about it from a secret policeman's point of view: A Soviet citizen who spoke good English (both my mother and I do) was likely to meet more people, learn more, and enjoy more in English-speaking countries than she would if she spoke only Russian. As for an English-speaking Russian with live American relatives: God only knows what might happen! Such an unreliable person might have decided to become a spy, or at the very least to defect to the West.

Thanks to this paranoid thinking, my mother never managed to travel to any of the African countries where her scholarly articles had been widely published and appreciated. (From Africa, after all, one may telephone freely and take a plane to any country in the world. The pre-*glasnost* Soviet system couldn't tolerate such a possibility.)

As a fledgling journalist. I had even less hope of getting permission to travel. In the first place, foreign assignments were reserved for men: for men, for party members (which neither my mother nor I were), and for people with spotless (usually meaning Russian or Ukranian) ethnic backgrounds. With luck, I might hope to turn the modest column I was writing about tourists into a real reporting job. Whenever I interviewed American tourists at that time, I was careful not to get too close, not to give them my home phone number or go out with them in the evening. That's the way things were; that's the way I assumed they would be for the rest of my life. I had no premonition that I was about to embark on a journey resembling nothing so much as Alice's fall through the looking glass.

I was hired to work for *Moscow News* in 1984, in the twilight of the old regime, by Gennadi Ivanovich Gerasimov. Gerasimov's face and voice would eventually become known to millions around the world when he became Gorbachev's personal spokesman. Looking back, I wonder if Gennadi Ivanovich may have sensed that a black Russian with American connections would soon be regarded in a far more positive light.

I owe a great deal to my first boss; many years later, I learned he had to fight hard, sticking out his neck with his own superiors, to hire me. Without his help, I might well have wound up working for a trade-union newspaper in some dismal backwater, far from the exciting political changes in the capital.

As *glasnost* gathered steam, Gennadi Ivanovich was succeeded as editor of *Moscow News* by Yegor Vladimirovich Yakovlev, who set about transforming the once-stolid publication into a voice for democratization. Even for the young—and I was only twenty-four when Yegor Vladimirovich took over the editorship of the paper—it was a wrenching experience to change the passive habits of a lifetime. In the journalism department of Moscow State University, I was trained not to investigate real news but to produce whatever stories were demanded by my bosses and, ultimately, by the political authorities. Individual initiative comes hard when it has always been discouraged.

But I did change; the freedom to say and write what you think is an addiction. The experience is not mine alone but the story of an entire generation of Russians; we have learned, in Chekhov's famous phrase, to squeeze the slave out of ourselves "drop by drop."

Part of the change in me is connected with America. In 1987, the unimaginable happened: I was chosen as the first Soviet journalist to visit the United States on an exchange program. Before *glasnost,* there was no possibility that someone like me—young, female, a non-Party member, and, horror of horrors!, the granddaughter of Americans, would ever have been selected to represent her country abroad.

I could hardly believe my good luck when I found myself on a plane headed for the land my grandparents left behind more than half a century earlier. I was to spend several months working at the *Christian Science Monitor* in Boston.

As a Soviet citizen and a journalist, one of my proudest moments came when I found myself attending the first Washington summit meeting between Gorbachev and President Reagan. I even became something of a hot story myself, as American reporters discovered a black Russian in their midst. This was more interesting than boring old arms control—a young black woman talking casually about "we Russians."

"You've got to be kidding," said the American correspondent in the next seat. "There aren't any blacks in Russia."

"Well, you can see for yourself I'm not white," I replied.

Surrounded by hundreds of reporters from every country in the world, listening to Gennadi Ivanovich, announce a tentative agreement on strategic arms control (START), I glowed with the knowledge that I was fulfilling several of my grandparents' dreams in ways they could scarcely imagine.

Oliver and Bertha had dreamed of Soviet-American cooperation, and here were two leaders moving beyond the rhetoric of "evil empire" and "capitalist imperialism" in order to make the fragile world a slightly safer place.

They dreamed of a life in which their children and grandchildren would not be crippled by bigotry—and here I was, functioning in my profession at a level impossible for a black woman in the America they left behind (though not, I was beginning to understand, in the America of the eighties).

On that first trip to the United States, I made no effort to find either my black or white relatives. But I did speak to a number of community groups and gave several interviews about my unusual family history. As a result of the publicity, some of my relatives began looking for me.

On the black side of the family, my Golden relations began tracking me down after I was interviewed on the ABC newsmagazine program "20/20." In Chicago, my grandfather's aged niece, Mamie Golden, cried out in recognition when Oliver's picture flashed across the screen. "That's my Uncle Buck," she said with tears in her eyes. Mamie, who lived with my grandfather and his parents in Memphis when she was a girl, remembered her uncle as a smiling young man, always handing out silver dollars to children (hence, the nickname

"Uncle Buck"). Delores Harris, Mamie's niece, was able to track down our Moscow address and phone number through ABC. A week later, the phone rang in Moscow, and my mother listened in amazement as Delores introduced herself and explained that her grandmother, Rebecca, had been my grandfather's oldest sister. My grandmother, Mama, and I always thought of ourselves as an isolated family of three. In the span of one phone call, Mama and I started to see ourselves as two Russian offshoots of a large family tree. Mamie and Delores informed us that we had at least a hundred Golden cousins in the United States.

Finding my black relatives was an uncomplicated joy, but I experienced great ambivalence when I began looking into the white side of my family. My grandmother's pain at her old estrangement from her relatives was never far from my mind. With the exception of one brother, Jack, no one in the Bialek family maintained contact with Bertha after she left for the Soviet Union with my grandfather. Jack was considered the most liberal member of the family; he'd drawn his younger sister into the Communist Party during the twenties. But he wasn't able to come to terms with his sister's love for a black man and told his son that Bertha married a Russian in Russia.

By the time I got to the United States, only one person in Jack's branch of the Bialek family—his widow, Minnie—knew the real story. Most of the family lives in Los Angeles, and in 1988 an article about me—in which I mentioned my grandmother's maiden name—appeared in the Los Angeles *Times*. At that point, Minnie decided it was time to tell her son about his aunt's long-ago marriage to a black American, since it seemed likely the secret would come out anyway.

When they finally learned their Aunt Bertha had married not a Russian but a black man, neither Jack's son Eugene, nor his grandchildren could understand the reasons for the long secrecy. My cousin Nancy, just a year older than I—her warm, sparkling brown eyes remind me of my grandmother—can't imagine being upset by the existence of a black cousin.

As it turns out, my mother and I weren't a total family secret. Although Jack didn't tell his children about us, my grandmother's older brothers, Marcus and Sidney, didn't keep the secret from their families. But it seems the brothers had their own disagreements, so information didn't travel from one branch of the family to the other.

After more than seventy years, who can know all of the explanations for family feuds and family secrets in the older generation? I do know that I have many second- and third-generation Bialek cousins who are pleased and fascinated to have reconnected with the two black Russians in the family. Black Bialeks! In fact, my relatives have pointed out a marked resemblance between my mother's features and those of the Hebrew poet Chaim Nachman Bialik. Like the poet, my great-grandfather's family originally came from Odessa, and Bialek family tradition maintains that Chaim Nachman and my great-grandfather Isaac were distant cousins.

My grandmother died in Moscow on the same day her brother Jack died in Los Angeles in 1985. I'm sad she didn't live long enough to see her young relatives in America move beyond the prejudices and fears that cut her off from her own generation. Even though she rarely talked about her pain, I felt it and to some degree still do. When I returned to the United States in 1990 to investigate my family history on a Rockefeller Foundation fellowship, I probably would not have looked for my white relatives were it not for the insistence of my supervisor at the foundation. I was still afraid—afraid my living relatives would reject me as the dead had denied my grandmother. A part of me is still surprised that my white cousins are pleased rather than dismayed to have found me.

Americans talk a great deal about "putting the past where it belongs—in the past." Raised in a country that has suffered so much by lying about its past, I cannot leave history behind. I prefer the concept embodied in a quotation, passed on to me by an American friend, from the international lawyer and Holocaust survivor Samuel Pisar: "We may not have to live in the past, but the past lives in us."

Only by confronting history courageously, by uncovering wounds most of us would rather forget, does it become possible truly to put the past "where it belongs." That is what I have tried to do during the last five years. My journey has taken me from Tashkent to Tanzania, from London to Los Angeles, from Chicago to the Mississippi cotton fields where my grandfather was born and raised. I am searching for the past that lives not only in me but in the two great countries lodged deep in my heart.

CHAPTER TWO

SOUTH TOWARD HOME

I am looking at a turn-of-the-century photograph, so faded and creased that it must have been lying at the bottom of a drawer for the last fifty years. I feel my hands trembling as I take the snapshot from my cousin Mamie, who inherited it from her aunt Viola, who was my grandfather's youngest sister. These are my great-grandparents, Hilliard and Catherine Golden, and this piece of paper tells me more than I have ever known about how our family got its start. This is the legacy I have come to America to find.

In an era when having one's picture taken was no casual act, Hilliard and Catherine posed with Viola, the baby of the family, for a portrait outside their home in Yazoo County, Mississippi. Catherine is a formidable-looking matriarch whose combination of dark skin and high, slightly slanted cheekbones clearly reveals both her black and Native American ancestry. She stands a head taller than her wiry, white-haired husband. Both wear staid, late Victorian Sunday-go-to-meeting clothes—he a long suitcoat, starched white shirt, and cravat, she a dark, high-collared dress and jacket.

The focus of the picture, though, is not on the family members—they stand off to one side—but on a large, white, two-story house, with long verandas on both floors. The picture gives substance to the Golden family legend of a "big house," burned down at some point by the Ku Klux Klan. In the Mississippi delta, where most blacks (and whites) lived in poverty in spite of being surrounded by some of the richest land in the state, such a house could only have belonged to a man of substance. Here a man and his wife could raise eight children, as my great-grandparents did, in comfort. To have built this impressive structure, on a spread of his own land that eventually exceeded six hundred acres, must have been an achievement of the most profound meaning for a man born into slavery in 1844. So it's not surprising that Hilliard Golden chose to emphasize his house, the physical representation of a lifetime of work, rather than himself in a portrait for posterity.

But that house was surely a source of bitter envy for whites determined to keep blacks in their place. After Reconstruction, it would have been perfectly natural for night-riders to put the torch to the Golden house in an effort to obliterate everything the structure implied about black intelligence, persistence, and achievement. In fact, the story handed down in the family is that my great-grandfather was burned out of not one but two homes he had built. When I visited Yazoo, I didn't meet anyone (black or white) who questioned the plausibility of the account. Neither house burnings nor lynchings, one old man pointed out in a wry, matter-of-fact voice, were reported along with weddings and engagements in the local papers.

What I was able to establish with certainty, thanks to help from indefatigable local historians of both races, is that Hilliard Golden was as prominent a citizen as a black man could be in Yazoo after the Civil War. Many blacks managed to acquire land during the immediate postwar era, but most of them lost their property soon after the end of Reconstruction. My great-grandfather, who kept his holdings until 1909, was one of a very few who managed to hang on for decades after the return of white supremacy in the South. Several years ago, a list of black landowners, beginning in 1866, was compiled for the Yazoo Historical Society by Harvey Perry. Mr. Perry, who was nearly one hundred years old when he set down the list from memory, lived in Yazoo County most of his life. The first name that sprang into his mind was Hilliard Golden.

> Out in the distance, as far as the eye can see, the
> land is flat, dark, and unbroken, sweeping away
> in a faint misty haze to the limits of the horizon.
> This is the great delta . . . a dark shadowy
> swampland, fetid and rich.
>
> —Willie Morris,
> *North Toward Home*

In February of 1991, I drove north from Yazoo City in search of my great-grandfather's land. My guides were the writer Willie Morris and his wife, JoAnne Prichard, who had prepared themselves for the search with copies of nineteenth-century as well as modern maps. Even when you know exactly what you are looking for, finding a piece of farmland is a more complicated enterprise than finding a city block; we found ourselves stopping and starting, squinting at old and new boundaries on the maps.

I reached this point only after a number of false starts. Neither my mother and I nor our Chicago relations knew exactly where the Goldens had lived in Mississippi. My mother mistakenly thought her father had grown up in Clarksdale (north of Yazoo), because the town was mentioned on his U.S. Army record book. In fact, Clarksdale was simply the place where he reported for basic training after being drafted in 1918.

The real trail emerged only when, through the Rockefeller Foundation, I was able to enlist the help of scholars in Mississippi. JoAnne, an editor with the University Press of Mississippi, found the first clue. It was a reference to my great-grandfather's votes when he served on the Yazoo board of supervisors during Reconstruction in a book she edited in 1976.*

---

*Harriet DeCell and JoAnne Prichard, *Yazoo: Its Legends and Legacies* (Yazoo, Mississippi: Yazoo Delta Press), 1976.

At the B. S. Ricks Memorial Library in Yazoo City, librarians Linda Crawford and Darlene Johnson took up the search as soon as they knew Hilliard Golden had indeed lived in Yazoo. Sifting through mildewed census records and property deeds in basements and even in an airplane hanger, they located the Golden property on an 1874 map so fragile they were afraid to hold it up to the light. Gradually these researchers put together a remarkable picture of what my great-grandfather achieved in his first decade after slavery.*

Hilliard Golden's name appears for the first time in the 1870 census, which reports that he already owned land valued at seven hundred dollars, a considerable amount of money at the time. That plot of land—moist, reddish-brown earth near the Yazoo River in the northeast section of the county—is exactly what we found on our drive.

It was a bitter-sweet moment when I stepped onto the land and ran my fingers through the soil. Now owned by whites, the land was being tilled by black workers. When I told them my great-grandfather had once owned this farm, they didn't believe me. They simply couldn't imagine that it had been possible for a black in the last century to own anything. I began to understand that the history of black landowners like my great-grandfather is as obscure to many Americans, even blacks, as it was to me when I was growing up in Moscow. Furthermore, the men refused to believe me until Willie and JoAnne backed me up; they needed the word of whites to convince them I was telling the truth. Once they believed me, they insisted I must carry away a piece of "my" earth. The workers loosened small pieces of soil, carefully packed them in a jar, and solemnly placed the glass container in my hands.

---

*JoAnne and Linda are white and Darlene is black—a fact I mention only because I had been misled by Soviet stereotypes about America, especially about the South, into assuming that only black historians would be interested in pursuing the story of a black family. On my trip to Mississippi, it was a pleasurable reeducation to discover so much interest on the part of scholars of both races.

The discovery of my great-grandfather's land held a special poi-
gnancy for me not only as a woman of African-American ancestry but
as a black Russian. Family history and background are extremely
important to Russians—more so, I believe, than to most white or
black Americans (although the contemporary revival of interest in
"roots" is certainly making inroads on the cheerful imperviousness to
genealogy that strikes me as an American national trait).

Many of my Russian friends come from distinguished prerevolutionary families, and they treasure the pictures, books, and artifacts
that their parents and grandparents managed to preserve through the
upheavals of the Soviet twentieth century. I never envied my friends
their *things*, but I did envy them their certain knowledge of who their
ancestors were and what they accomplished.

When I was growing up, it seemed to me that history began with
my grandmother (and, of course, with the grandfather I never knew).
How could I have had any real sense of my family's existence before
we found ourselves in the Soviet Union? Emigration and the Cold
War had shattered the family's links with America; if the rules of
Soviet society had not changed dramatically in recent years, my
mother and I would have gone to our graves knowing almost nothing
about our American family.

My pride upon finding my great-grandfather's land has nothing to
do with the sort of nonsensical ancestor worship in which people puff
themselves up like pouter pigeons at the discovery of "noble" blood
in their lineage. (In my country, the craze to uncover a Romanov or,
at the very least, a Tsar's mistress in one's family tree is a comic
by-product of the collapse of communism.) The Golden land tells me
nothing about my ancestors' blood and everything about their character and persistence as they rose from slavery. From that Mississippi
earth, even though it was eventually mortgaged and lost (probably to
bankers), came the money for the private education of eight black
children. In a real sense, it is one of the reasons my mother is a
historian and I am a journalist. It is why Hilliard Golden's third- and
fourth-generation descendants in Chicago are dentists and teachers
and government administrators. The land gave us our start as a family.

Because I knew so little of my family's past when I was growing up in the Soviet Union, I always felt at some level that I was a nobody from nowhere. In Mississippi I understood—not merely in my brain, but in the deepest recesses of my soul—that I come from a long line of somebodies. And I began to care for and identify not only with my own grandfather and great-grandparents but with all of the black men and women of past generations. My trip to Mississippi seemed to unlock a secret chamber in my heart. A part of me—the black part—was being reborn.

At every turn, I have tried to verify family legends, to be what Americans call a "hard-nosed reporter." Before I began spending time in America, my knowledge of the South was not second-hand but third-hand. My grandmother never traveled to Mississippi with my grandfather before they left for the Soviet Union; that would have been an invitation to a lynching in the twenties. Everything she knew of the South, she learned from her husband. Her picture of the South and of Mississippi—of lynchings, of absolute segregation, of every extreme form of racial oppression—was to a great extent frozen in time. In Moscow we knew about the civil rights movement of the sixties, but the knowledge was abstract.

As I made arrangements to visit Yazoo, I was somewhat afraid, not of physical violence, but of the subtle condescension I expected to see in the eyes of white southerners. I anticipated a look, as painful and difficult for me to describe as it is for me to see, that clearly telegraphs this message: "We tolerate you because you are a black Russian, an exotic member of your species. If you were an ordinary black American, we wouldn't be interested in you." I had seen that look flicker across the faces of certain northern whites, whose indifferent demeanor changed to bemused respect when I explained that I was Russian. In the South, I expected even more frequent encounters with what I have simply come to think of as The Look.

I was wrong. What I found in certain white southerners was an attitude of deep respect for both the white and black history of their region. I do not mean to suggest that the South lacks its full quota of white racists or that the whites I met were typical. The point is that neither my Soviet preconceptions nor the parochial (I now understand) warnings of certain northern American acquaintances had prepared me for the kind of white southerners who have pondered, understood, and grieved over the long, often tragic interaction between the races. In many respects—not the least of them being a willingness to sit, eat, drink, and endlessly debate obscure historical questions—these liberal southern intellectuals bear a marked resemblance to the best specimens of the Russian *intelligentsia*. I must explain that there is no precise American equivalent for the Russian term *intelligent,* which is usually translated as "intellectual" but means more: someone with a deep attachment to humanistic values and history. Mississippi's great native son, William Faulkner, is one of two or three American writers whose sensibility appeals most strongly to the true *intelligentsia* of my country.★ I sensed this cultural affinity in certain conversations in Mississippi and realized at the same time that such encounters would have been impossible in the South my grandfather knew.

There was also something very familiar to me—very Russian, if you will—about the pride taken by both blacks and whites in their particular corner of the world. In Yazoo, people place a high value on hospitality, and they all do their best to make a stranger feel at home. In truth, it's difficult to feel like a stranger for long. People who know about my family refer to me as "our Yelena"; if you have an ancestor who once lived in Yazoo, Yazoo continues to claim you as its own.

One night, Darlene and I were driving along the back roads and lost our way in a blinding rain. Darlene was relieved when we crossed

---

★Nearly all of Faulkner's novels have been translated into Russian. In the pre-*glasnost* era, passages from his 1950 Nobel Prize acceptance speech frequently turned up in dissident *samizdat* (self-published) writings. One oft-quoted passage was: "I believe that man will not merely endure: he will prevail. . . . It is [the writer's] privilege to help man by lifting his heart, by reminding him of the courage and honor and hope and pride and compassion and pity and sacrifice which have been the glory of his past."—S.J.

paths with a local sheriff, who happened to be black. (The sight of black policemen in the South was another surprise for me. My mental image had been formed by old pictures of white sheriffs beating up civil rights demonstrators in the sixties.) The sheriff knew Darlene, but he immediately spotted me as a stranger because I was wearing my conservative New York work clothes. "You're not from around here, are you?" he commented, waiting for me to explain my presence. "I'm from Russia," I replied. His eyes widened. "Russia? I thought everyone there was white." I assured him once again that I really did come from Russia and explained that I had found my great-grandfather's land. After I pulled out the map and showed him where the land was located, he seemed happier. "So your folks were really from around here," he said in a tone evincing considerable satisfaction at having placed me in a known universe.

While Yazoo's hospitality and intense interest in history reminded me of Russia in a positive way, certain other aspects of life evoked a negative déjà vu. The rural poverty around Yazoo—the sight of dull-eyed people sitting outside shacks that seemed to promise little more in the way of material comfort than antebellum slave quarters—truly shocked me. I hadn't encountered anything like it in America.

I have seen impoverished, drug-ravaged neighborhoods in America's cities, but rural poverty still conveys a special quality of isolation and despair to me. Both Russian and American cities—in spite of their very different economic and political circumstances—are filled with energy. In my native Moscow and my adopted New York, hopeful people on the move rub shoulders on a daily basis with those lacking any realistic prospect of improving their lot.

But on the way to my great-grandfather's land in Yazoo, I was oppressed by the sight of exhausted-looking laborers, working land they didn't own or sitting outside shacks and giving off a palpable aura of having nowhere to go and nothing to do. This brand of rural apathy is familiar to me, because I encountered it repeatedly in the Russian villages where I began my training as a reporter. For many years under the Soviet regime, villagers and farm workers were bound to the land by law as well as by poverty. The old laws required elaborate job and residency permits before anyone could move from the countryside to a large city, or even from a small city to a bigger one. (When I was born in 1962, my mother had to struggle with bureaucrats for months to arrange an apartment exchange that enabled my grandmother to move from Tashkent to Moscow to help take care of me.) The old Soviet system trapped farm workers in a static universe; villagers' lives were as far removed from the life of an educated Muscovite as a Yazoo farm laborer's life is from that of a Rockefeller.

I met so many helpful, hospitable people in Yazoo that I began to daydream about how nice it would be to live in a place close to my family roots and far from the competitive pressures of New York. The sight of rural poverty made me rethink this sentimental fantasy and reminded me why my ancestors left. How fortunate for the Golden family that my great-grandfather managed to educate his children before he lost his land! On the back roads, I watched young mothers, some of them teenagers, sit outside their rickety houses and stare into space as their children played in the dirt. With a different twist of fate, with a different great-grandfather, I might have been born into poverty myself. I might have been one of those vacant-eyed girls, growing old too soon and looking forward to nothing.

One question no historical document has answered is exactly how Hilliard Golden acquired his first piece of land after the Civil War. But I can make a well-educated guess, based on family stories, Yazoo records, and the general experience of southern black landowners during Reconstruction.

In many instances, the first black landowners were "favorite slaves" (an expression I learned in America), who received their first pieces of land from former masters. These masters were undoubtedly motivated by a complex mixture of guilt, a genuine desire to help their most trusted servants, and the near-impossibility of maintaining large plantations in a devastated economy (and in the absence of slave labor). The land was not necessarily an outright gift; many new black owners had to pay for their farms with their first crops. Hilliard probably acquired his original land in this way, not only because it was a relatively common occurrence but because the children in the family were always told that their great-grandfather had been a trusted slave whose master taught him to read.

In Yazoo, local historians think Hilliard's owner might have been the prominent B. S. Ricks (for whom the Yazoo library is named). Ricks owned 113 slaves—the seventh-largest number in Yazoo—in 1850.★ His prewar plantation covered an area close to my great-grandfather's first plot of land. Although there are no pre-1870 records involving the Golden land, county property deeds show that Hilliard added to his holdings by business dealings with Ricks after 1870. Finally, my great-grandfather was a member of the Yazoo County board of supervisors during Reconstruction, and Ricks supported him when he ran for office. All of this suggests the two men had a longstanding relationship, and there was only one relationship between a black man and a white man in Mississippi before the war.

On one important point the census records contradict family accounts of my great-grandfather's life. The 1870 census reported that Hilliard was illiterate, but the family believed his master taught him to read while cautioning him against revealing his literacy to anyone else. That counsel would have been eminently wise, in view of southern laws prohibiting teaching slaves to read.

It seems clear to me that family tradition is right on this point. Hilliard's granddaughter Mamie, whom I was able to interview before she died in 1991 at the age of eighty-three, knew her grandfather well and said flatly that he could read. Furthermore, all of Hilliard's and Catherine's children could read and were sent away to school as soon as they were old enough. Illiteracy was the rule rather than the exception among both whites and blacks in the South of that time; it seems highly implausible that all of Hilliard's and Catherine's children would have been taught to read if both of their parents were illiterate.

D. W. Wilburn, an eighty-one-year-old Yazoo City resident

★Unfortunately, the Ricks plantation records, which would have shown whether Hilliard was listed as "property," have been destroyed.

whose grandfather also owned land in Yazoo during Reconstruction (and received his first plot from his former master) told me he thought it would have been impossible for Hilliard to hang on to his property for forty years without being able to read and write. "You're talking about maybe 2 percent of the black population at that time," he said. "The people who could read were the ones who owned something, and the people who owned something could read. They were lucky, the ones who had decent masters during slavery. They got a better start after the war than the blacks whose masters had done everything possible to crush their slaves' spirits."

Only five years after the end of the Civil War, it seems entirely reasonable that a prudent black man—and my great-grandfather was certainly that—would have followed the customs of the past and kept his literacy to himself when the official census taker came to call.★ What good could have come to a black from letting a white stranger in on his private business?

One final, highly suggestive piece of evidence: My great-grandfather was a preacher, and Mamie remembered him carrying a well-thumbed Bible. I know there were illiterate preachers who knew much of the Bible by heart—nearly every good Christian did in the nineteenth century—but I am certain that Hilliard Golden could read. I like to think of the slight figure in the corner of that tattered photograph, a man the census simply described as a "farm laborer," knowing the joy of opening his Bible and reading anew the words he carried in his heart.

There are several explanations—and every one may be true—of how and why my great-grandfather ultimately lost the land he had acquired through such diligent effort.

★Yazoo librarian Linda Crawford points out that many census takers probably failed to ask blacks if they could read and simply checked "no" on the census form. Then, she notes, a question can be put in an intimidating way: "You can't read, boy, can you?"

During the early 1870s, as the rich delta farming area began to recover from the devastation of the war, Hilliard was doing well enough to add to his land. County records show that on Jan. 31, 1871, he bought a 161-acre tract of land from Isaac H. and Carrie Hunter for $900—a sum larger than the value of his entire holdings in 1870. He kept buying more land from white owners in the same area of the county and eventually held title to more than a section (approximately one square mile, or 640 acres).

The Goldens had acquired some of the best cotton-growing land in the state. The thick, fluffy crop commands higher prices than scragglier cotton grown on less fertile soil. Nevertheless, farming was, and to this day remains, a risky business on low-lying land subject to periodic flooding. In the nineteenth century, before a system of levees was built to control flooding along the river, life was even riskier for a farmer than it is today: An entire year of work could be wiped out by one torrential rain. Borrowing was a way of life; farmers took out loans and repaid what they owed from the next year's crop. If the crop was wiped out, the land was of course lost.

Before 1895, my great-grandfather managed to avoid the kind of debt that would threaten his ownership of his land. At that point, though, he obviously encountered financial difficulties and began mortgaging his property. In 1909, his borrowing culminated in the loss of the land, probably to local banks. In the 1900 census, the Goldens appear as prominent landowners. In 1910, the family name disappears.

Economic realities aside, the racial politics of life in post-Reconstruction Yazoo must have played an important role in the family's fate. Most black landowners acquired their property during Reconstruction and lost what they had when "local control"—and white domination—were restored in 1876. According to Mamie, Hilliard Golden managed to cling to his land in spite of unremitting white hostility. Family legend maintains that the Golden "big house" was burned down once in the 1890s and again in 1909. The Klan was angered, so the story goes, because my great-grandfather employed both whites and blacks on his farm. (The well-informed Mr. Wilburn told me the latter part of this saga is probably a tall tale. He has little doubt that the house was burned down by the Klan but says it would have been impossible for my great-grandfather to have employed whites in the nineteenth century. "No matter how poor he was, no white man would have worked for a black at that time," Mr. Wilburn said.)

After Hilliard lost his property—when he was nearly seventy—the family embarked on a northward migration that would eventually scatter its members throughout the United States and the world. My great-grandfather's descendants can be found today in Los Angeles, Omaha, Chicago, Detroit, and, most improbably, in Moscow. I have often wondered about the emotional and intellectual impact on my grandfather of *his* father's loss of hard-earned property. After all, Hilliard Golden played by the rules of laissez-faire capitalism (rigged though they were by systematic racial discrimination). He played, and he lost. In view of his own family's experience, my grandfather had no reason to view the acquisition of private property as either a guarantee of future success or a bulwark against disaster.

My grandfather, Oliver, was born on Nov. 15, 1887, the sixth child and second son of Hilliard and Catherine. (Hilliard also had three daughters by a first wife. That marriage ended at some point in the 1870s, when my great-grandmother Catherine, born in Texas in 1858, appeared on the scene and set her sights on Hilliard. Catherine's determination and forcefulness—probably a nice way of saying she was overbearing—were legendary in the family. "When that lady put her mind to something, she usually got what she wanted," was the blunt way Mamie put it. At any rate, she obviously wanted and got my great-grandfather.) At least two of the three daughters by his first wife remained in the "big house" and were raised by Hilliard and Catherine. Their descendants are active members of the Golden clan in Chicago; my mother met them at a family reunion in 1990.

In 1909, when Hilliard was losing the struggle to keep his land, my grandfather, Oliver, was living in Memphis, Tennessee, and working as a tailor along with his older brother, Hilliard (Hillary) Jr. Oliver was twenty-two; he had already studied at Alcorn College and would enter Tuskegee in 1912. Neither institution has any of my grandfather's academic records; the likeliest explanation is that he did not graduate. Oliver later told friends he was expelled from Tuskegee after getting into a brawl with a white man in town. That explanation is plausible, because the last thing black colleges wanted at the turn of the century was any trouble between a student and a local white. After he moved North, my grandfather maintained contact with a number of Tuskegee classmates. He also knew George Washington Carver well enough to ask for and get his help in organizing a group of black agricultural specialists to work in the Soviet Union.

In Memphis, my grandfather was occupied mainly with making a living and helping family members who had fallen on hard times. At first, Oliver made clothes on a piecework basis for another shop owner; eventually he and his brother Hillary opened their own business.

Mamie, the oldest of Hillary's three children, was able to give me a vivid picture of the man the youngsters in the family knew as "Uncle Buck." In 1915, disaster struck Mamie's family. Her father died of tuberculosis, a disease that killed swiftly and surely in that era if the patient was too poor to go away to a sanatarium in a drier climate. Her account is a testament to precarious economic existence, in an age without any social safety net for those on the lowest rungs of the middle-class ladder.

> We lost my father and then my brother and then my baby sister in that terrible, terrible year. When my father died, Uncle Buck had to stand for the funeral; no one else in the family could afford it. After that, we went back to Mississippi and my mother found work, first on a farm and then as a cook in town. It was on the farm that the babies died. I know the filthy water from the pump was what caused their death. I guess because I was older and stronger, I didn't get so sick. My mother was half out of her mind with grief. Then she remarried; I don't think she knew what else to do. That was when Uncle Buck brought me back to live with him in Memphis. I was glad to go. I was a happy little girl in Memphis; Mississippi seemed like a bad dream.

The house where Mamie lived with my grandfather (and with his parents, who joined him in Memphis after they lost the farm) was an eleven-room structure at 805 Saxon Avenue. It had indoor toilets and hot and cold running water—the first time Mamie had encountered these luxuries.

Mamie remembers the Saxon Avenue household as a happy one, though domestic tensions sometimes surfaced as a result of Catherine's desire to rule with an iron hand. (She had, after all, been mistress of her own house for more than three decades.) My grandfather's habits already departed in certain respects from those of the rural world where he was born and raised. Oliver did not go to church, even though his parents and everyone else in the family did. Hilliard would lead prayers at Sunday breakfast and Oliver would usually remain silent but bow his head out of respect for his father. At age seven, Mamie was fully aware of this difference between my grandfather and the rest of the family; it must have been a source of considerable comment and friction in a preacher's household.

For the most part, though, everyone in the family loved Uncle Buck, a tall, slim, very dark-skinned young man who was known for his wit and generosity. Mamie described him as a man "who really knew how to enjoy life."

> Your grandfather was so good-looking, a real ladies man. He made his own beautiful clothes, waistcoats out of pure silk and vests out of 100 percent wool—the kind of thing you don't see nowadays. Women were just crazy about him, and he surely liked them. He was so *good* to everyone. Before he had his own shop, he would take the vests he had finished during the week to Mr. Fox—that was the tailor he worked for at the time—and get paid every Saturday afternoon. When he came back home on the streetcar, he'd always be carrying something for Grandpa, Grandma, and me, whatever we liked most of all: chocolate for me, peppermint for Grandma, shelled pecans for Grandpa. Uncle Buck didn't go to the dimestore to buy candy; he always went to a real old-fashioned candy store, where they made

everything themselves and wrapped it up in beautiful paper. That was the kind of man he was. He was really like a daddy to me after my own passed on.

My grandfather insisted on paying Mamie's tuition for private school, even though her mother thought public school was good enough. "He wanted me to have the best education possible," she said. "He always said you couldn't spend too much money on schooling. The whole Golden family set a great store on education; I think maybe my mother came from a family where just being able to read and write was enough."

For both my mother and me, Mamie's memories of the young Oliver are priceless treasures, offering us glimpses of his life in a time and place so far from the Soviet world of our upbringing. As I learn more about my grandfather's early years, it occurs to me that his background parallels, in several important ways, the lives of revolutionaries in turn-of-the-century Russia.

Like many Russian radicals, he came not from the lowest level of society but from a family of middle-class (communists would say bourgeois) aspirations and achievements. Oliver's color surely sensitized him to injustice in ways not unlike the experience of Russian Jewish radicals with prerevolutionary anti-Semitism. The Golden family stories include not only the burning of the "big house" but the rape of one sister by a white man and the threat of a lynching for a brother who apparently attracted the attention of a white woman. Whatever their achievements in the nineteenth century, the Goldens were always outsiders and hostages to racial obsessions. It's not surprising that at least one child of such a family would pin his hopes on another kind of system, a new world in which a man's fate would be sealed neither by the color of his skin nor the contents of his wallet.

In any event, the First World War intervened decisively in my grandfather's life. He was drafted into the army and reported to Clarksdale for basic training on March 31, 1918. Then he was shipped out to France. U.S. armed forces were entirely segregated at the time, and the 370,000 blacks made up a total of about 11 percent of those on active duty. Some black soldiers distinguished themselves in combat; the ninety-second and ninety-third Infantry Divisions served with French troops (who, unlike Americans at the time, had no objection to fighting side-by-side with blacks) and were awarded the croix de guerre by the French government. Most black soldiers, though, were restricted to behind-the-lines jobs as stevedores on the French docks or as cooks and janitors. That was the case with my grandfather, who was a cook and waiter.

My mother believes her father's tour of duty in France had an important impact on his thinking. In a fashion both humorous and sad, she learned about his French sojourn shortly after his death in 1940.

When my grandparents first arrived in the Soviet Union, they lived in a small village near an agricultural station. My creative grandfather, who enjoyed cooking throughout his life, believed in using local ingredients, so he caught frogs and prepared them as the French had taught him. He enjoyed offering this Gallic delicacy to unsuspecting guests, watching them wolf down the food and then eliciting horrified reactions when he informed them they had just eaten "gourmet" frogs. After Bertha and Oliver moved back to the city, the villagers—who appreciated the joke and enjoyed this strange black American even though he could not speak their native Uzbek and pronounced Russian with a Mississippi accent—would bring him fresh frogs so he could try out his specialty on guests in Tashkent.

My six-year-old mother learned about the French background to this family joke—and about my grandfather's stay in that alluring land—when the unsuspecting villagers brought a new consignment of frogs to the apartment shortly after my grandfather's death. They didn't know, of course, that Oliver had died and were chagrined when my grandmother burst into tears and told them to throw the frogs away.

As a historian, my mother is convinced that France gave Oliver much more than a recipe for frog's legs.

> He could speak French quite well—it was one of the things
> that impressed my mother's girlfriends back in New

York—so he must have spent a fair amount of his spare time socializing with French people. At that time, the French did not treat blacks the way white Americans did; a black American soldier could get on the train, go to a restaurant with white people—things that must have seemed very foreign, and very liberating, to a black man who grew up in Mississippi. France would have shown him there was another way for blacks and whites to be with one another. Some black American soldiers, you know, liked the feeling of being treated as equal human beings so much that they never returned to America after the war. They married French girls and stayed.

In his segregated army unit, my grandfather had another important experience. He made a close friend in James Ford, later one of the founders of the U.S. Communist Party and a two-time candidate for the vice-presidency on the Communist ticket (with William Foster and Earl Browder) during the thirties. It's certainly one of the more ironic twists of my family history that the U.S. Army provided the setting for the first stage of my grandfather's education in communism.

After finishing his stint in the Army, my grandfather headed for Chicago in 1920. Many of his relatives had settled there in the years immediately around World War I, which marked the beginning of the first great wave of black migration from the rural South. The only job my grandfather could find in Chicago was that of a Pullman dining-car waiter, one of the few possibilities for steady work open to blacks at the time.

The life of a Pullman waiter did not suit my grandfather. He was, after all, a proud individualist who had already refused to live by the code of deference to whites required of blacks in the South. But he had married a lovely black woman in Chicago (her name was Bessie, but everyone called her Jane), and any job was better than none for the head of a new family. Some years later, he told a fellow American student in the Soviet Union—he was there for an extended stay as a student before returning with my grandmother for the second time in 1931—that his desire to "get off those dining cars" played a major role in his decision to accept a Soviet invitation to study in Moscow. The story is recounted by Harry Haywood in *Black Bolshevik: The Autobiography of An Afro-American Communist.*★

We students were a fairly congenial lot and in particular I got to know the other Black students quite well. Golden was a handsome, jet-Black man; a former Tuskegee student and a dining car waiter. He was not a member of the Communist Party (in 1921), but was a good friend of Lovett Fort-Whiteman, head of the Party's Afro-American work.

Golden told me that his coming to the Soviet Union had been accidental. He had run into Fort-Whiteman, a fellow student at Tuskegee, on the streets of Chicago. Fort-Whiteman had just returned from Russia and was dressed in a Russian blouse and boots.

As Golden related it: "I asked Fort-Whiteman what the hell he was wearing. Had he come off the stage and forgotten to change clothes? He informed me that these were Russian clothes and that he had just returned from that country."

Golden at first thought it was a put-on, but became interested as Fort-Whiteman talked about his experiences. "Then out of the blue, he asks me if I want to go to Russia as a student. At first, I thought he was kidding, but man, I would have done anything to get off those dining cars! I was finally convinced that he was serious. 'But I'm mar-

---

★Published by the Liberator Press (Chicago, 1978), *Black Bolshevik* provides an entertaining as well as informative account of the lives and ideals of foreigners (not only American blacks) in Russia during the twenties and early thirties. Although Haywood lapses into tedious jargon when he talks about Communist ideology, his description of personalities and individual experiences is free of cant. His recounting of this conversation with my grandfather appears on p. 154.

ried,' I told him. 'What about my wife?' 'Why, bring her along too,' he replied. He took me to his office at the American Negro Labor Congress, an impressive set-up with a secretary, and I was convinced. Fort-Whiteman gave me money to get passports, and the next thing I knew, a couple of weeks later we were on the boat . . . on the way to Russia. And here I am now.''

I suspect that my grandfather's decision to study in Moscow the first time wasn't quite as casual as he made it sound to Haywood. He was a mature man of thirty-three when he finished his army service and must certainly have had many discussions about communism with his friend Ford. From the time of its founding in Chicago in 1919, the U.S. Party, with strong support from Moscow, made serious efforts to interest black Americans in its program. Oliver once told my grandmother that the first white American to take his hand and shake it as an equal was a Communist. All of this, reinforced by what I see as my grandfather's lifelong taste for adventure and travel, fed into his decision to take a look at the "Reds" in Moscow.

My grandfather and Haywood were students at a special university established to train Party agitators from ethnic minorities inside the boundaries of the former Tsarist empire as well as those from foreign countries. Known by the Russian acronym KUTV (which stood for University of the Toilers of the East) the institution included students from many colonial empires, along with numerous representatives of racial and ethnic minorities within the borders of the newly established Soviet state. American blacks were also considered to be under the yoke of "colonialist oppressors" because of their low status in American society.

The real purpose of KUTV was to train students to return to their respective countries and overthrow the yoke of colonialism (and, of course, to install Communist rule). It would have been interesting to sit in on the lectures of these Bolshevik theoreticians during the thirties and hear them try to explain the failure of the Party to exert any widespread impact on the views of working-class Americans during the Depression. Of course, by that time a good portion of the university faculty—loaded as it was with suspect foreigners, Jews, and Russians with foreign connections—had been dispatched to the gulag as the great purges began.

While he was in Moscow in the early twenties, my grandfather suffered a personal tragedy when his wife, Jane, died of a kidney ailment. Jane (like my grandfather at that time) was not a Party member but was extremely popular with the KUTV students, who regarded her as a kind of den mother.

When Haywood met my grandfather for the first time, he was in a state of shock after witnessing his wife's death in a Moscow hospital. The next day, the entire student body marched out Tverskaya Street to bury Jane in a municipal cemetery. After the funeral, where Jane was eulogized as one of the first women of her race to come to the land of socialism (though she probably came only because she loved Oliver), the other students tried to comfort him. "Golden had borne himself well at the graveside," Haywood remembers, "but we didn't want him to return to his room in the students' dormitory, which would only remind him of his grievous loss. So we went to the apartment of MacCloud, an old Wobbly friend of ours from Philadelphia, who had attended the funeral and who lived in the Zarechnaya District, across the river. . . . There we tried to drown our sorrows in good old Russian vodka, which was in plentiful supply."

After Jane's death, my grandfather continued studying in the Soviet Union until 1927, when he returned to the United States. In the late twenties, he tried to recruit Pittsburgh steelworkers for the communist cause but found himself ill-suited to the Party's bureaucratic structure.

Everything I know about my grandfather labels him as a man who always went his own way. I'm certain he would have found it difficult to mold himself to what was then called "Party discipline." His outstanding quality was not collective-mindedness but individual initiative, which he displayed in full measure when he came up with the idea of organizing black agricultural specialists to go to the Soviet Union in 1931.

My grandfather may have had a tough time fitting into the U.S. Party (which was already showing strong signs of the Moscow-inspired rigidity and conformity that would become even more marked in the thirties. Even so, there is no question that Oliver was a committed Marxist, thoroughly enmeshed in the flourishing American "progressive" subculture of the twenties. This child of Mississippi—a man whose father fought to hang on to his own land—was by then committed to a belief in a world in which all property would be held in common, one without extremes of wealth or poverty.

This philosophy appealed just as strongly to young Bertha Bialek, the Warsaw rabbi's daughter who became involved in left-wing union activities just a few years after she passed through the portals of Ellis Island into the energetic, hopeful world of immigrant Jewish New York.

CHAPTER THREE

BERTHA AND OLIVER

Even today, the Great Hall on Ellis Island is an intimidating place. As I followed in my grandmother's footsteps through what is now a highly evocative museum, one thought dominated my mind: How dearly she must have loved my grandfather to turn back, little more than a decade after coming to America, and retrace the uncertain immigrant's journey to yet another unknown land!

Stand in the island's beautifully restored hall, look out a window, and you see two things every new arrival saw: the beckoning, overwhelming skyline of lower Manhattan and the forbidding dormitories, windows barred with heavy wire mesh, where many unlucky immigrants—rejected by U.S. officials for a variety of reasons—awaited the ships that would carry them back across the Atlantic. Like most immigrants, fifteen-year-old Bertha had never seen anything remotely resembling the glittering skyline, just a ten-minute ferry ride across the waters of New York Harbor. In 1920, the year Bertha arrived with her mother, Bessie, and two of her three older brothers, the sixty-story Woolworth Building was just as impressive to new-comers as the towers of the World Trade Center are to visitors today.

Inside the Great Hall, Bertha awaited a medical inspection and crucial questions (including those designed to determine whether a pretty young girl was entering the United States for purposes of pros-titution) that would decide whether she might be allowed to live beneath the enchanting skyline.

Until I visited Ellis Island, I don't think I fully understood how much courage it must take to leave one's native land, even accompa-nied by family, for an entirely alien world. Neither Bertha nor her brothers spoke a word of English when they arrived at Ellis Island. Many immigrant memoirs have described the Great Hall as a veritable Tower of Babel. That's easy to believe. In this cavernous space, today's tourists—though most of them are speaking the same lan-guage—create an almost unbearable, ear-splitting cacophony. How disorienting it must have been to wait, surrounded by thousands of fellow immigrants speaking dozens of languages, and move slowly in line toward officials who held, if not the power of life and death, the power to decide what sort of life you would be allowed to live. Being accompanied by relatives was no guarantee of admission to the United States; the annals of immigration are filled with agonizing stories of families forced to split up because one member failed the health test.

I shivered at the sight of a buttonhook, the instrument used to lift up each eyelid in search of trachoma (a contagious eye disease that was a common cause of rejection for immigrants). My grandmother also had to pass a brief literacy test, introduced for the first time in 1917. That was no problem for Bertha, because she read both Yiddish and Polish (and probably German as well).

Finally, there were questions designed primarily to find out whether the prospective immigrants had any way of supporting themselves. By 1920, with Russia torn by civil war between the Bolsheviks and their opponents, and the Red Scare in full swing in America, there were other, specifically political questions: "Are you an anarchist?" "Are you a Communist?" I was astonished at the notion that any prospective immigrant would have answered these questions in the affirmative, but a National Park Service librarian assured me that some of the political émigrés were men and women of such staunch principle that they refused to lie in order to gain entry into the United States. It was a shame these anarchists and Communists couldn't bring themselves to lie, because a great many of them eventually perished under the Nazi or Stalinist regimes.

At any rate, my grandmother was neither an anarchist nor a Communist at age fifteen; her political radicalism was truly "made in America." She passed every test and became one of more than 225,-000 immigrants admitted through Ellis Island in the first year after the end of World War I.★

The war that swept away so many European empires was undoubtedly the reason my great-grandfather, Isaac, was separated from his wife and children for several years. He left Warsaw in 1915—one step ahead of the Tsar's army "recruiters," as Bialek family legend has it—and established himself in a Jewish immigrant neighborhood in the Bronx. In the normal course of events, the family would have followed soon afterward, but the war put an end to transatlantic migration until the armistice was signed in November 1919.

I wish I knew much, much more about my grandmother's girlhood in Warsaw. Although she helped raise me from the day I was born and was a second parent to me—not *like* a second parent—she told me almost nothing about that period of her life. Perhaps it was too painful for her to discuss her childhood, in view of the break with her family after she fell in love with my grandfather. It's also possible that later experiences—passionate politics and passionate love in New York in the twenties, her adventurous life with my grandfather in Uzbekistan, and her lonely struggle to raise my mother after his death—were far more vivid in her memory than a girlhood closed off by not one but two immigrant doors.

★According to U.S. Immigration and Naturalization Service figures, more than 430,000 immigrants entered the United States through all ports of entry in that year.

On the Bialek side of the family, no piece of earth evokes a sense of my grandmother's origins in the way that the soil of Yazoo gave me a feeling for my grandfather's beginnings. The Jewish world Bertha knew in Warsaw perished in the ashes of the Holocaust. But my Bialek relatives did manage to unearth one treasure from our family's past: a 1907 portrait of Isaac (Yitzhak), Bessie (an Americanization of her original name, Pesa), and their four children—Bertha (called Bessie in Poland), Jack (originally Jacob), Sidney (Solomon), and Marcus (Moishe). My great-grandfather Bialek is dressed in a formal suitcoat and starched shirt that bears a strong resemblance to the finery my great-grandfather Golden wore for his picture. Whether in the Mississippi cotton fields or the Jewish quarter of Warsaw, families donned their best attire when leaving a visual record for posterity.

The Bialek family portrait clearly shows that these were educated, acculturated Jews who were participants in the secular as well as the Judaic culture of their times. My great-grandfather's head is bare, his beard short and neatly trimmed in characteristic Edwardian style. This secular appearance suggests that he was a rabbi of the so-called German school associated with the Jewish Enlightenment.* My great-grandmother wears no wig, as strict adherence to Jewish Orthodox tradition would have required; her face is framed with her own curly, slightly unruly hair, which seems determined to escape from its sculptured topknot. The boys wear suits that might have been school uniforms, and two-year-old Bertha, clad in a starched white linen frock, looks like a character from a Victorian children's story.

When my grandmother told me her father had been a rabbi—one of the few facts she revealed about her family—I envisioned a figure from a Chagall painting or a Sholom Aleichem tale. My Soviet education provided almost no information about the breadth of Jewish cultural history, and the only sort of rabbi I could imagine before I

---

*According to scholars at New York's Yivo Institute for Jewish Research, there were numerous rabbis of the German school in Warsaw at the turn of the century, and they would have been dressed exactly as my great-grandfather was.

came to America was someone completely out of touch with secular education, manners, and social thought. I now understand that there were many turn-of-the-century European Jews like the Bialeks, assimilated into the larger culture yet retaining their religious identity and practices. While such Jews were not unheard-of in prerevolutionary Russia, they were extremely rare. Russian Jewish assimilation before the revolution was generally associated either with conversion to Russian Orthodoxy or with proscribed political radicalism; there was no significant community of assimilated Jews who also practiced their religion.

My newly acquired knowledge of Jewish history (and it still has huge gaps) has helped me solve a riddle created not only by the omissions of Soviet education but by my grandmother's reticence on the subject of her Jewishness. I never quite understood how the daughter of a rabbi could have become involved in radical politics; it seemed to me, from my limited perspective, that such activism would have meant a break with her family long before she fell in love with my grandfather. I now realize that a rabbi of my great-grandfather's bent (and his family) were not severed from but enmeshed in contemporary secular culture in both Europe and America. I don't know if my great-grandfather was pleased (somehow I doubt it) when his son Jack and his only daughter became involved with American communism, but he could hardly have been surprised.

Because my grandmother was an atheist, I assumed that being a Jew in the cultural sense (as that phrase is understood by Americans who take pride in their ethnic heritage) had no meaning for her. It came as a great surprise to me to learn, via the Bialek family network in America, that my grandmother spoke, read, and wrote Yiddish. When I sing the lullaby my grandmother sang to me—I always assumed the words were German—many American Jews instantly recognize it as the same song their grandmothers used to coax them to sleep.

Bertha Bialek came of age, intellectually and politically, in the rich cultural soil of *Yiddishkeit* (a word I never heard in Russia). This exciting period is described by Irving Howe in *World of Our Fathers*. (I'm going to need more than one lifetime to make it through a pile of books by scholars of African-American and Jewish life, explaining the cultural forces that have shaped both sides of my family. "You've got to read Howe to understand your grandmother," orders one friend. Another presses *The Autobiography of Malcolm X,* several novels by Isaac Bashevis Singer, and the poetry of Alice Walker into my hands. This ever-growing stack attests to and symbolizes the richness or my family's history. How will I ever find time to get through all of them? How can I not make the time?) Howe describes my grandmother's world as one where "Jewish intellectuals find themselves torn by conflicting claims: those of an alien world, whether in the guise of accomplished cultures or revolutionary movements, and those of their native tradition, as it tugs upon their loyalties and hopes for renewal. . . . The sufferings of an oppressed people rub against and contribute to utopian expectations and secularized messianic fervor."★ In short, this was a world in which my great-grandfather might teach Hebrew school and two of his children might just as readily be drawn to communism.

Seven years would pass before my grandmother and grandfather met in 1927. While Oliver studied Marxist theory at a university in Moscow, Bertha began adjusting to the New World. In Poland, she was still a schoolgirl; in New York, she quickly found work in an embroidery factory to help support her family. Like so many other immigrants, she was an avid reader of the *Jewish Daily Forward,* the most popular and influential Yiddish-language newspaper in the United States. (Bertha's attachment to the *Forward* suggests that she was not a particularly doctrinaire Communist, at least not in her early years in the United States, since the hard-line Party types regarded the democratic socialist *Forward* as the devil's own herald.) A friend of my grandmother's told me how much they enjoyed the *Forward*'s famous

---

★Irving Howe, *World of Our Fathers* (New York: Harcourt Brace Jovanovich, 1976), p. 16.

"Bintel Brief," a Yiddish "Dear Abby" for immigrants seeking advice on how to handle life in American society. The "Bintel Brief" was filled with material that was directly pertinent to Bertha's life; one recurring theme, I noticed with amusement in my readings at the New York Public Library, was the dismay of immigrant parents when their children began dating and contemplating marriage with non-Jews. ("My daughter argues with me," wrote one unhappy mother in the year Bertha and Oliver were married. " 'Why? [she says] You used to say that all people are equal.' . . . When one is young and in love, one is in the clouds and sees no flaws. But when love cools down, she will see it's no good. I see it in advance. True, it could happen that she could marry a Jewish man and after the wedding not be able to stand him. But with a Jew it's still different."★) The usual stance of the "Bintel Brief" was to sympathize with the parent's distress but caution against cutting off the errant child (advice my great-grandmother ignored). Of course, the *Forward*'s correspondents were only concerned with white gentiles as undesirable mates; as far as I know, no one ever wrote and asked what to do about a prospective match with someone who was neither white nor Jewish.

But marriage was the last thing on Bertha's mind in the early years after her arrival in America. She concentrated on making a living, learning English, and organizing garment workers. Bertha joined the Communist side of the labor struggle along with her favorite brother, Jack. Five years separated them, but Bertha and Jack shared a strong concern for social justice and a rebellion against their Orthodox Jewish upbringing. (Their absolute rejection of observant Judaism separated the two not only from their parents but from the other brothers.) Although Jack introduced his sister to the Party, he backed off from Communist activism in the mid-twenties while she plunged in deeper. (From her later Soviet perspective, my grandmother thought her brother had abandoned his interest in and devotion to left-wing social ideals along with his involvement in the Party. This wasn't

---

★*A Bintel Brief,* Isaac Metzker, ed. (New York: Ballantine, 1972), pp. 147–48.

entirely true. Jack's wife, Minnie, says he subscribed to *Freiheit,* the Yiddish-language Communist newspaper, until his death. Perhaps his subscription to the newspaper was nothing more than a reminder of the heady days of his youth. Still, there must have been more entertaining ways to recall youthful enthusiasms than to read a dreary, Moscow-oriented publication that lost most of its readers as it hewed faithfully to the Party line over many decades.)

As a worker in an embroidery factory (Jack was a pocketbook maker), Bertha naturally belonged to the International Ladies' Garment Workers' Union (ILGWU). The bitter struggle between leftist and rightist union factions fueled my grandmother's political activism throughout the twenties. She clearly relished her memories of union activism in New York and told me stories of rising at dawn to walk picket lines, of occasionally landing in jail, with all of the enthusiasm that other women bestow on memories of dances and romances. Of course, jail was romantic as far as Bertha was concerned, because that was where she eventually met the great love of her life.

Bertha was already a dedicated Communist, though perhaps not yet a Party member, when she met Pearl Steinhardt around 1924. Pearl, now 85, is the only friend of my grandmother's whom I was able to find in the United States. She occupied a special place in my grandmother's life because she and her late husband, Misha (my grandmother's first cousin) were the only white, non-Communist friends who continued to see Bertha regularly after she moved in with Oliver Golden. After my grandmother left for the Soviet Union, she and Pearl kept in touch by letters—albeit on the sporadic basis dictated by Soviet censorship, World War II, FBI monitoring of Soviet-American correspondence, and the generally slow communication of that era. In the mid-sixties, Pearl and Misha visited my grandmother in Moscow. My mother and I always knew about Pearl, because my grandmother proudly told us we had a relative who was a world-famed violinist. Pearl's son, my cousin, is Arnold Steinhardt of the Guarneri Quartet. When I came to the United States, I found Pearl by looking up her number in the Los Angeles telephone book, an act that would be impossible in my country because it is still impossible to buy comprehensive phone directories.

Pearl's generosity with her memories filled in many of the gaps in my image of my grandmother as a young woman. After talking with Pearl, I began to understand much more about the links between her political activism in America and the social consciousness that originated in the experiences of a Jewish girl in Warsaw. It was vital for me to realize, Pearl said, that even the most assimilated Jews in Poland were deeply affected by anti-Semitism.

> Your grandmother and I were alike in one important way: We had both seen a lot of injustice, anti-Semitism, and discrimination in Poland. You couldn't imagine how bad it was. Out of that memory of injustice came the desire of Jews to make a better world in America. That's why there were so many immigrant Jews not just among the Communists but among the Socialists and all other reformers. Jews allied themselves with just causes, and communism seemed like a just cause at the time. It was for equal rights for everyone and a better life for workers. Equal rights: Think what that meant to people who had grown up afraid to go out in the street at night because they were Jews. And that is what the immigrant Jews had in common with the blacks, who had also known fear in America. One of the saddest things to me today is that so many Americans have forgotten what the black and Jewish people had in common. Bertha would be shocked, I think.
>
> I wasn't a Communist in the twenties—not because I disagreed with any of those ideas but because I was, frankly, more selfish than your grandmother. I wanted to have some fun; I was young; I didn't want to devote all of my time to demonstrations and picketing. Your grandmother was always working for a cause; that was her idea of fun. Nothing was too much work in the fight for justice. She was a very, very serious person.

"Serious" is the adjective everyone applied to my grandmother throughout her life. Throughout my childhood, I never saw her without a book or magazine in her hands unless she was cooking or getting ready for bed. Still, the young Bertha also knew how to have fun in the conventional sense. She and Pearl met at a party, and America had liberated them (another source of regret for mothers writing the "Bintel Brief") from the close family and community supervision that ruled the lives of well–brought-up Jewish girls in Poland. Bertha adopted the dress and hairstyle of an emancipated New Woman of the twenties: Her curly brown hair was fashionably bobbed and photographs show her wearing the typical flapper costume of short skirt (short by the standards of those days) and T-strap shoes. Although several young men were interested in Bertha ("Of course she had boyfriends," was Pearl's indignant reply to my question), she does not seem to have seriously considered marriage until she met Oliver.

> She met your grandfather through their work in the Party. How else for your grandmother? I know she wasn't especially looking for a husband—black, yellow, or white. This was around 1927, and your grandmother was earning enough money to have her own apartment. This was very unusual at the time, and I don't suppose her family could have approved of it.
>
> Bertha and your grandfather had a shared belief in equal justice for all, regardless of race, color, or creed. She didn't fall in love with Golden *because* he was a black man. It's just that Bertha wouldn't have let his color stop her from seeing the person inside.
>
> Of course, you know there were people who found it impossible to understand how Bertha could love a black man. But my dear, he was very handsome, very charming and interesting, much older and more sophisticated than we were. He had been all over the world. He could even cook! If he had been a white man, no one would have asked how someone could fall in love with him.

When Bertha and Oliver met, she was twenty-two and he was nearly forty. As far as she was concerned, there could have been no better matchmaker than the New York City police. Picketing, followed by a few hours in jail, was her idea of a proper introduction. How else, and where else, would she have been as likely to find a man who shared her values?

Their meeting seems to have been a case of love at first sight. Bertha was not beautiful in the conventional sense, but her face had a tender, soulful quality that revealed gentleness as well as strength. In a picture taken around that time, her shoulders are bared in a low-necked dress with a portrait neckline. She gazes into the camera with a dreamy expression: a young woman ready for love. And Oliver was a man who needed to love and be loved in a serious way. Although he was extremely attractive to (and attracted by) many women, he eschewed casual relationships. In current parlance, he was a man who wanted commitment—in the language of my grandmother's day, "the marrying kind."

Although Oliver was as politically dedicated as my grandmother, he possessed a more spontaneous, ebullient personality. Everyone who actually knew my grandfather, from his niece Mamie to his old Bolshevik comrades, made a point of mentioning his wit and gift for laughter, a zest for life as well as politics. This quality appealed enormously to my serious grandmother; with Oliver, she was able to express the usually submerged, fun-loving side of her own nature. When I was a little girl, I found it almost impossible to imagine my grandmother dancing the night away in her T-strap shoes or sitting in on jam sessions. What was a "jam session," I asked, bewildered by the image of grownups sitting around all night eating bread and preserves. My grandmother laughingly explained that this sort of "jam" meant music and that she had heard the best jazz musicians in the world in New York. "It was such fun, you can't imagine," she would say. Her face lit up and grew younger, as it always did when she talked about my grandfather. Theirs was a successful union based on a complementary meshing of very different personalities. From an adult perspective, I see that my grandmother lost an important part of herself when Oliver died young. No other man managed to bring out the spontaneous, joyful elements in her character.

Not long after their meeting in 1927, Bertha took a step that was socially daring even for a young woman in progressive circles: She began living with Oliver in a one-room apartment in Harlem. I suspect my grandmother's earnest, intense nature would have precluded dating in the ordinary sense when she found herself deeply in love. Furthermore, a black man and white woman almost *had* to set up housekeeping in order to see much of each other, since they would hardly be welcome in most apartment buildings, eating establishments, or even in many public places. And Bertha would surely have been evicted from her old apartment in the Bronx if a black man came calling with any regularity.

Many Americans are surprised to hear that even in the famous bohemian atmosphere of Greenwich Village during the twenties, blacks were usually unwelcome as tenants or customers. While rehearsing *The Emperor Jones* in the Village in 1924, Paul Robeson found the nearest place he could order and be served a full meal was Pennsylvania Station, a fifteen-minute taxi ride away in midtown Manhattan.* The father-in-law of a white acquaintance of mine had the same experience in the Village with his friend, the poet Countee Cullen. They had to go to Grand Central Station to order a sandwich, sit at a table, and talk. (It seems that blacks in the North had reason to be grateful for restaurants in railroad stations.)

Harlem was really the only place where an interracial couple of modest means and no celebrity could hope to live with safety and tolerance. Even there, Oliver and Bertha had to pay twice as much for one room as they would have had to pay in another neighborhood for a five-room apartment—if only they had not been a mixed couple. "It made me furious," recalls Pearl. "Just like in Poland, people made to live in a ghetto."

When Bertha introduced Pearl to my grandfather, he was working at a coffee shop on Fourteenth Street as a short-order cook. It was the story of the Pullman dining car all over again. When Americans ask

---

*This incident ·is is recounted by Martin Bauml Duberman in *Paul Robeson,* (New York: Ballantine, 1989), p. 87.

me how such an intelligent man could have been "duped" by communism—and they do ask—I remind them that the Communist Party was the only institution in white America that recognized Oliver Golden's unusual capabilities and saw him as something more than a potential cook or waiter.

In Harlem nightclubs, one setting where blacks and whites mingled freely, Oliver and Bertha met Misha and Pearl for evenings of dancing and listening to jazz. But, whenever they ventured outside their small circle of progressive friends, pain and humiliation awaited them. My grandmother once told my mother a story that reveals the intense pressure she felt at those times. It hurt my mother to hear the story, and the pain was still fresh in her voice when she retold it to me:

> My mother and father wanted to go to a Broadway theater to hear a black vaudeville group that usually played in Harlem. My mother went downtown to the box office to buy the tickets, and they were the best orchestra seats. When she and my father came to take their seats—they were dressed in their best clothes—the other people in the row, all of them white, stood up and left. They weren't going to sit in the same row with a black man. My mother hadn't expected trouble, I suppose because it was a nice theater and the performing group was black. But it was one thing for whites to go to a black nightclub—that was all right— but another thing for a black to come to a white theater. I don't know, I can't imagine how proud people would react to that kind of thing on a daily basis. As a white person, you wouldn't know how it was unless you fell in love with and lived with someone who was black.

Unlike Pearl, most of my grandmother's girlfriends from the garment factories dropped out of her life when she moved in with Oliver. At first she made an effort to invite them to her apartment, presumably to show them that the man she loved was not a member of another species but a captivating human being. On one occasion she invited several of her friends for dinner—Oliver cooked, as usual—and they went away wide-eyed with admiration at his charm, his sophistication, his command of several foreign languages, and his stories about travels around the world. They told Bertha they understood why she had fallen in love with Oliver, that they would do the same if they could muster up the courage to defy their families. But they didn't call, didn't come back, and, of course, didn't invite Bertha and Oliver to their homes. My grandmother would say—did say, later in life—that such behavior demonstrated small-mindedness and intolerance, that those "friends" weren't worth keeping. Still, such incidents must have wounded Bertha at age twenty-two, a time in life when it's far from easy to make a choice that cuts you off from friends as well as family.

Indeed, Bertha's health nearly broke under the strain of trying to decide whether to listen to her heart or to her family. After nearly a year of living with Oliver, she had no illusions about the everyday difficulties facing an interracial couple (and it's important to remember that Oliver and Bertha were planning to spend their lives not in the Soviet Union but the United States). My grandmother suffered from frequent fainting spells, high blood pressure, an erratic heartbeat, icy sweats, and what was diagnosed even then as "nervous depression." Oliver, whose first wife had died in Moscow, feared he would lose Bertha too.

After months of fainting spells, Bertha heard about a doctor who specialized in nervous disorders and took the subway downtown to speak with him. She described her relationship with Oliver and the attitude of her friends and family. She told the doctor she loved Oliver and he wanted to marry her, but she couldn't make up her mind because she knew marriage would mean a final break with her family. The physician gave my grandmother wise and compassionate advice: He told her she was sick from indecision and that her physical symptoms would disappear as soon as she made up her mind. "I wouldn't presume to tell you what to do," he advised her, "but you say you love this man. Only you can know if you love him enough."

Bertha did, of course, decide she loved Oliver enough, and she never had a sick day in her life from that point until just before her death in 1985. She forgot that doctor's name, but she never forgot his humanity in dealing with a young girl in a delicate predicament. "I learned a lesson that stayed with me the rest of my life," she once said. "Avoiding difficult decisions makes you sick; facing them gives you strength."

My grandmother told us her own mother never spoke to her again after she refused to leave Oliver. Even so, she sent baby pictures of my mother from Tashkent during the thirties. Bessie never answered, and it's just as well. An aging relative,★ whose own mother knew Bessie well, told me how my great-grandmother reacted when she received a letter from her daughter in the Soviet Union. Bessie opened the envelope and said, "So here's a letter from my daughter in Russia." Seeing a snapshot inside, she said, "That must be Bertha's baby." Without looking at the picture, she handed it to another woman (my relative's mother) and asked, "Is the child a *shvartse?* Told her granddaughter was indeed black, Bessie grabbed the snapshot and tore in up in front of several family members.

I'm very happy Bertha was spared the knowledge that her own mother refused even to *look* at a snapshot of her black granddaughter. In America, many whites have tried to convince me that my Bialek great-grandparents were motivated not by racism but by religious opposition to any involvement between a child of theirs and a gentile. I know that some Jewish families sat *shivah* for a child who married out of the faith—and Isaac and Bessie were observant Orthodox Jews—but the account of my great-grandmother's tearing up the snapshot suggests that racism was also at work. The elder Bialeks left Poland to escape the virulent anti–Semitism of the Old World, only to adopt the prejudices of their new world.

When she talked about her family, my grandmother rarely mentioned her brothers Marcus and Sidney. They didn't write her in Russia; Jack was the only member of the family who kept up contact

---

★She prefers that her name not be used. I consider her account absolutely reliable.

with his sister over the years (which makes it all the more puzzling that Marcus and Sidney made no secret of Aunt Bertha's marriage to a black man, while Jack concealed the fact from his son). Unlike the other two brothers, Jack and Bertha were united by their involvement in left-wing politics during the twenties and by their rejection of religious Judaism. I think my grandmother expected Jack to support her decision to stay with my grandfather. Because he was her favorite brother, his coolness caused her more grief than the reactions of any other family members.

Still, Jack cared enough to visit my grandmother in Moscow in the mid-sixties. Only then did she learn that Jack and his wife, Minnie, had never told their son the truth about his aunt's marriage to a black American. There was some talk about my grandmother coming to Los Angeles for a visit, and Jack admitted that his son, Eugene, didn't know he had a black Russian cousin. "But what about all the pictures I sent you?" my grandmother asked. They, too, had been destroyed. (Eugene and his wife, Sheila, didn't find a single picture of my mother or me when they went through old papers and documents in Jack's house after Minnie finally told them about our existence.)

In any event, young Bertha made a complete recovery from her psychosomatic ailments as soon as she decided to stay with Oliver and accept the estrangement from her family. She and Oliver lived a quiet life, devoted to their Party work and to each other. Bertha kept the books at local Party headquarters in New York, while Oliver participated in Communist-led strikes (including the war that raged between left and right* in the largely Jewish garment district).

Although Oliver was fulfilled in his private life, he never managed to carve out a satisfying niche in his American work life, either inside or outside the Party. That dissatisfaction served as one motive for his

---

*I'm told that "left," in this context, means Communists and "right" means Socialists—some of whom later became doctrinaire anti-Communists. It's difficult for someone brought up in Russia to keep track of what "left" and "right" mean in different historical settings.

effort to organize a group of black agricultural specialists who would help develop the Soviet Union. By virtue of his upbringing and education, he was better suited to put together an agricultural aid mission than to dispense agitprop in the streets of New York.

I don't mean to leave the impression that my grandparents' life in New York was all work (though many of the Party meetings they attended must have been the dullest sort of labor imaginable). It was exciting and energizing to play a role in the left-wing culture of that generation, and progressive social circles afforded a welcome respite—indeed, the only respite—from the larger society's intolerance toward an interracial couple. With groups of Party friends, they visited Niagara Falls and went camping in the Adirondacks. (Camping seems to have been a popular left-wing activity. Socialists and Communists maintained separate camps, in both the literal and metaphoric senses.) In the city, they particularly enjoyed eating out in Chinese restaurants. There was no trouble about being served, because the Chinese regarded both blacks and whites as strange-looking foreigners, equally odd as human specimens and equally desirable as customers.

I once asked my grandmother why she was so happy with my grandfather (a child's question) and she replied that happiness was much more difficult to describe than unhappiness. But she did tell me one story that illuminated their shared values.

When they first met, Oliver had naturally told Bertha about his marriage to Jane and her tragic death in Moscow. He also told her about another important woman in his life. Anya, as he called her, was a Soviet woman who had helped him recover from his grief after Jane's death. She was an Udmurt, from the far northeast, and was also been studying in Moscow. Oliver owed her a great deal, he told Bertha, because she had loved and cared for him even though he told her he could not marry her because he would soon be returning to the United States to carry on Party work in his native land. (He could not have brought Anya with him; by the mid-twenties it was already becoming extremely difficult for any Soviet citizen to leave the country.) But it had not been a casual relationship on either side.

And there was more: Anya loved Oliver so much that she had

wanted to have his child even though she knew he was leaving. She gave birth to a son in the mid-twenties and named him after his father.

My grandmother's reaction was not that of an ordinary twenty-two year old. Instead of being taken aback to learn that her husband-to-be had a baby by another woman in a far-off land, her reaction was that they must try to help that unknown woman and child if the occasion ever arose. And when they left for the Soviet Union in 1931, Bertha carried a sack of presents in hopes of locating Anya and Oliver's son. They were not, however, to meet for many years; the chaos of the great purges and World War II meant that the bag of toys and clothes remained undelivered in my grandmother's closet. But Anya did reappear in my family's life many years later, in an entirely unexpected way. That is another chapter in my family's complicated history and is, as Americans say, a tease—to be continued.

For me, the sweetness of this story lies in its decency, in the trust and mutual respect that underlay my grandparents' love. Bertha made it clear to my grandfather that he owed her no explanations about any women in his life before her and that she was glad he had found consolation after his wife's death. Oliver never thought he owed Bertha an explanation; he simply loved her so much that he wanted to share his past as well as his present with her. And he didn't want to begin their marriage with any important secrets between them.

Family secrets! Sometimes, it's hard to figure out how they start and why they last. I stumbled across yet another secret while I was trying to learn more about my grandparents' life in New York. Trying to find out when and where my grandparents were married, I asked my mother if she had ever seen their marriage license. "Well," she said, "they didn't actually go through a wedding ceremony. After my father died, my mother obtained a certificate from the Soviet government entitling her to the legal status and pension of a widow."

"Why didn't you ever tell me that?" I asked Mama. "It just didn't seem important," she replied. "They were as married as two people can be, so what difference does it make when they got a piece of paper?"

Until the day of her death, my grandmother referred to my grandfather as her beloved husband. I wanted to understand why two people, who defied society to be together, who lived in harmony for thirteen years, who brought a much-loved child into the world, didn't formalize their union. At first, I jumped to the mistaken conclusion that their decision had something to do with laws against miscegenation in the United States. It's worth noting that miscegenation, at the time Bertha and Oliver fell in love, was not only a potentially lethal violation of social mores but a crime in many states, North and South. The ethos of the era is summed up in a line from the musical *Show Boat:* "One drop of black blood makes you black in these parts."

At one time, thirty-eight states had laws prohibiting interracial sex or marriage. (When the U.S. Supreme Court declared these laws unconstitutional in 1967, twenty-one states still had such statutes on the books.) But New York didn't have any such law, and my grandparents weren't the sort of people to be deterred by disapproving looks from officials at City Hall.

My grandparents' decision not to enter into a formal marriage contract had nothing to do with American racial attitudes and everything to do with their own political beliefs. Like many radicals of their generation, they considered marriage a bourgeois economic institution, something they didn't need to sanctify their love. In recent years, some aging Moscow survivors of their political generation have gone through a wedding ceremony in order to emigrate from the Soviet Union. After living together for decades and raising a family, they finally submitted to the formalities required to leave Russia.

Knowing my grandmother's stubbornness, I suspect she would have remained defiantly, legally "free" until the end, bound to her beloved husband not by bureaucracy but by their mutual devotion. They were truly married.

So I cherish the image of Oliver and Bertha as a pair of lovers, eating Chinese food, sharing secrets, holding each other in their small room, believing in the struggle for a better world in spite of (or perhaps because of) the bigotry that surrounded them. In my dreams, I see them not as Black Man and White Woman but simply as a man and a woman. I need the voice of a poet to describe them: the voice of Langston Hughes, one of my grandfather's favorites.

Come,
Let us roam the night together
Singing.

I love you.

Across
The Harlem roof-tops
Moon is shining.
Night sky is blue.
Stars are great drops
Of golden dew.

Down the street
A band is playing.

I love you.

Come,
Let us roam the night together
Singing.

—Harlem Night Song

CHAPTER FOUR

THE SOVIET JOURNEY:
ADVENTURE AND ANGUISH

I ever had.
We gonna pal around together from now on . . .
—Langston Hughes

This hymn of praise to the young Soviet state sounds almost unbearably naive in light of what we know today about the toll the
revolution exacted in human lives, but the poem accurately represents my grandparents' frame of mind when they sailed into Leningrad on the German ship *Deutschland*. The ship, which left New York
Harbor four weeks earlier, arrived at the birthplace of the revolution
on November 7, 1931—the fourteenth anniversary of the Bolshevik
seizure of power. Trying to figure out what people were thinking
long ago is a risky business, but I am certain of one thing: My grandparents could never have imagined that in less than sixty years the
inhabitants of revolutionary Leningrad would vote to return their city
to its Tsarist name of St. Petersburg.

The sixteen Americans on board the *Deutschland* were embarking
on an adventure in what was, for everyone except my grandfather, an
unknown land. (The fate of this ship, by the way, took as many

unusual twists as the fate of my family during the next sixty years. In 1945, Germany handed over the *Deutschland* as part of its war reparation to the Soviet Union; a few years ago, still wheezing along in the service of my country's equally feeble economy, the vessel caught fire and sank in the Black Sea.)

On that 1931 transatlantic voyage, my grandmother brought along only two important personal possessions: a Singer sewing machine and a Smith-Corona typewriter. The typewriter is now my mother's most cherished memento, because it is the only remaining object that actually belonged to my grandmother.

I once asked my grandmother why she brought so little with her—she might have crammed her trunk with every imaginable possession, given the poverty that awaited her at her Soviet destination—and she explained that she traveled light precisely because she was bound for a poor country. She said she had no desire to flaunt the kind of material well-being enjoyed by most Americans, even during the Depression, in comparison to most Soviet citizens.

The men who sailed into Leningrad with my grandparents were a varied lot. (Some had brought along their American wives, while others would marry Russian women. My grandmother was the only white woman in the group.) George Tynes, my grandfather's closest friend in the group (and the first to volunteer to go), was a football star and graduate of Wilberforce University in Ohio. In Uzbekistan, Tynes began breeding Peking ducks and eventually became an award-winning, nationally recognized expert on water fowl. (The Soviet economic system never managed to find a way to get Tynes's fine ducks from the collective farms where they were raised to ordinary city markets and the tables of hungry Russian consumers. But his birds did turn up in the best Moscow restaurants.) John Sutton, a Tuskegee graduate, was personally recommended by his former teacher, George Washington Carver. The son of a junior high school principal from San Antonio, Texas, he was the oldest of fifteen children, all of whom graduated from college. His youngest brother is Percy Sutton, who grew up to become the borough president of Manhattan and now owns the famed Apollo Theatre.

Also on board the *Deutschland* was Joseph Roane, a specialist in cotton cultivation born, fortuitously, in the tiny town of Kremlin, Virginia. A graduate of Virginia Normal College (now Virginia State University), the twenty-six-year-old Roane was newly married and regarded the trip as one long, grand honeymoon.

My grandfather was probably the only card-carrying Communist (to use the description literally, rather than in the pejorative sense popularized during the McCarthy era) in the group. A few of the men certainly sympathized with Marxism (what they knew of it), while others had no particular interest in communism and no knowledge whatsoever about the Soviet Union.

These men agreed to go to the Soviet Union, and signed work contracts with the Soviet government, because they needed jobs. In 1931, when my grandfather was doing his recruiting, America offered even gloomier prospects for blacks than for whites. How could a college-educated black man find a job commensurate with his training when millions of educated white men were out of work too?

The Soviets were offering good jobs and good pay by anyone's standards. The agricultural specialists would earn the equivalent of several hundred dollars a month, a fortune by Depression-era standards. In the Soviet Union, their money could be used in special stores offering foreign customers a wide variety of goods unavailable to ordinary citizens. The Americans would also enjoy a month's free vacation, in Crimean resorts reserved for foreigners and the Soviet Party elite.

In spite of the obvious economic incentives, it would have been difficult to put together this group without the assistance of George Washington Carver. On December 12, 1930, my grandfather wrote to Carver in Tuskegee and asked for his help in organizing a group of "Negro specialists" to assist the Soviet Union in developing a cotton industry. The letter noted that during the 1920s, "50 of America's largest industrial concerns have sent 2000 of their representatives to Soviet Russia to help develop the Russian industry. Yet so far we have not on record any Negro specialists in Russia." On January 24, 1931, Carver responded and said he would seek out twenty-five to thirty experts in cotton breeding and production.

My mother and I knew about Carver's role in the project—my

grandmother typed Oliver's letters on her Smith-Corona—but we had never seen the actual correspondence until we came to America. When she learned the originals could be found among Carver's papers in the Tuskegee archives, Mama made a special trip south to see the documents. Unexpected tears came to her eyes as she read the old, yellowing letters, with the initials "B. B." in the lower left corner to show that Bertha Bialek typed them. As a historian unable to travel outside the Soviet Union for so many years, my mother never expected to see any documentation concerning the dream that brought her parents to the Soviet Union. I understand her emotions very well; I too experience a combination of excitement and sadness whenever I uncover another piece of the family puzzle. What could be more exciting than the discovery of your heritage? And what could be sadder than the knowledge that much of your family history is lost forever because, for so long, your country discouraged international travel and the free exchange of information?

Carver was exactly the right person for my grandfather to consult. Of course, he possessed an eminent reputation among educated blacks, those W. E. B. Du Bois called "the talented tenth." As a respected educator uninvolved with left-wing politics, Carver could open doors that might have been slammed in the face of Oliver Golden, Communist organizer. And Carver did help, not because he had any special interest in the future of the Soviet Union, but because he cared about finding jobs for educated young black men in their chosen fields.

The Carver-Golden correspondence★ shows a shrewd old man, intrigued by the prospect of good jobs and pay for former students, intent on helping while simultaneously sidestepping any political agenda. The Soviet government wanted Carver to make an all-expenses-paid tour of the country to demonstrate his agricultural research findings. In a letter dated April 15, 1931, my grandfather says it

★Eight letters survive among Carver's papers in the Tuskegee archives.

is "absolutely necessary" for Carver to accompany the group to the Soviet Union. "Tuskegee is nationally and somewhat internationally known," he argues, "but your going to the U.S.S.R. and the success of these men [agricultural specialists] will give Tuskegee an international character." Then my grandfather flatly declares, "You owe it [a trip to Russia] to your race." He tells his old teacher that Russia is the only country in the world to provide equal opportunity for all races.

But Carver adroitly avoided making a direct response. Pleading ill health, he told my grandfather his doctor had prescribed complete rest. A long journey would be impossible. (Carver was then seventy and in poor health, but he lived another twelve years.) Clearly, Carver did not number a trip to the Soviet Union among the debts he owed his race. He must have known that a widely publicized official visit would be a propaganda coup for the Soviets (however much they really did need his professional expertise). At that time, few black educators would have been willing to identify themselves with a Communist-led venture. Although the Party made serious attempts to gain support among working-class blacks, these efforts succeeded only with a small group of intellectuals and artists. Most blacks found communism a bewildering, alien ideology that did not address itself to their plight as second-class citizens in their own country. Administrators of Negro colleges certainly had nothing to gain, and much to lose, by identifying with a political movement that had already aroused fear and loathing among native white Americans.

Still, Carver did make every effort to help my grandfather by recommending and writing to outstanding former students about the Soviet project. For several of the men sailing on the *Deutschland,* the Soviet offer meant their first, and only, chance to work as professionals rather than waiters.

For my grandfather, racial pride played a critical role in his desire to organize a black agricultural mission to the Soviets. He wanted the Soviets to see blacks as givers and contributors, not only as oppressed people in need of liberation from afar. During the twenties, thousands of progressive Americans and Europeans, skilled in every field from construction to food canning, responded to Lenin's call for foreign assistance to the world's first Communist state. Most (though not all) of these skilled foreigners were white. My grandmother always told me that my grandfather was particularly excited by the prospect of working with non-whites in the former colonies of the Tsarist empire. "It meant something special to him for a black to help other people of color," she said. "It would mean more to an Uzbek, he thought, to see an educated, skilled black American than to see only white specialists. It would show what was possible when people pulled themselves out of oppression."

I've occasionally heard patronizing suggestions about the propaganda value of these black American agronomists. There's no doubt that certain Party hacks did want to display blacks as propaganda trophies, but any well-informed Soviet agricultural official certainly understood how well-trained these men were by any standard and how rare their skills would be in a primitive agricultural economy. The Soviets needed cotton breeders and irrigation experts, of whatever color, as badly as they needed engineers and auto workers in other parts of the country. That's why they were willing to pay foreigners in precious hard currency. Propaganda was just a bonus.

Few voyagers on the *Deutschland* had any idea what to expect in Uzbekistan; most of them adopted the practical attitude that any job, anywhere, was better than no job at home.

"I hardly knew where the Soviet Union was when Golden came to my college to speak," is the recollection of eighty-six-year-old Joseph Roane, the only surviving member of the original group. "No one called me a Communist for going, because no one in my circle knew exactly what a Communist was. I didn't either. I signed on with Golden for two reasons. In the first place, Amtorg★ was offering better pay for a month than a lot of people would make in a year in the Depression. Secondly, I was young and I wanted to see the world. I thought this might be the only chance I'd ever get."

Roane had tracked me down to tell his tale after an article about

---

★The official Soviet agency hiring foreign workers and managing foreign trade.

me appeared in a Washington newspaper. When I interviewed Roane at his home, I also met his son, the first child born on Soviet soil to a member of the American group. "What's your name?" I asked innocently. "Joseph Stalin Roane," he replied, obviously expecting an amazed (or shocked) reaction. He got it. A friend who accompanied me said the pupils of my eyes widened visibly (and that's not easy for anyone to see when your eyes are as dark as mine). Roane and his wife decided to name their son Joseph when he was born in 1932. Their Soviet interpreter (the Roanes' Russian was still shaky) added the middle name "Stalin" on the birth certificate. The younger Roane considers this a good joke on every new, unsuspecting acquaintance. (For a Russian of my generation, the joke is, to say the least, unsettling.)

The four-week voyage on the *Deutschland,* with a stop in London, was a vacation for the young men and women. Many of them were enjoying their first taste of life outside the rural South. They passed time on the ship with convivial games of shuffleboard and cards, and with dancing. They toasted one another with vodka, an unfamiliar drink lavishly provided by their Soviet hosts. They also took Russian lessons—the Soviets had supplied a tutor—so they would at least be able to ask for directions and say "please" *(pozhaluysta),* "thank you" *(spasibo),* and "bottoms–up" *(do dna)* when they arrived.

But Joe Roane says he and his wife didn't learn much Russian on shipboard, because the trip was one long party:

> We had just gotten married, so this was our honeymoon. The first stop was London, where we ran around looking at all of those places from storybooks and buying long underwear, because we were told it was very cold in Russia and you couldn't get it there. The wonderful thing about London was that we could do whatever we wanted, go wherever we wanted. There was no back of the bus, you could just get on and ride. For those of us who'd spent our lives in the South, always taking a back seat, this was really something. I was already glad I'd come, and I hadn't even gotten to Russia. I'd never in my life, you see, been able to walk

into a restaurant and know I would be served food, and treated like any other customer.

Getting on a train and sitting anywhere, walking into a hotel through the front door, ordering food in a restaurant (when there was food) and being routinely served: All of these experiences would continue in the Soviet Union and would deeply affect each member of the group, including those who had scant interest in communism. Several of the men, including Roane and Sutton, returned to the United States in 1937 when the Soviets, at the beginning of the purges, offered them a choice of giving up their American citizenship or getting out of the U.S.S.R. Unwilling to relinquish their U.S. citizenship, these men nevertheless regretted a return to segregation.

"In just a few years—you'd be surprised—you could forget what segregation was like," recalls Roane. "When Golden spoke at my college, I didn't believe him when he said there was no segregation in the Soviet Union. Why should I? But it proved to be absolutely true." Roane remembers encountering only one incident of raw racism during his years in the Soviet Union, and white Americans were the instigators. In Moscow, Roane and a friend from the ship entered a hotel barber shop and asked for a haircut. Two white American visitors, who happened to be having their hair cut at the time, said, "What are you niggers doing here? Get out." The Russian barbers didn't understand a word of the argument, but when Roane explained what had happened, they threw the whites out of the shop with lather still on their faces. I offer these reminiscences not to suggest that the Soviet Union was a racial paradise at that time, but to underline the importance, for men as different as Roane and my grandfather, of having escaped American-style segregation.

Happy as they were to leave segregation behind, the Americans realized they were also leaving modern civilization behind as they traveled more than 1,900 miles by train from European Russia to Tashkent, a six-day journey. In his recruiting lectures, my grandfather stressed the primitive nature of the economy in Soviet central Asia, but his listeners had envisioned something along the lines of a small American town. What they found instead in Uzbekistan was a rural, tribal, traditional Muslim society struggling to emerge from near-feudalism.

On his second day in Tashkent, Joe Roane pondered whether he had wandered onto a movie set when he got lost in a snowstorm and was suddenly confronted by an Uzbek riding a camel and brandishing a saber. This romantic apparition spoke neither Russian nor English, and Roane spoke no Uzbek, so he was unable to ask for directions back to his hotel. On the streets of Tashkent in 1931, a driver in a car was a more remarkable sight than a driver on a camel.

At the Tashkent station, the group was met by drivers in *arby,* traditional open-air Uzbek carts pulled by donkeys. The absence of cars surprised Roane, though my grandfather had warned his recruits that all modern conveniences, from automobiles to telephones, were in short supply. One thing struck Roane forcefully on the ride from the station to the hotel: Every house was built extremely low to the ground. He asked the interpreter for an explanation. *"Tovarishch* Roane," he replied, "don't you know that we have frequent earthquakes here?" That small fact, Roane told me dryly, was something Oliver Golden failed to mention in his orientation lectures. (My grandfather, who had never been in Tashkent himself, didn't know that Uzbekistan was earthquake country.)

Soon after the group's arrival in Tashkent, officials dispatched most of the Americans to a small agricultural station in the Uzbek village of Yangiyul, about forty miles away. In the countryside, many aspects of life had not changed for centuries. Polygamy was common and a great many women wore veils over their faces (though both practices had been abolished by Soviet law). My grandmother took on the task of persuading women to shed their veils; she encountered resistance from older women and men of all ages, but young women liked the novelty of the sun and wind on their bare faces. The Soviet government's attempts to improve the status of women, through compulsory elementary schooling for both sexes and laws prohibiting the sale of girls into marriage, generated fierce opposition among religious and tribal leaders. Gradually, however, the status of women did change for the better—and I consider this a genuine achievement of the revolution. Even before *glasnost,* I would rather have been born a woman in Uzbekistan than, say, in Pakistan or Afghanistan. If that places me in opposition to so-called sacred ethnic and religious traditions, so be it. Freedom of religion is being restored throughout the former Soviet Union now—and that's wonderful—but I don't want priests, rabbis, or imams to write laws controlling my destiny. The men who framed the American constitution had the right idea: freedom of religion on the one hand, strict separation of church and state on the other.

Unlike traditional practices regarding women, formal prerevolutionary barriers separating Asians from Europeans collapsed immediately. Langston Hughes, who visited Yangiyul in 1932 and spent Christmas in my grandparents' home, noticed fading signs on Tashkent streetcars and trains designating sections for "Europeans" and "non-Europeans." No one paid any attention to the old signs by the time the Americans arrived, though, in a typical display of Soviet inefficiency, no one had bothered to take them down. For black Americans, the contrast with the American South was as striking as in London, Leningrad, and Moscow, even more striking, perhaps, because Uzbekistan had a large colored population.

Hughes described his reaction in an autobiography containing a lengthy account of his picaresque journey through the Asian republics. "In Tashkent, whenever I got on a street car and saw the old partitions, I could not help but remember Atlanta, Birmingham and Houston in my own country where, when I got on a tram or a bus or a train, I had to sit in the COLORED section. The natives of Tashkent, about my own shade of brown, once had to sit in a COLORED section, too. But not any more. So I was happy for them."*

Hughes traveled by train through central Asia with his friend, the journalist Arthur Koestler. Koestler attended several early political trials (still open to observers at the time). As a result, he began to adopt a far more critical attitude toward the Soviet state.†

In Hughes's view, his color made him more tolerant of everything

---

I Wonder As I Wander (New York: Thunder's Mouth Press, 1956), p. 172.
†Hughes believes Koestler began gathering material for *Darkness at Noon* during this period.

Soviet—from filth on the trains to political trials—than he would otherwise have been. Of course, a great many whites, both Soviets and foreigners, also excused government abuses of power "for the good of the cause" (the title of a famous—in my country, at least—short story by Alexander Solzhenitsyn).

Hughes noted that "in the old days, Koestler and I could not have stayed together in the same hotels in Turkestan, nor ridden in the same railway compartments. . . . Koestler perhaps could not understand why I did not complain as often as he did, nor why I was not quite so impatient with the maid who refused to set our bags over the doorsill in Bukhara. . . ."★

Hughes's 1932 visit to Yangiyul was a high point for my grandfather, who greatly admired his poetry. In this remote outpost of the new Soviet empire, my grandparents missed the cultural and intellectual life of New York. There were no libraries or movie theaters within driving distance (if anyone could manage to scare up a working car), no bookstores, no Chinese restaurants, no live jazz. The nearest real city, Tashkent, was a two-hour ride away on the abysmal Soviet trains of the day. Miserable travelers had to stand in line for days to buy train tickets. (This crazily disordered system of selling plane and train tickets prevails in my country to this day. It's still impossible to pay for a ticket by mail or reserve one by phone. Now people camp outside airline offices or in airports.)

My grandfather and Joe Roane met Hughes as he was sinking into the ankle-deep slush and mud alongside the train track. Because Yangiyul was so small, the trains didn't actually stop there; travelers were simply advised to jump and take their chances. At first, Hughes—not a "good sport" or a gracious guest—was so infuriated by this typical Soviet travel experience that he refused to join in the Christmas merry-making planned by the Americans. By Christmas Day, though, he had thawed out and thoroughly enjoyed the dinner of

---

★*I Wonder As I Wander,* p. 211.

pumpkin pie and as many traditional dishes as the wives could manage to concoct out of Soviet ingredients. When he woke up, he had found a stocking filled with halvah, and cashew and pistachio nuts hanging over his bed. Gazing out the window, he saw dark-skinned Uzbeks, clad in traditional long robes, doing their chores outside the stables. He thought they looked "just like Bible characters on Sunday-school cards" and "imagined in their stable a Manger and a Child."

The food and physical comforts of my grandparents' apartment attested to the fact that contract workers from abroad were not expected to live like ordinary Soviet citizens. The Americans had a large house, divided into separate apartments. They were able to supplement food supplies with purchases from special, well-stocked stores open only to foreigners. This was important, because forced collectivization of the land created famines in Uzbekistan and many other areas during the thirties.

Elite stores have been a feature of life under every Soviet government. Today, when foreigners are no more willing to live like ordinary Russians than they would have been in my grandfather's day, the *valuta* shops take American Express, Visa, and MasterCard. Elite travel, too, has always been a feature of Soviet life. Back in the thirties, my grandparents rarely had to endure the horrors of Soviet-style train travel. They were encouraged to jump to the head of lines and were able to buy tickets even when there were none for sale to Soviet passengers. Again, the system of "foreigners first" is exactly the same for plane tickets today.

These kinds of privileges, taken for granted by both foreigners and Party leaders (who had their own private stores), were obviously at odds with my grandparents' commitment to egalitarianism. They received fewer privileges when they took Soviet citizenship in 1936, but some distinctions remained. No ordinary Soviet, for instance, could hope to vacation at the best resorts in the Crimea. I don't know, can't know, how my grandfather rationalized the contradictions—any more than I know how his views would have changed if he had lived beyond the Stalin era.

I do know that my grandmother, who remained a True Believer

until the end of her life, was extremely uncomfortable whenever she was exposed to any special privileges enjoyed by the Soviet elite. When I was about four, my mother's friend Svetlana Alliluyeva offered us the use of her dacha at Zhukhovka, a luxurious resort for the Communist elite. Svetlana and my mother had been friends since they were in their early twenties. (This relationship would cause my mother serious problems with the authorities after Svetlana's defection in 1966). The dacha, in a wooded area reserved for high Party officials and their relatives, was part of Svetlana's legacy as Joseph Stalin's daughter. My mother packed me off with my grandmother to spend several summer weeks there, but my grandmother disliked the luxurious house, surrounded by KGB guards. She told my mother she wanted to return to Moscow, something I doubt she would ever have done (since it meant depriving her baby of a vacation in the country) if she hadn't been deeply disturbed by the evidence of both privilege and police control.

On a cotton-growing collective in the thirties, my grandmother had no idea that she was helping to build a society in which Party bigshots, like the old capitalist robber barons she detested, would bequeath lives of luxury to their descendants.

In Yangiyul, the Americans strove to develop a new breed of cotton, one capable of maturing in the relatively short Uzbek growing season. For nearly three years, the men painstakingly crossed Uzbek seeds with American seeds, which they brought over on the *Deutschland*. The experiments finally succeeded; by 1935, Uzbek collective farms were producing a new strain of cotton that took 25 percent less time to mature than cotton in the American South.

Roane vividly recalls the manual labor involved in every phase of the cotton experiments. "It was backbreaking for the people who actually tilled the soil," he says. "The Uzbeks were tireless workers. They could almost make water run uphill. I'd seen something like this in the South, but irrigation didn't pose the same kind of problem back home; we always had lots of rivers near the best growing land."

The Americans envisioned cotton as only one crop among many, but Soviet authorities turned Uzbekistan into a one-crop republic. They ignored the Americans' advice about rotating crops to avoid wearing out the land. The irrigation channels Roane remembers so vividly are now loaded with pesticides that have polluted the Uzbek soil. This environmental disaster, which began with the introduction of stronger pesticides in the fifties, became a matter of public record only when scientists started to publish honest research findings during the *glasnost* era. Today, health officials repeatedly warn against eating fruit grown in Uzbekistan. (Although King Cotton dominated the economy, fruit was an important minor export to the rest of the Soviet Union.) Uzbeks themselves suffer from an unusually high rate of birth defects. Trained in classical methods of plant breeding and careful soil management techniques, my grandfather's generation of agronomists would be horrified by the misuse of their pioneering work in the Uzbek cotton fields.

Stalinist politics—what else?—ruined the Uzbek agricultural economy. By the late thirties, when most of the black Americans had already returned to the United States, Trofim D. Lysenko had become Stalin's favorite biologist. Lysenko insisted that Soviet scientists could create a new, genetically distinct Soviet man by altering his environment, and he extended his crackpot Lamarckian theories to plant and animal breeding. Courageous Soviet scientists and agronomists, who spoke up and defended Mendelian genetics, wound up in the gulag. Pliant Party functionaries, who knew nothing about agriculture, replaced the real scientists. Had the Lysenkoists controlled Soviet agriculture in 1931, men like Joe Roane wouldn't have been free to conduct their cotton breeding experiments as they saw fit.

In 1934, the Americans' first three-year work contract expired. Everyone signed up for another three-year stint and received a raise; many of the men knew that needy relatives in America were depending on them to send home part of their salaries (which the Soviets allowed the Americans to do). Although Soviet officials were pressuring the Americans to abandon their U.S. citizenship, few were willing.

The establishment of U.S.-USSR diplomatic relations after Roosevelt's election made the Americans feel more secure about their legal status vis à vis the Soviets and their own government. They traveled to the newly established American embassy in Moscow to have their American papers renewed. Only Joe Roane had a problem, when a junior-grade diplomat refused to believe there was a town in Virginia named "Kremlin." Looking out the diplomat's window overlooking the Russian Kremlin, Roane tried without success to convince the bureaucrat that he had in fact been born in an American Kremlin. At least two cables to the State Department in Washington were required to back up Roane's story. The young diplomat, miffed at being proved wrong, broke off the point of his fountain pen while signing Roane's papers.

In 1934, the group broke up when many were sent from Yangiyul to other areas in need of their skills. Roane knew something about food preservation because his father once owned a small canning factory. He was sent to the Caucasus to help the Georgians operate a tomato-canning plant. George Tynes went off to breed poultry on numerous farms. John Sutton continued working on a process for making a new kind of rope. By this time, both Sutton and Tynes had married Russian women.

My grandfather was sent from Yangiyul to the Institute of Irrigation and Mechanization in Tashkent, where he taught until his death in 1940. My grandmother was happy to move to the city, not least because of its better medical facilities, because by then she was pregnant.

On July 19, 1934, my mother, Lily, was born in Tashkent. This was the decisive event in my family's history; without a child, my grandparents would have returned to the United States in 1937. In spite of their hatred of racism at home, they considered themselves Americans. This was no less true of my grandmother, even though she had only lived in the United States for eleven years: Consider the fact that English remained her preferred language for the next fifty years of her life in the Soviet Union.

My grandparents decided to become Soviet citizens because they did not want to raise a racially mixed child in America. In the Soviet

Union, regardless of the strong prejudices Russians might hold toward various ethnic minorities, and those minorities toward one another (and toward Russians themselves), there would at least be no legal discrimination against their daughter. It would be presumptuous of me, with the advantage of hindsight, to pass judgment on their decision. I find what they did completely understandable in view of hostile American attitudes (black and white) toward interracial marriage in their generation. What they could not have realized at the time was how much discrimination my mother would encounter not because she was dark-skinned but because she was the child of foreigners. In 1935, the worst of Stalin's terror was still in the future. The suspicion and paranoia that would soon be directed toward all foreigners was something my grandparents could not have predicted.

Because her father died when she was just six, my mother has only fragmentary memories of him and of life as a family. They lived in a four-story apartment house called the House of Foreign Specialists, inhabited by a few foreigners and many highly placed Party functionaries. The apartments were luxurious by Soviet standards, even without hot water. To have cold running water as well as separate kitchens and bathrooms was luxury enough.

Throughout my mother's childhood, her family shared its apartment with a Ukranian woman, Mama's "Aunt Nadya." Since both of my grandparents spoke Russian poorly, they invited Aunt Nadya to live with them because they wanted their daughter to have the daily experience of talking with a native Russian-speaker. Aunt Nadya, of course, spoke Russian with a Ukranian accent, but that was a lot closer to good Russian than my grandfather's Mississippi accent. And it's no wonder that my grandmother didn't feel totally comfortable speaking Russian, since it was her fourth language, after Yiddish, Polish, and English. Because my grandparents spoke English to each other, it was Mama's "cradle language." Unlike me, she has never had any formal instruction in English—yet she speaks it extremely well.

Aunt Nadya had been an actress in Kiev, but my mother never found out exactly why she ended up in Tashkent. It could have been anything: Her family might have been fleeing civil war after the revolution or the subsequent purges of Ukranian nationalists or the brutal dekulakization campaign that uprooted millions of peasants from their lands. Who knows? People without pasts—or with pasts they wished to forget—were wandering the length and breadth of the country in those days. Our family became Aunt Nadya's family.

My mother has only a few clear, precious memories of her father. She remembers Sunday dinners, which he prepared with ingredients bought at the huge, open-air Alaisky Bazaar in Tashkent. This market is famous throughout the Soviet Union; foreign tourists who come to Tashkent always ask to stop at the Alaisky. One stall after another bursts with plump fruits—grapes, strawberries, melons, figs of a kind seen almost nowhere else in the country. Uzbek farmers used to load up suitcases with fruit grown on tiny private plots (these were permitted on most collective farms), fly to the cold cities of European Russia, and sell their produce at an enormous profit. These days, though, the pollution warnings have hurt out-of-town business.

Every Sunday morning, my grandfather set out for the bazaar in search of the best fresh food in town. He would return triumphantly in a taxi loaded with watermelons, lamb, grapes, tomatoes, rice, nuts, baklava, and anything else that struck his fancy.

Although my mother was still very young, the details of happiness impressed themselves upon her memory. "As soon as Papa came home," she recalls, "he would get to work in the kitchen. Women absolutely weren't allowed. Sunday was my mama's day to be treated like a queen. As soon as the meal was ready, he would yell, 'Baby, dinner's on,' pick up Mama, and carry her to the table in his arms. Then he would come for me, scoop me up and say, 'Now you too, Baby.' This is one of my earliest memories. It seemed that all the love and security in the world was in those arms."

"Baby" is a nickname that followed my mother into adulthood and eventually stuck to me too. It comes not only from my grandfather's endearments but also from Paul Robeson, who picked my mother up during a concert in the Soviet Union during the thirties, cradled her in his arms and sang, "sleep, baby, sleep" to her in English. Everyone at the concert remembered Robeson, an idol to Soviets of all ethnic groups, crooning to the toddler in his low, rich tones. And all of my grandparents' friends called my mother "Baby" until the end of their lives. Since I have been a reporter for *Moscow News,* many people have sought me out and introduced themselves as friends of my grandparents. If they call my mother "Baby," I know they're telling the truth.

So my mother's earliest memories are all good ones—of parents who loved each other, of a house filled with Soviet friends and visitors from their old life in America, of picnics in the countryside around Tashkent, of her much-loved Aunt Nadya teaching her Ukranian songs.

But life outside the family circle was already beginning to change for the worse, and my mother was able to sense the difference as she moved out of babyhood toward the age of reason. She noticed, first of all, that her home, which had always been open to friends, was often empty. "They say a very young child can't remember such things, that I must have been told later," my mother says, "but I absolutely don't agree. A child, however small, can feel a change in atmosphere. I know that when I was very young, there were always people in our house. Then I remember wondering where all the people had gone, why the house was so empty, why Papa smiled so rarely when he used to be so cheerful. The answer—this I did learn later, of course—was that a lot of friends were being arrested and others were afraid to come to us because of our American background."

In the summer of 1937, my grandparents took a vacation in the Caucasus with Robeson, his wife, Eslanda, and their son, ten-year-old Paul, Jr. Robeson, who was deeply sympathetic to Soviet communism even though he never joined the Party,[*] had seen to it that his son spent several years living in Moscow attending Russian-language schools. During the month the Robeson and Golden families spent at a spa in Kislovodsk, my mother overheard her father and

---

[*]See Martin Bauml Duberman, *Paul Robeson: A Biography,* (New York: Knopf), 1988.

Paul, Sr., in heated political discussions. She had no idea what they were talking about. Years later, she learned that Robeson could not locate many of his old friends on this 1937 trip. They were already dead or in labor camps, cut down at the beginning of the purges. This was the first but far from the last time Robeson would come to the Soviet Union to find that old friends had vanished. The only thing Mama understood as a child was that both her father and Robeson were deeply upset.

After this unsettling vacation in an elite rest home (named for Felix Dzerzhinsky, the founder of the Soviet secret police), Mama and my grandparents returned home to a shocking sight at the House of Foreign Specialists. When they climbed to the second floor and arrived at their apartment, they saw that the door next to theirs was sealed with strips of paper. Those paper strips were a dreaded sight throughout the country during the Stalin years. They meant one thing only—that the apartment's occupants had been arrested and everyone else was forbidden to enter the room.

And that wasn't all. While the family was away in Kislovodsk, the police had also come in a dark unmarked car for my grandfather himself. The family learned this from neighbors; my grandmother didn't tell my mother until she was an adult.

While living in Tashkent, my father also traveled widely, delivering lectures in remote areas of Uzbekistan on the plight of black Americans in general and the case of the Scottsboro boys in particular.* The police issued him a pistol to protect himself from bandits, who lurked in these regions and preyed on outsiders. When my father heard that the unmarked car had come for him in the middle of the

---

*The Scottsboro boys were sentenced to death by an Alabama jury in 1931 after being falsely accused of raping two white women. Their case is well-known in the Soviet Union. I have been interested to learn in the United States that many American historians also give the Communists a fair share of credit for keeping the men alive through unrelenting international publicity. After a series of appeals, the last man was freed in 1953.

night, he took the pistol to the office of the NKVD (the 1930s equivalent of the KGB).

"You came for me," he said. "Arrest me if you think I'm an enemy of the people." The genial police official replied, "Comrade Golden, don't get so upset. We've already fulfilled the plan of arrests for your area. Go home and work in peace."

This story sounds strange, perhaps apocryphal, to anyone who didn't grow up in the Soviet Union. But it's a fact of Soviet history that arrests were made according to plan—that numbers arrested, not merely individuals, counted in the overall scheme of things. And some people did manage to avoid arrest simply because they didn't happen to be home when the police arrived at the door. Still others, like Nadezhda Mandelstam, widow of the great poet Osip Mandelstam, moved around in a deliberate strategy to stay one step ahead of the police. In her memoir *Vospominaniye* (published in English under the title *Hope against Hope*), Madame Mandelstam describes a life spent moving from town to town after her husband (who had written a derisive poem about Stalin) died in a camp. She considered it a sacred duty to stay alive and preserve his poetry, and she managed to do this. From such memoirs, it's easy for me to believe in my grandfather's stroke of luck.

It's also possible, given the fact that the Tashkent NKVD probably had fulfilled its plan for that month, that some official thought better of arresting a well-connected black American Communist. Although many foreigners (including longtime Party members who had fled Nazi Germany) were arrested in 1937 and 1938, no blacks who came on the *Deutschland* were sent to prison.

What did happen, though, was that every non–Soviet citizen in the group was ordered to leave the country, sometimes on forty-eight hours notice, unless he was willing to give up his American citizenship on the spot. Among those who returned were Roane, with his wife, Sadie, and their son, Joseph Stalin, and John Sutton. Sutton, like many of those forced to leave abruptly, left behind a Russian wife and son. He was trying to bring his son to America in 1939 when the Germans invaded the Soviet Union. All contact was lost for thirty years and John Sutton died. But then, in another twist of fate, John's brother, Percy Sutton, discovered the whereabouts of his nephew in the 1970s.

When I came to New York in 1990, Percy Sutton's name was in my notebook under the heading of "possible American relatives" of the *Deutschland* group. I had no idea who he was when I looked up his number in the Manhattan phonebook. I don't know what I expected, but the Soviet part of me is still surprised when I meet an extremely successful black American. For my grandparents, I'm sure the idea of a black capitalist was a contradiction in terms. In any event, Percy Sutton owns several radio stations and a record company in addition to the Apollo Theatre. As Manhattan Borough President he learned the whereabouts of his long-lost nephew.

As Sutton tells the story, he was sitting in the United Nations dining room when he was approached by a Nigerian diplomat, recently returned from Moscow. "Your son is looking for you," the diplomat told Sutton, who immediately realized that the man looking for him in Moscow must be his nephew. Percy used his political connections to track down Juan, by then a man in his forties. Juan (his father, who spoke perfect Spanish, gave him the Latino form of John) has now visited his American relatives many times, but his story in Russia was essentially a sad one. Juan's mother died during the war, and he wound up in a state orphanage. He suffered from epilepsy and was shuttled among several different foster families, never knowing that his American father was trying to find him.

There were other tragedies among Russian wives and children left behind in 1937. When the women tried to reestablish contact with their husbands in the United States, Soviet authorities told them the men had been arrested upon their return and died in American prisons. This lie sounded perfectly reasonable to Russians who had no other source of information and who had already heard many true stories of American racial injustices from their husbands. After the war, a number of the American men, in turn, tried to locate their wives and children—only to be told by the Soviets that their families were dead. During the Khrushchev years, some of these men returned to the Soviet Union, revisiting the scenes of their youth and looking up friends who had taken Soviet citizenship.

Many of these men or their relatives turned up at our home in Moscow. My mother always told them not to take the word of officials that their families were dead. Keep looking, she advised them, go to the last known address you have, dial the last known phone number. Several unexpected reunions occurred in this fashion; that's how, after more than thirty-five years, the Russian wives learned their husbands had been alive all along. Most of the men, having been told by the Soviets that their Russian wives were dead, had started new families in the United States. The lies these women were told—for no reason other than the Stalinist system's paranoia concerning contacts between foreigners and Soviet citizens—offer yet another example of the absolute indifference to human dignity and ordinary human feeling that characterized the darkest years of my country's history.

As young as she was, my mother sensed a change in her father between 1937 and his death three years later. She noticed that he stopped telling jokes. He also gave up his favorite game of quoits, an old-fashioned amusement in which rope rings were thrown at an upright peg. Oliver Golden died of kidney and heart failure—he told my grandmother his kidneys had never been the same since a a New York policeman kicked him in the back during a demonstration— but my mother firmly believes that her father's ability to resist disease was impaired by the terror around him.

Some of my grandfather's closest Uzbek friends had been among the first arrested. Their names mean nothing to Americans, but to me it's somehow important to remember the individuals who perished. One of them was Faizul Khodzayev, chairman of the Uzbek council of commissars, who was charged with "bourgeois nationalism." Another was the Uzbek Party head Kamil Ikramov, arrested not long after he made a personal phone call to Stalin to question the validity of other arrests. Both were accused of having ties to Nikolai Bukharin, who was of course one of the most prominent figures at the Moscow show trials in 1938.

Because Party members were the first to go in the purges of the late thirties, my grandparents had reason to be grateful that their application to join the Soviet Communist Party was turned down. After they became Soviet citizens, these old American Bolsheviks naturally assumed they would be welcomed into the Party in their new country. Nothing doing, they were told. You may have belonged to the Party in decadent America, but that doesn't make you good enough to belong to our glorious Party here. So much for Communist internationalism. It makes me shudder to imagine that my mother might have wound up in an orphanage for "children of enemies of the people," the official designation for those whose parents disappeared into the frozen waste.

In the general suspicion of foreigners, the contributions of my father and his colleagues to Uzbek agriculture—the fact that "Soviet" cotton was now an American-Uzbek hybrid—were largely erased from official history. My grandfather was an extremely popular man in Tashkent, partly because his friendly, informal relations with his students were such a departure from the rigid relations that generally prevailed in Soviet classrooms. He was also a member of the Tashkent City Soviet. When he died, thousands turned out for his burial in what is known as the "Communist cemetery." His grave disappeared during World War II, when Tashkent was so crowded with refugees that new graves were dug on top of old ones.

In Uzbekistan as elsewhere, *glasnost* brought about a renewal of interest in local culture and history. In 1987, my mother learned that high school and college students in Tashkent were beginning to investigate the contributions of black Americans to agricultural development in the area. Supervised by archeologists, they went digging in the cemetery in hopes of finding the graves of prominent historical figures. Two years ago, a fifteen-year-old high school student found the grave of Oliver Golden. When my black American relatives visited us in Moscow, Mama was able to take them to Tashkent to visit her father's grave. Thanks to my country's reexamination of its history, a piece of our family history was restored to us. But the discovery came too late for my grandmother, who died in 1985. She would have liked the fact that young students, searching for lost parts of their own past, were the ones to rediscover my grandfather's final resting place.

CHAPTER FIVE

NO-NONSENSE WOMEN

We were always an odd couple, my grandmother and I. When she walked me to school, strangers would turn to stare. Why was this short, plump, white *babuska* clutching the hand of a very brown little girl? "Baby," my grandmother would say in the heavily accented English that still came more naturally to her lips than Russian, "Baby, have you finished all of your English homework? English is a piece of bread." I would speak to her in English at home, but on the street I would answer in Russian. I wanted to be like everyone else, a Russian girl speaking Russian with her Russian granny.

In certain ways, both my mother and grandmother were dedicated to the belief that we were indeed like everyone else, with all of the rights and duties (more duties than rights) of every Soviet citizen. "No excuses" was the consistent, powerful message I received throughout childhood from the most important people in my life. Yes, I was black, and, yes, that might occasionally cause me a problem or two with ignorant people. Yes, I was the granddaughter of Americans and the daughter of an African, and that might render me suspect among the large numbers of my countrymen who distrusted all foreigners.

But no excuses, Yelena. I would make a place for myself in Soviet society, just as they had done. And it would be a better place than theirs, because I had them to help me.

Of course, there were two sides to the "no excuses" message. The first was "you *are* like everyone else," and the flip side was "but you are better. You are special. You must work harder, achieve more, show the world what you can do."

Now that I understand much more about American influences on my family, I'm struck by how very un-Russian and un-Soviet the latter half of this message was. From the ambitious passions of Jewish immigrants and the strivings of the black "talented tenth," my grandmother and mother had forged an ethic of individual responsibility very much at odds with Soviet culture. Other people we knew might blame their laziness or their drunkenness or their failures on "the system," but not Oliver Golden's and Bertha Bialek's descendants. We were special. No excuses.

Throughout my childhood, I simply referred to my mother and grandmother as "my parents," because I never felt the three of us were anything other than a complete and normal family. Not that I wouldn't like to have known my father or to have had a father in my life. But the two female powerhouses who determined my destiny made certain I never felt less secure because there was no man in our home. I was raised with a triple dose of the pushiness and protectiveness traditionally associated with black, Jewish, and Russian mamas. These ladies wove their cocoon so cleverly that I never sensed any fragility or marginality to our existence. Our family's position in Soviet society was in fact quite precarious and had been so since my grandfather's death. But my two mamas (at one point I called my grandmother "Mama" and my mother "Baby-Mama," probably because Bertha called us both "baby" in slightly different, instantly recognizable tones) never let me know about all the unsettling turns of their lives until I was old enough to understand and cope with the realities of Soviet society.

As I grew up and heard more about my grandmother's life in Uzbekistan after her husband's death, it became clear to me that she could never have raised my mother during those years if *she* had made any excuses. While Aunt Nadya took care of my mother and the household chores, my grandmother held down several jobs. She taught English at Central Asian State University in Tashkent, gave private lessons at home, and translated articles for the Soviet radio network's English broadcasting service. She also worked as an announcer on broadcasts aimed at India; her low, accented voice so charmed her listeners that many wrote letters begging her to marry them.

At the beginning of World War II, when the Nazis were overrunning the Ukraine and laying siege to Leningrad, my grandmother gave her last $600—she had brought it from America and saved it for an emergency—to help pay for a Soviet tank. Later in the war, she needed that money desperately when my mother fell ill with a severe vitamin deficiency. The doctor told Bertha that her daughter could only be restored to health through a high-fat, high-calorie, high-priced diet. Although the population of Tashkent wasn't starving during the war, butter and meat were distant memories for most civilians. Nearly everything produced in the area around the "bread city" (Tashkent's designation in wartime) was shipped west to feed the Red Army. My grandmother scraped together the money for food by selling her few remaining American possessions: the sewing machine, a small ice-cream maker that had given her great delight, and most of her clothes. (When I was a girl in Moscow, she was still wearing two cotton dresses she bought before leaving New York.) The sewing machine may have saved my mother's young life. It brought my grandmother 200 grams (less than half a pound) of butter, which she fed my mother at a rate of 10 grams a day. If your body is literally starving, such small amounts of fat can make the difference between life and death, not just between health and sickness. By the end of the war, my grandmother had only the faithful Smith-Corona. If she hadn't needed it for work, she would have sold it along with every other reminder of American affluence.

Young Lily studied by candlelight, for there was seldom electricity. She would look up from her homework at the silhouettes of her mother and Aunt Nadya, gesturing and talking about which possessions to keep and which to sell, how to acquire enough food to live until the next payday. Like me, she never felt insecure. "It never occurred to me that Mama wouldn't find a way to keep us going," she says.

Fortunately, there was plenty of translating and teaching for Bertha in a city bursting with refugees as a result of the war. Since Tsarist times, Tashkent had been a magnet for all kinds of refugees and political exiles. In the nineteenth century, nobles who had incurred the Tsar's displeasure, but not enough displeasure to land them in Siberia, were dispatched to warmer exile in Tashkent. Some Jews fled east from programs in the Ukraine. After the revolution, the city attracted a steady stream of refugees, like Aunt Nadya, who were running away from god-knows-what twists of state policy and police terror.

With the war came a new wave of the displaced, including a large component of Jews who had the foresight to abandon their homes ahead of the advancing Nazi troops. When the government began evacuating Leningrad after the "starvation winter" of 1941–42, many of that city's most distinguished artists and intellectuals, among them the great poet Anna Akhmatova, took up residence in Tashkent until the end of the war. This contingent also included many musicians and professors, and Tashkent's musical life became that of a capital rather than a provincial town.

My mother had displayed musical aptitude from earliest childhood. Now she had the chance to study under teachers she never would have met if Tashkent had not become a cultural center during the war. She eventually became an accomplished classical pianist and singer. (She wanted to learn more about jazz improvisation, but that was not considered a respectable academic subject.)

At age sixteen in 1950, my mother won a piano competition, playing Bach preludes. She insists that this competition was the only occasion in her girlhood when she gave any thought to the effect of her color on other people's judgments of her. The judges were all well-known professors from the Moscow conservatory, and for some reason my mother thought they might have awarded her first prize because she was black—not because she was the best musician.

No matter: Young Lily marched up to the judges and asked them point-blank whether they awarded her first prize because of her color. They seemed dumbfounded by the question and assured her she had been the best pianist in the competition. They said she should seriously consider continuing her studies in Moscow, where she would be exposed to better teachers and a broader musical life. My mother was relieved. She'd been brought up with her parents' conviction that all blacks needed was an equal chance in society, and she didn't want any special favors—no excuses.

This unusual incident notwithstanding, it's clear to me that my mother did not think about her race, at least when she was young, as often as I did. Of course, her color didn't stand out in Uzbekistan as sharply as mine did in Moscow. Although my mother is unmistakably a black woman (by Russian as well as American standards), her complexion is in fact lighter than that of many Uzbeks. Tashkent, as a focal point for refugees from many areas, has always been ethnically diverse. Moscow, in contrast, has a strongly Slavic flavor (and this was even more true when I was young than it is today). In a city of blue-eyed blonds, I have always attracted stares. In a city of many colors, my mother was just another shade of brown.

When she was thirteen, Mama began taking tennis lessons from a local coach. His eyes lit up at the sight of her long arms and tall, wiry frame. (She was well on her way to her adult height of five feet eight inches.) Height, not color, was her most distinctive feature as a teenager. "From the time I was a baby," Mama remembers, "Russians and Uzbeks were always oohing and aahing because I was the tallest little girl they had ever seen. I was proud of my height because papa was tall, but after he died I felt like a Gulliver. The tennis coach, who was a very short fellow, saw me as a freak of nature too, but a very good freak, someone who could cover the court with ease."

Mama made rapid progress and was soon chosen to travel with the Uzbek tennis team. In the early years after the war, with the train system in ruins, ordinary citizens couldn't travel for pleasure. Tennis gave Mama her first chance to see what was happening in the rest of the country. In 1947, when she took part in her first national competition, she understood for the first time how much European Russia had suffered during the war. Stopping at Saratov on the Volga River, the ship was surrounded by starving beggars. "They grabbed at us with shaking hands," Mama says, "asking for bread, a piece of fruit, anything. And I realized how lucky we had been to escape this devastation in Tashkent."

During her travels, Mama made tennis friendships that would last a lifetime. She was the first black girl to compete in Soviet tennis matches, and her color made her a celebrity. In her tennis life, my mother was living out one of her father's thwarted dreams; he had always wanted to play the game, but it was a white, upper-class sport in the America of his youth. That's probably why my mother saw to it that I received tennis instruction in Moscow on a much higher level than the coaching available to her in Uzbekistan. But tennis was not my dream. I succeeded in competition up to a point, but I never had the drive that makes a true champion. Mama gave up without a fight when I entered college and decided that going on with tennis was incompatible with seriously applying myself to my studies in journalism.

My grandmother was only thirty-five at the time of my grandfather's death, and she might easily have married again. My mother remembers many a suitor who tried to woo Bertha through her daughter. One of them was a general who would have been able to end their financial struggles and, quite possibly, to shield Bertha from the political problems that arose from her American background. The general's desire to marry Bertha, in spite of the obvious liability posed by her foreign connections, attests to her powerful feminine charm. Even so, she refused all of these offers. As she explained to my mother, she didn't think she could ever love another man as much as she loved my grandfather.

If the general had known what lay ahead for my grandmother, and the Soviet Union, in the late forties, he might have thought better of asking her to marry him. During the war, Stalin appealed to Russian patriotism to sustain the level of sacrifice needed to defeat the Germans. And Russians responded, in spite of their exhaustion after years of political terror. As long as the war lasted and the entire country's energies were focused on beating back the Nazis, the domestic political atmosphere remained more relaxed than it had been in years. Some prisoners were even released from camps in order to fight with the army. All of that changed almost as soon as the last shot was fired. Former prisoners who had fought for their country were resentenced and sent back to camps. Stalin also launched a campaign against "rootless cosmopolitans"—Jews and foreigners—that did not end until his death in 1953. My grandmother, a rootless cosmopolitan on both counts, suddenly found herself vulnerable.

Mama first understood what the term "cosmopolitan" meant when she learned to dance while she and my grandmother were vacationing in the Crimea. Friends took turns guiding twelve-year-old Lily around the floor. When the band played, my grandmother dropped her serious demeanor and began tapping her foot. Mama could see flashes of the young woman in love, whirling around the floor of a Harlem nightclub in her T-strap sandals.

But this wasn't Harlem. As Lily enthusiastically learned the steps, her elders quietly cautioned her against calling the tango and fox trot by their real names. Instead, she should say "slow dance" and "fast dance." When Mama innocently asked why, my grandmother explained that "tango" and "fox trot" were foreign expressions. If she used them, someone might overhear and get the wrong idea about her political reliability.

Later, after returning to Tashkent, Mama was trying to improvise a jazz tune on the piano. My grandmother walked into the room and closed the windows so no sound could be heard from the street. She then explained that people were actually being sent to jail for playing jazz. Lily mustn't display any knowledge of "Western" music to strangers. Only their closest, most trusted friends could know that Oliver Golden's widow and daughter hadn't abandoned their love of American jazz.

In 1948, my grandmother was fired from her job as an English teacher at Tashkent's Institute of Foreign Languages. She was told her "American credentials" weren't good enough to merit a teaching job. Never mind that she was one of the few people at the institute with any knowledge of the spoken language. During those years, universities were ordered by the political authorities to fire thousands of distinguished teachers in the sciences and humanities. Most were Soviet Jews, whom Stalin had come to regard as a Fifth Column, but many non-Jews with foreign associations were also fired.

In 1949, the papers were filled with stories about a pro-American Jewish conspiracy in the Soviet Union. Scores of leading Jewish public figures were arrested and shot, including nearly every member of the Jewish Antifascist Committee, which had conducted effective international propaganda on behalf of the government during the war.★ The Yiddish-language theater, which had been a vibrant cultural institution, was destroyed. When Paul Robeson made his first postwar visit to the Soviet Union, he found (as he had in 1937) that more of his old friends, this time in the arts, were missing. One of them was the writer Itzik Feffer, who had visited Robeson in New York in 1943 along with the actor Solomon Mikhoels. While he was in Moscow at the end of 1948, Robeson made persistent inquiries on Feffer's behalf. He didn't know that his old friend had already been arrested. Stalin, who had every reason to want to placate Robeson,

---

★Roy Medvedev's *Let History Judge* (New York: Columbia University Press, 1989) contains the most complete account by a Russian historian of the campaign against cosmopolitans. Medvedev's massive account of the Stalinist system, published in the West long before it appeared in my country, can now be read in Russian.

arranged for Feffer to be temporarily released from jail and brought to his hotel room. Robeson later told his son that Feffer, with gestures, was able to let him know the room was bugged. Through hand signals and notes, Robeson learned that the secret police had killed his friend Mikhoels and that Feffer himself expected to die. He was eventually shot.

In this fear-filled atmosphere, my mother came of age. When my grandmother talked about life in Uzbekistan, she concentrated on her life with my grandfather, on their shared dream of helping the Uzbeks, on the joy of my mother's birth. She almost never talked about her struggles after Oliver's death. It pains me to think about the fear my grandmother must have felt, especially for her child, when the arrests started again in the forties. How did she live with the contradiction between the terror around her and her old Bolshevik dreams?

Pearl Steinhardt told me that when she visited Moscow during the sixties, my grandmother deflected her attempts to discuss the destruction of Yiddish culture "Bertha said she'd never even heard anything about these writers like Mikhoels," Pearl recalls. "I couldn't believe it, that someone who loved reading all the Yiddish writers in the *Forward* wouldn't know about what happened to such people in the Soviet Union. I didn't know what to make of your grandmother's attitude."

I know what to make of it. By the time my grandmother was reunited with her old friend, she had been living in the Soviet Union for more than thirty years. Pearl was an American; how could she fully comprehend what an injudicious word might mean to a Soviet of my grandmother's generation? Whatever my grandmother knew, didn't know, or didn't *want* to know, the fate of Jewish culture in the late forties would not have been a safe topic of conversation, even with a friend who shared the Yiddish-speaking world of her girlhood. Keeping her daughter and granddaughter safe was her main goal.

My mother, in spite of having come to maturity in this same repressive climate, was and is a much less cautious person than my grandmother. In any system, certain people stand out from the crowd by force of personality. They open their mouths and argue when others remain silent. No one ever wins an argument with my mother—not even the most recalcitrant bureaucrat.

When she was sixteen, my mother presented herself at the Tashkent police station to receive her internal passport, a document then required of all Soviet adults. For more than sixty years, Soviet citizens had to show passports to the authorities on just about every significant or insignificant occasion in life—entering a university, applying for a job, moving from one city to another, changing apartments, getting married or buried. On this vital document was stamped every citizen's nationality, which means something very different to Soviets than it does to Americans. The Soviet nationality designation most closely approximates what Americans call "ethnicity." "Jewish" was considered a nationality in the old Soviet Union, as were Russian, Georgian, Amenian, and hundreds of other ethnic groups. The child of a mixed marriage could choose the nationality of either parent. Many children of Russian-Jewish intermarriages, for instance, used to take the Russian nationality on their passports in order to minimize the impact of anti-Semitism on their lives. But as more Jews were allowed to emigrate during the seventies and eighties, children of mixed marriages began to take the opposite tack: They had "Jewish" stamped on their passports because this official designation improved their chances of being allowed to leave.

But what nationality should be stamped on the passport of a child born to Americans—one black, one white?

The police in Tashkent wanted to close the matter by stamping "American" on my mother's passport. My mother didn't care for this idea: because she knew that the adjective "American" was used to designate citizenship—not what Soviets call nationality. Fine, said the police chief, who suggested that she pick either Russian or Uzbek as a nationality. Mama didn't like this idea, either. Uzbeks and Russians are among the few ethnic groups *not* represented in our complicated family lineage. She didn't want to play the Soviet game of picking the "best" nationality available; she wanted her documents to reflect her actual ancestry. So she asked the police chief to write "black" or "Negro" on the passport.

The police chief countered with the statement that *Negro* was not a nationality but a race. Okay, said Mama, then just put my race on the passport. But the policeman wasn't giving in so easily. Even though he was looking directly at her dark features and natural Afro hairstyle, he demanded that she prove she was a Negro. Anyone could come along and try to trick the authorities by claiming to be a Negro. If he made an exception, he carefully explained, he might be inundated by Uzbeks and Russians attempting to pass themselves off as Negros on their passports.

Finally, Mama went home and found an old newspaper article describing my grandfather as a Negro. That piece of proof satisfied the policeman, who agreed to stamp *Negrityanka* (Negro woman) on her documents. This same classification is used on my passport. It's utterly silly, of course, but what other classification would describe me better? My father was a Zanzibani, but Zanzibar (I can imagine some police officer saying) is not a nationality but an island. Terms like African-American and Italian-American, which sound so natural in the United States, simply don't work in Russia. And "black" is considered somewhat rude by many Russians, who are unfamiliar with the way Americans associate its use with racial pride. (It's interesting that Soviet newspapers often referred to black Americans as Afro-Americans long before the term became fashionable in the United States.)

This argument over a passport may sound trivial to Americans, but it was not trivial in Soviet terms. My mother was raised in a country paralyzed by fear of authority. To talk back to any bureaucrat over a small matter of principle was not such a small matter. He probably gave in because he had never met anyone, especially a girl, who refused to take no for an answer.

Two years later, my mother's determination was tested again when she traveled to the capital to take the entrance exams for Moscow State University (MGU). MGU is often described as the Harvard of Russia, but it's much easier for a bright American student to get into Harvard than it was, in Mama's day, for a bright Soviet student to get into MGU. Being smart and prepared isn't enough, not if you come from a provincial town or are of the wrong nationality. In 1952, when Mama went to Moscow to take her exams, the MGU student body was heavily weighted in favor of ethnic Russians. Muscovites had the best chances of getting admitted. Quotas against Jews, at the height of the anticosmopolitan campaign, were especially restrictive. Students from Asian or southern republics were barely represented; they were expected to enter universities in their own republics. My mother already had one big, black mark against her because she grew up in Tashkent.

When Mama presented herself at the MGU admissions office, the academic bureaucrats waved her away and refused even to look at the documents certifying her academic preparation for the exams. She didn't give up. Armed with a list of names of her father's old acquaintances, she made one phone call after another until she found a friend who had a friend in the central committee. She asked this man to use his connections simply to get her a chance to take the entrance exam.

The next time my mother returned to the admissions office, it was obvious that the nasty educational *apparatchiki* had received a call from higher up. They grudgingly agreed to let this nobody from Tashkent take the exams, and she passed with top scores. I wonder how many young men and women, just as intelligent as my mother but lacking connections or the aggressiveness to use them, were turned away at the door in those years by indifferent guardians of privilege in what was supposed to be a land of equality?

Although my mother wanted very much to live in the nation's cultural capital and to obtain the best education possible, her years at MGU were not happy ones. In the early 1980s, when I was a student in the MGU journalism department, the moribund politics of our society only rarely intruded on my consciousness. In my department, there were a few students who planned to build themselves fine official careers and who pretended, at least in front of their superiors, to take Soviet orthodoxy seriously. For the most part, these students were simply disliked and ignored. The rest of us went our own way, preparing ourselves for less ambitious careers, which we hoped would give us some measure of personal satisfaction without compromising our principles. In my mother's generation, it was impossible to relax and ignore the political situation.

Informers were everywhere. "The professors were afraid of the students, the students were afraid of the professors, and everyone was afraid of everyone else" is the way my mother describes the academic atmosphere. When she entered the university in 1952, older students would tell her in lowered voices, "You should have been here when Professor X was teaching, he was one of the most brilliant men I ever met." (Professor X, more often than not Jewish, had either been fired or arrested in the anticosmopolitan campaign.)

According to my mother, Stalin's death in 1953 did little to change the workings of a frightened, supine academic community. "There was a brief period, from around 1954 until the Hungarian Revolution in 1956, when students began to talk more openly about their doubts," my mother says. "All of that ended when the Soviet tanks rolled into Budapest. The last time I remember any open discussion of a political event was when we first heard the news of the revolt and were arguing about whether the Soviet government had been right to end it. What strikes me now is how little information we had, how dependent we were on the Soviet press, how little we really understood of the feelings of people in other countries."

Around this time, twenty history students, many of them personally known to my mother, were arrested for meeting in a group to discuss Lenin's writings (a truly dangerous topic). My mother heard the discussions were interesting—the group was taking up the question of whether Soviet society bore any resemblance to Lenin's original vision—and she planned to drop by as soon as her exams were finished. Before she had a chance to do so, everyone in the group was arrested.

"They were the most brilliant students in the history faculty," she recalls. "Imagine what that meant to everyone else. One friend of mine was there because he disagreed with what the others were saying, and he was arrested too. He was eventually released—apparently some of those good, honorable kids told their interrogators he was arguing with them—but his life was ruined. There was no chance of his being allowed to get a job or continue his studies. Everyone knew an informer among the students had to have told the KGB about the group. It's impossible to breathe in such air. No, I don't look back on my student days with any nostalgia at all."

During those student years, Mama survived a private tragedy. Not long after beginning her studies, she met and fell in love with Nikolai Makarov,★ a music student and pianist. Nikolai belonged to one of the most distinguished intellectual families in Russia. For generations before the revolution, the Makarov family produced eminent scholars, writers, musicians: creative and performing artists of every variety. Read Vladimir Nabokov's memoirs, and you have a good idea of the level of Russian culture represented by the Makarovs.

Mama's background couldn't have been further removed from that world, but Nikolai fell deeply in love with the tall, dark-skinned girl, with the strange-sounding last name, who shared his passion for music. Over the fierce objections of his parents, they soon married. To this point, the story sounds like a case of history repeating itself, a replay, in a very different cultural setting, of my grandparents' experience. But my mother and her first husband never had a real chance to build a life together: He was killed in a car accident only a few months after their marriage. Nevertheless, this short, intense love affair changed my mother's life. It is her story, and she should be the one to tell it.

> The first thing: I absolutely wouldn't be the person I am today if I hadn't known Nikolai. He lived in a wide world I didn't imagine in Tashkent. Remember, at school, my education was Soviet, censored, very limited. And my mother, because of her unusual background, couldn't

---

★This name has been changed to protect privacy.

make up for it. She couldn't know much about Russian literature, because so many important books had just disappeared by the time she came to Russia. And she wasn't widely read in English literature because, remember, she only lived in America for eleven years. American culture, for her, was frozen in time. She knew the jazz of the twenties, for example, but nothing later. An example: The first time I ever heard Gershwin's "Rhapsody In Blue," Nikolai played it for me. I was enchanted. It was never played on Soviet radio, so how could I know it? He knew because he lived in the musical world of Moscow, and even in those years, some foreign compositions got through.

And his family had books I'd never seen—in English, German, French, and Russian. He introduced me to Bulgakov and the satirists Ilf and Petrov,* all of these things that just disappeared from Soviet bookstores during the thirties. I was hungry, so hungry, for all of these things, and I never knew it.

Oh yes, and he could quote pages and pages of poetry by heart. At that age, you're like a sponge. You can take in everything in the world. Nikolai was just as interested in my family, and in the things I knew about America that he didn't, as I was in everything he knew. And of course we both loved music more than almost anything else. We were in love—minds, bodies, everything—in the way that's only possible when you're very young.

---

*Mikhail Bulgakov, an outstanding Russian novelist, died in 1940. His most famous novel, *The Master and Margarita,* was published in his own country for the first time (in censored form) in 1967. The uncensored version was only published three years ago. Ilf and Petrov are the authors of *The Twelve Chairs,* an immensely popular satirical novel about Soviet life in the twenties. Ilf and Petrov's works were banned during the Stalin era and published again during the Khrushchev thaw.

But Nikolai's family, most of the family at least, wasn't in love with
Mama.

> Nothing was ever said directly to my face—people of this
> kind wouldn't behave so crudely—but I understood that
> the family felt I wasn't good enough for Nikolai. And it
> wasn't because I was black, though that certainly didn't
> help. First of all, I was a girl from the provinces. At that
> time there were a lot of young people who wanted to
> marry someone, anyone, in Moscow just to get a *propiska*
> (permit) to live in the capital. I was seen as some kind of
> adventuress, looking to move up in the world by attaching
> herself to their son. Also, people like the [Makarovs] marry
> people like themselves. What on earth was a "Golden" to
> them? I was something like a Gypsy as far as they were
> concerned; and if you know how Gypsies are looked upon
> in Russia, you know what that means. They wouldn't have
> been quite as unhappy if I were white, but they certainly
> wouldn't have been thrilled no matter what color I was.
> With his mother feeling the way she did, I could hardly live
> in their apartment. If I should have a child, she made it
> clear, we would be on our own. For Russian mothers, who
> always help with children, that's quite a statement.

Nor could Mama's husband live with her in a student hostel.
Members of the opposite sex, married or not, weren't allowed to
occupy the same room. *Nyelzya:* another official "don't."

So Mama and Nikolai had to snatch small moments of time, whenever and wherever they could be together. One of Nikolai's uncles
looked kindly upon my mother and the unorthodox match, and he
bought the couple a car, an unheard of gesture in those days. Nikolai
was driving when he had his fatal accident. Fortunately, Mama wasn't
with him.

"When I think about that time in my life," Mama says, "it's almost
as if I'm reading a book about another person: So much beauty and so
much pain. And some of my memories of that family are good. True,

many of the Makarovs looked down on me, but others were kind, recognized my special qualities, and helped me move into a whole new world. Some of those people remain close to me till this day. This was also another lesson for me—this time not from my mother's teachings, but from my own experience—that you must judge people not as types but as individuals."

Private sorrow notwithstanding, Mama still had to grapple with the question facing every honest young person: how to support herself, with some measure of integrity, in a poisonous political climate. She did what all true intellectuals did throughout the Soviet period. Abandoning any hopes of a successful career, as Americans understand the idea, she carved out a niche for herself in an obscure (to Russians) area of culture: the history of African music.

When it came time for my mother to defend her dissertation (the equivalent of an American Ph.D.), it was almost impossible to assemble a panel of judges because no one knew anything about her topic. The musicians knew nothing about African history, and the Africanists knew nothing about music. Finally someone managed to dig up one judge, a member of the USSR Academy of Sciences, who was a specialist in the music of Australian aborigines. Aborigines, Africans: They were all the same to the fools in charge of Soviet academic bureaucracy.

Like my grandmother, Mama supported herself by taking on a variety of odd intellectual jobs. In addition to working at the African Institute (the one created by Khrushchev at the suggestion of W. E. B. Du Bois), she wrote articles on African culture that were circulated by Soviet agencies and published abroad in African newspapers and magazines. Of course, she was never allowed to visit Africa to pursue her own research: That privilege was reserved for Party members of proven political reliability (and scant knowledge of Africa). Mama's one way to pursue her cultural interests was by acting as a trouble-shooter, organizer, and interpreter for the growing number of official visitors from newly independent African nations. That's how she met my father, Abdullah Khanga, a former secondary-school teacher who became a Marxist revolutionary committed to independence for his native Zanzibar. He eventually became the first vice-president of the independent republic of Zanzibar, which was soon unified with the former British colony of Tanganyika in the newly created state of Tanzania. In 1965, shortly after the union took effect, my father's political enemies murdered him, in part because of his longstanding ties to Moscow. All of this took place several years after he left Moscow, without my mother and me (though originally, my mother had planned to join him in Africa).

It speaks volumes about my mother's character that she made every effort to give me a balanced, honest picture of her complicated relationship with my father. When a mother is raising a child alone—I saw this in many of my girlfriends' homes—it's easy to give way to the temptation to make the absent father sound like a god or a devil. (This was an even easier course to take for a Soviet woman with a child by a foreigner, because the man was unlikely to turn up to tell his side of the story.)

My mother knew my father for several years before she agreed to marry him. She had met many of his Zanzibari friends while taking charge of African delegates to an international festival in Moscow, and they told him about the beautiful black, English-speaking woman they had encountered in Russia. One night, he turned up at her door with a proposal of marriage. His friends had told him, he informed my mother, that she would be exactly the right sort of educated, politically aware wife for him. My mother naturally received this proposal in a humorous rather than a serious vein; an independent Soviet woman was not about to marry a stranger from a strange land simply to become his political asset. But my father persisted, courting Mama for two years while studying in Moscow. He was a man with a political mission; he couldn't have differed more markedly from the artistic, nonpolitical Russian intellectuals who made up my mother's circle of friends. In temperament, education, and interests, he bore no resemblance at all to my mother's dreamy, musical first husband. He asked Mama to make up lists of Soviet films essential to his political education, movies like Eisenstein's *Potemkin* and *Ten Days That Shook the World*. Mama says my father never went to a movie for pure enjoyment, only to learn something. During their courtship, Mama and my father had long talks about his dreams for the development of his country. My grandmother urged my mother to marry Abdullah and accompany him to Africa. She would tell Mama, "It's your duty to help the Africans, as it was your father's and my duty to come here." Finally, Mama accepted Abdullah's proposal and embarked on what she thought would be a union of intellectual and political equals.

After the marriage, though, my father's behavior changed overnight. He was not a religious believer, but he nevertheless wanted my mother to follow many of the customs of a traditional Muslim wife: to avoid any contacts with men (even professional colleagues) unless her husband was present, to ask his permission when she wanted to leave the house, to remain silent when male guests visited their home.

My father was frequently away during this period, in both England and Africa, but whenever he was in Moscow, the couple lived in a special government house reserved for important foreign visitors. There my mother was exposed to luxuries she had never seen in Soviet life. An endless supply of fruits and fresh meats turned up even in the middle of Russian winter. Servants saw to the guests' every need. The bedroom came complete with a movie screen and heating ducts that enabled the residents to walk barefoot while blizzards raged outside in sub-zero weather.

But the luxurious house became my mother's prison. Fiercely jealous, my father would lock her inside when he went out. Nor did he want her to go to her office while he was in town; fortunately, her boss let her bring work home from the African Institute. If my father had dinner guests, she was allowed to serve them but not to speak. (When I visited Zanzibar last year, I found this traditional practice unchanged. As a Western woman, I was permitted to speak at formal dinners, but the African wives—with whom I'd had lively conversations while we were alone—were sentenced to silence in the presence of men.)

My mother particularly recalls one dinner where my father gave her a special dispensation to sit at the table with his important African guests. "Those men had never been to Russia before," she remembers, "and they were saying all sorts of things that made me want to answer and argue. And I couldn't say one word. The sense of humiliation was so deep that I asked myself, 'Why am I here?' " You would have to know my mother as I do to realize what it meant to her not to be able to raise her voice in argument.

After I was born, the cultural rift between my parents grew into a chasm. My father had expected a son, and he was disappointed and angry when their first-born turned out to be a girl. He even refused to pick my mother and me up and take us home from the Moscow maternity hospital where I was born. An old friend from the university, who didn't want my mother to be embarrassed in front of the hospital staff, came to fetch us. I was named Yelena after another friend of my mother's; my father didn't care what I was called.

For the next two years, my father traveled back and forth between the Soviet Union and England, where he was studying economics. He and my mother continued to talk about her joining him in Africa after his country gained its independence, but I don't think there was any real possibility of that after his reaction to my birth. "If you had been a boy," my mother told me, "things might have worked out differently. I felt it was my duty to give you every opportunity I possibly could. How could I do that in a society in which women aren't allowed to speak in the presence of men? How would you be educated? Your father's behavior toward me had changed so much while we were still in Russia, I could only imagine what it would be like in his own environment, with all of the force of his own culture."

When my mother told me about my father, she explained to me that his attitudes toward women were the product of a culture very different from our own. She did not criticize that culture but emphasized that she, brought up with a very different way of thinking about women's possibilities, could not adapt to his attitudes. And she also told me a good deal about my father's dreams for an independent, modern Africa. The result of her sensible, honest approach was that I was able to think about this long-dead father and to respect certain aspects of his character, without turning him into a figure of romantic fantasy. Along with no excuses, she handed me no fairy tales.

There was, and is, nothing unusual about an all-female Russian household. My mother's generation experienced a man shortage because the country lost 15 million soldiers in World War II. This scarcity of men in the postwar years made it easy for dissatisfied husbands to abandon their families and begin new lives with other women. (The official divorce rate is even higher today. As in the United States, about half of all new Russian marriages are expected to end in divorce.)

Even when there is a man in the house, Russian women assume the responsibility for nearly everything, particularly the care of children. Women simply assume men are incompetent when it comes to children (and the men like it that way, because they have much more free time than their wives). The American idea of joint custody of children after a divorce sounds ludicrous to Russians; no one expects a father to take any day-to-day responsibility if he is no longer married to the mother of his child. Married or divorced, babushka and mama rule the roost—and do the work.

In spite of the matriarchal character of Russian private life, many girls are still raised on the hope that a man will come along to take care of them. This was absolutely not the case with me. In our house of women, self-reliance was the main theme. My grandmother had an extremely happy marriage with a man she loved passionately, but he died when she was only thirty-five and their child was only six. My mother had a troubled marriage with a man from another culture but she too was left with a child to raise by herself. From the very different experiences of the two women closest to me, I learned the lesson that security was not to be found in a man. To love a man and be loved was wonderful, but you must not believe that love frees you from responsibility for your own life. Both my grandmother and mother insisted that I prepare to support myself. Prince Charming and magic carpets were for fairy tales.

All of the "magic" in our home was the result of hard work and resourcefulness. Consider the first year of my life, when I came close to death. The trouble began in the maternity hospital, where I contracted some sort of infection. (Russian hospitals often lack sterilization equipment and ignore routine sanitary precautions, such as not using the same gauze on two different patients. No wonder it's common for newborn babies to leave the hospital with a variety of infectious diseases. This is even more true today than it was when I was a baby, because the economic crisis of the past few years has left the country with a catastrophic shortage of antibiotics. Babies have become infected with the AIDS virus because there are no disposable hypodermic needles and proper sterilization procedures aren't followed with the old-fashioned syringes.)

To my mother's dismay, I remained weak and sickly even after I recovered from the infection I brought home from the hospital. The year I was born, 1962, was the rainiest in the memory of living Muscovites; my mother says the sun hardly shone at all during the usually clear months of June, July, and August. In spite of regular doses of cod liver oil, I developed rickets. On my first birthday, I could barely lift my head. It always surprises Americans to hear that a child from an educated, urban Russian family could suffer from rickets. This softening of the bones, a disease associated with poverty around the world, is easily correctible with proper nutrition. But severe vitamin deficiencies are common in northern Russia, where fresh fruits and vegetables are virtually nonexistent in the winter months. Furthermore, the nation has no frozen food industry to deliver summer's vitamins in winter.

In May of 1963, my pediatrician told Mama he feared I would die if she did not somehow manage to take me to a warmer climate, where I could eat nutritious foods and be exposed to the sun's rays. Under Soviet conditions, giving this advice to a single mother was like telling her to fly her child to Mars for a vacation. Hotel rooms in resort areas were reserved for Party bigshots (and sometimes for foreign tourists). Large spas of the kind my grandparents visited in the thirties were entirely booked by factories for their workers, who had no choice about when to take their vacations. One neat twist of the system, calculated to make family life a pure joy, is that husbands and wives are rarely able to vacation together because time off is determined entirely by their employers.

No matter: The doctor said I needed sun to live, and sun I would have. Mama got on the phone and spoke with everyone from her past who happened to live in a warm area of the country. She looked up friends from her tennis-playing days and people she met while she was singing and traveling with a jazz group in the mid-fifties. Somehow, she managed to book us a berth on a Black Sea cruise ship and a hotel room in the Black Sea port of Batumi, the warmest city in the country. She piled up freelance translation work so she could continue to earn money while we were away and borrowed the rest of what she needed from friends. For Russians, unlike Americans, no social stigma is attached to borrowing from friends. Everyone does it, and everyone assumes that he himself will one day need to borrow. Not to give to the limit of one's ability would be considered a gross breach of friendship. Russians do expect to be paid back (when the borrower can afford it), but no one would ever expect a friend to sign a note. A demand for a promise in writing, something that seems quite common in America even between relatives, would be considered an insult in Russia.

Two weeks after we arrived in Batumi, I lifted my head for the first time. By the end of the summer, I was walking as if I had never been sick at all. A visitor from a remote area of Georgia was so entranced by my beauty and liveliness that he begged my mother to sell me to him. (This is Mama's story, anyway.)

This episode from the first, precarious year of my life naturally acquired a mythic quality as time passed. At the core of the myth, though, was the truth of my childhood: If there was a threat to any of our lives or well-being, my grandmother and mother would find a way to vanquish it. We would take care of our own, and I would grow up to take my place in this self-reliant scheme of things.

As if these two powerful personalities weren't enough, there was a third important woman in my life, my *baba* Anya, grandmother Anya. She was the lover whose existence my grandfather revealed to my grandmother when they were beginning their lives together in New York.

How we found Anya, and why it took so long, is another tale from the Stalinist chamber of horrors. In 1953, when my mother was singing with her jazz group, a friend came up and told her he knew a young man in Leningrad who looked exactly like her, "close enough to be a twin." My mother wasn't surprised. She and my grandmother had never forgotten about the son Oliver Golden fathered in the mid-twenties; my mother quickly and correctly concluded that the man who resembled her must be her half-brother.

When they arrived in the Soviet Union, my grandparents attempted to track down Anya and her son, Olava, the child named for my grandfather. The authorities finally told my grandfather that Anya was dead and Olava had disappeared after being sent to an orphans' home. (In the chaos of the thirties, when so many people were being arrested, it was extremely difficult to locate a child assigned to a state home. Institutions were overloaded and many children simply ran away. They were known as *bezprizorniki,* literally, "shelterless ones," and many fell into lives of crime to survive). After the war began, it seemed impossible to locate a child who was said to have disappeared from a home. Still, my mother always had the feeling that her brother might find her someday. Olava's mother, Anya, was also very much alive when the authorities were telling my grandfather she was dead.

What was the point of such cruel behavior? Racism had nothing to do with it: Russians involved with white foreigners were subjected to the same lies and threats. The only point was the Soviet police state's paranoia about contacts between Russians and foreigners, and the need of its representatives to assert government control over every aspect of private life. These pieces of official scum—for that is what they were—couldn't have cared less about millions of broken families and broken hearts.

And yet, Baba Anya—like my grandmother—remained absolutely loyal to the Soviet state. How was it possible for good people to tolerate, even to justify, the actions of this state? Most of these old-line Communists told themselves and one another that mistakes were inevitable in the building of a completely new society: "You can't make an omelet without breaking eggs." To this day, many members of their generation cannot understand that "mistakes" were not simply flaws in the system: They were the system.

Although Baba Anya and my grandmother were both committed Communists, they were so different that it was hard for me to understand how they could have both loved, and been loved by, the same man. Baba Anya, whose straight, steel-gray hair showed that she had never seen the inside of a beauty parlor, wore severely tailored dark jackets, covered with the military medals she earned fighting with Soviet partisans behind German lines during the war. Her looks were cast in the utilitarian, frumpy mode exemplified by Lenin's wife, Nadezhda Krupskaya: A revolutionary woman must not wear frills. My grandmother (though she, too, eschewed makeup) presented a softer, more feminine image. Every month, even in the coldest depths of Moscow winter, she would take a taxi to the hairdresser for a shampoo and set. Until she weakened during the last year of her life, I never saw her without a perfectly combed, wavy coiffure. I could still catch glimpses of the dreamy, young woman who fell in love with my grandfather.

Whenever Baba Anya came to stay with us, something she did frequently when I was growing up, she would keep me awake at night with exciting stories of all the Germans she had killed and captured. "Your Uncle Olava stayed in the camp in the forest with me," she said. "We lived on berries we could gather in summer, on rabbits and squirrels we shot. Sometimes we were very hungry, because the Germans had taken everything from the farms, everything they could steal." Olava's life in the forest sounded unbelievably romantic to me; I never really thought about how scared he must have been. Baba Anya made guerrilla warfare sound like an adventure from a fairy tale. As I drifted off to sleep on my cot, my grandmother would come into the bedroom, hear us murmuring softly about those evil, dead Germans, and say, hands on hips, "What, back with the partisans again?"

I don't think my grandmother really approved of these late-night stories, but she loved Anya too much to stop her. Nor did my granny care for official symbols of ideology or enforced patriotism. Baba Anya would regularly take me to Red Square and point to Lenin's tomb, reminding me of all the deeds of *"Nash velikiy Lenin"* (our great Lenin). My grandmother never used the language of official propaganda and had no interest in visiting a mummy.

Yet she and Anya treated each other as sisters, sharing memories of the man they both adored. For a Party member like Anya, it took great courage to register the name of an American on her child's birth certificate. She could easily have put down someone else's name, or no name at all, and spared herself the attentions of the secret police. My grandmother's reaction, upon learning that Anya was alive in 1953, was one of characteristic compassion and generosity. She considered herself fortunate to have had thirteen years with my grandfather and six years of raising their child together. It caused her deep sorrow to think of the undelivered presents she brought for Olava in 1931, of the years when Anya knew the father of her child was back in the Soviet Union but was afraid to contact him. Like my grandmother, Anya led a life of love and self-sacrifice. These women provided the glue that held families together in a terrorized society, and my mother's generation was cast from the same mold. "No excuses, Yelena." How could it be otherwise, when the women who raised me never made excuses for themselves?

CHAPTER SIX

GROWING UP SOVIET

My best friend when I was a little girl was our next-door neighbor's son, Sasha. We were the same age, and Sasha's mother nursed me for several months when my own mother's milk dried up. The practice of wet-nursing, long gone in the baby formula–rich West, persists in Russian culture (though it's not as common today as it was when I was a baby). In Russia, nursing another woman's child is no longer a service the poor perform for the rich but a gesture of friendship and sisterhood, as American feminists say, in a country where breast milk is not only the preferred but often the only form of nutrition for infants. (Baby formula does exist in Russia today but supplies are erratic.) Incidentally, no one thought it at all unusual that a white woman would volunteer to nurse a black woman's child. I wonder whether there has ever been an American community, before or after slavery, northern or southern, in which the same situation could have evolved so naturally and attracted so little notice? A white American friend tells me it defies every aspect of her cultural conditioning even to imagine a white mother offering her own breast to a black baby. In Moscow, I never gave this aspect of my infancy a moment's thought.

Because Sasha and I were introduced in the cradle, he never seemed to see my color at all. He appointed himself my defender whenever other children would ask why I was so dark. They didn't inquire to be mean; they had never seen a black person in the flesh and were simply astounded by my appearance. Sasha would explain that I was black because my father came from Africa, where it is very hot and people grow very dark from the sun. No doubt this was the simple explanation his mother gave him when he was old enough to tell black from white and ask his own questions. But his answer failed to satisfy the other kids, who didn't understand why I hadn't turned white as a result of living in a cold country. (Genetics isn't the strongest point of four and five year olds. In truth, a great many Soviet adults wouldn't have been able to answer the question either, thanks to Lysenko's crackpot theories. According to Lysenko's notions, I should indeed have turned white, and eventually have produced white children, as a result of being exposed to Russian winters.) But there was nothing funny about the consequences of Lysenkoism. Thousands of distinguished scientists and agronomists were imprisoned or murdered for daring to challenge his ludicrous ideas.

In any event, Sasha quickly lost patience with the question of why I stubbornly remained brown. As my friend, he favored the direct approach: Anyone who persisted was apt to get a punch in the nose. Sasha also taught me to fight, an accomplishment I hid from my watchful grandmother. Her idea of womanhood, socialist or otherwise, didn't include punching, kicking, and biting. To be honest, both Sasha and I seized on any excuse to prove our prowess in battle. My grandmother considered us precocious *khuligany* (hooligans). And I was most certainly a full-blown *sorvanets* (tomboy).

My grandmother and mother played quite different roles in my upbringing. My grandmother's role was in many ways that of a traditional mama; she was usually the one who took me to school, saw that I did my homework, bandaged my skinned knees, and tucked me into bed at night. My mother was out in the world, working several jobs to provide for us and see that I had the very best a Soviet parent could offer. They made a formidable team. The American feminist joke that "every woman really needs one thing: a wife" was a precise description of our domestic setup. I consider my mother to have been the perfect single parent, but she was never alone in the way so many divorced American women are.

From the start, my two female parents raised me with three goals and three worlds in mind. First, they wanted me to get along in the Soviet system. Next, they wanted me to take pride in my blackness even though I was living in a virtually all-white world. Last but not least, they saw me as a classic Russian intellectual. My mother, in particular, was determined to give me the cultural and intellectual advantages she missed growing up in Tashkent.

Only now am I fully beginning to understand how lucky I was to have a mother whose experience spanned all three worlds. As much as I loved my grandmother, I could share my blackness only with Mama. She was my first, for a long time my only, image of black womanhood.

Mama understood how frustrating it was to have stubborn, kinky black hair (though mine was kinkier than hers) in a world of flaxen-tressed Ludmillas. I see myself as a small girl, sitting on the floor as Mama bent over to brush my hair every night. One stroke . . . two . . . three . . . fifty . . . my frizzy hair would come out in kinks as the relentless brush moved over my head. Sometimes the brushing hurt so much that tears sprang to my eyes. Why the pain? My Russian friends didn't seem to mind when their mamas brushed their hair before plaiting it in braids or pulling it back into a pony tail. Neither Mama nor I knew that black hair is far more delicate than white hair. The "hundred vigorous strokes a night" recommended by beauty advisers for whites is a recipe for ruining black hair, and that's why the more Mama tried to tend my "crowning glory," the more it fell out. In the early sixties, we couldn't get American magazines that would have told us how to take proper care of black hair. They wouldn't have helped, anyway, because where could we get the creams and conditioners needed for a healthy, shiny black head? Eventually, Mama gave up and cut my hair as short as possible. In my early school pictures, I would have looked like a boy if I weren't wearing the obligatory pinafore over my brown uniform. Whenever Mama cut my hair, she saved it and used it to stuff pillows around the house. My sheared kinks produced the most comfortable pillows in Moscow, but that didn't comfort me. I wanted people to compliment the hair on my head—not to lie down on it.

In spite of my hair woes, having a black mother made me more self-confident than many of the other black Russians I met while I was growing up. Most of these children came from unions between white Russian women and African students, who had long since returned to their own countries. The women did their best but were not equipped to transmit the pride in black heritage my mother was able to convey.

Mama once received a phone call from another single mother, a white woman, who begged us to visit her and her daughter because the child never had the chance to meet other blacks. This little girl, only three or four when I first met her, had developed a physical fear of black people. When she saw my mother and me, she hid under the sofa. Only after we had been sitting, talking, and drinking tea for several hours did she dare to crawl out from under the couch and touch me. She stroked my head and her eyes widened in amazement when she felt—I suppose for the first time—hair with the same texture as her own.

Because I had a black mother who was also firmly imbedded in Russian culture, most of the psychological issues surrounding my color remained on the back burner until I grew older and began thinking about boys, love, and marriage.

(There's another element to the story of the frightened little black girl that has nothing to do with race and everything to do with one of the many cultural differences between Russians and Americans. The child, who obviously had an African father, was abandoned by her biological mother—a Russian—and placed in a children's home. Mama's friend, who didn't have any children of her own, adopted the girl, but never told her about her true background. Americans, who take it for granted that parents should tell adopted children the truth are baffled by this story. In Russia, adoption is considered a slightly shameful secret. Adopted children are scorned and mocked if anyone knows about their origins. The girl's mother asked me to cut out a picture of a handsome African from one of my mother's magazines so that her daughter could have a mental image of her father. I did this, choosing a picture of some African rock star, without thinking twice about piling one lie on top of another. Many Russians consider it quite normal to lie to a child in this fashion; viewing this situation from an American perspective, I see that all of the lying might well have confused the child regardless of her color.)

For much of my childhood, we lived in a three-room apartment, plus kitchen and bath, on Profsoyuznaya (All-Union) Street. The five-story apartment buildings in our neighborhood, brand-new when we moved in, were known as *khrushchevki,* because they were built during Nikita Khrushchev's tenure as leader of the Soviet Union. Silvery birch forests surrounded blocks of new construction, but we children were told to play in the enclosed courtyard of our apartment because wolves had supposedly been sighted not far away.

My grandmother and I slept in the same room, while the living room doubled as Mama's bedroom and study. Through all those years, Mama never had a proper bed of her own because there wasn't enough space for one. At night, she curled up on the sofa. "If I ever get rich," she'd say, "I'm going to have a real bed." (She finally achieved this ambition in 1985, when we moved into a four-room apartment, palatial by Russian standards, in the House of Writers, after Mama's marriage to the well-known author Boris Yakovlev. Books, more than 30,000, by Mama's last count, covered every surface and filled every spare nook in our home. They jammed the two large steamer trunks my grandparents had brought over with them on the *Deutschland.* Our library included Russian translations of Cicero and Montaigne, everything from Galsworthy to Langston Hughes in English, rare prerevolutionary editions of Mandelstam and Akhamatova, proscribed political writings by Nikolai Bukharin, Russian translations of Maupassant, Flaubert, and Dumas. Books spilled out from under my bed and Mama's sofa, but we somehow managed to find space for new ones.

Mama's room housed our most prized possession: a Japanese-made phonograph given to us by an American friend. Thanks to that record player, I first heard the voices of Sarah Vaughan, Ella Fitzgerald, and Ray Charles. The phonograph, and our few records, were so precious that Mama wouldn't let me touch them until I was in my teens.

"Mama's room" was also a gallery of African art. African visitors brought her sculpture from many parts of the continent, and she showed them off to her friends. In our apartment, many Russians got their first look at West African masks, Benin bronzes, and *poto-poto* paintings, from a village near Brazzaville, capital of the Republic of Congo.

In this cramped but culturally rich setting, Mama began giving me lessons I could never have learned in school. She talked, for instance, about the good things Nikita Khrushchev had done. I was only two when Khrushchev was ousted from power, so I naturally had no memory of the roly-poly leader who started the task of de-Stalinization and gained international notoriety by pounding his shoe on a desk at the United Nations. By the time I began school, Khrushchev had either been dropped entirely from textbooks or was described as a "hare-brained schemer" who embarrassed the great Soviet people by behaving like a peasant. The fact that he was also responsible for bringing home millions from Stalin's labor camps was never mentioned.

My mother did mention this fact, along with the fact that the "peasant" was the first Soviet leader to make a real effort at dealing with the housing shortage in Russian cities. If it weren't for Khrushchev, she explained, we might have to share a kitchen and toilet with five or six other families. My mother's way of introducing me to the better side of the deposed leader was clever and effective. Some of my friends still lived in communal flats, and I had witnessed some hideous domestic arguments over stove and toilet time. I was grateful to this unknown Nikita Sergeyevich for starting the construction more Russians their privacy. My mother was careful to warn me that I should not repeat her favorable words about Khrushchev outside the house. For me, this was the beginning of the dual consciousness all honest Russian parents instilled in their children. I learned at a very early age that there were two realities: one for home and one for school. No area of life, from the roof over our heads to the books we read, was exempt from the need for these explanations. Mama made me understand that the reality of school was a game whose rules I had to know to get along in Soviet society. But there was no question in my mind that the truth was only to be found at home.

In our house, we lived with a triple consciousness, because my grandmother refused to listen to one bad word about communism in general or Soviet society in particular. Locked into the political beliefs of her youth, her mind could not be changed by new facts coming to light. This was not unusual in Russian homes; many in my mother's generation had old Bolshevik parents who spent time in Stalin's camps but still refused to acknowledge anything fundamentally wrong with the system. My mother dealt with this not by arguing with my grandmother, which would have filled our home with strife and gotten her nowhere, but by telling me we must respect her views even if we didn't agree with them.

Nevertheless, Mama was determined to communicate the truth to me as she saw it. She could remember using high-school textbooks with holes where the faces and names of purged revolutionary leaders used to be. In the years before *glasnost,* Soviet schoolchildren learned nothing about the role played by disgraced leaders like Trotsky and Bukharin; only when my mother became a historian and gained access to special libraries closed to average citizens was she finally able to fill in some of the gaps. She was determined that my own knowledge of history would not have as many blank pages as hers had, so she began with simple matters, easily understandable to a child, like Khrushchev's apartment buildings.

Beginning at age three, I spent most of the day at *detsky sad* (kindergarten). These communal institutions exist mainly to provide child care for working mothers who have no *babushka* to help out at home. I had a *babushka*, but she believed devoutly in collective nurseries as the cornerstone of socialist upbringing. In fact, nurseries serve the important social function of enabling otherwise isolated children to meet and play with one another. In Russian cities, the acute housing shortage has made one-child families the rule rather than the exception; nearly all of my friends were only children. Nurseries and kindergartens offer a supervised alternative to the street and courtyard; the frequency of my adventures with Sasha diminished markedly once we were both under the watchful eye of our kindergarten teachers.

Russian kindergartens do not stress the kind of "reading readiness" so common in American preschools. In the view of Russian educators, premature emphasis on academic instruction robs children of their childhood. But no child was ever too young for political education. Each of my nursery classrooms featured a small shrine to Lenin, consisting of a portrait surrounded by ribbons and fresh flowers. We children vied for the honor of bringing flowers and placing them on a small table underneath the picture; in this way, we were prepared for the more direct political education we would receive in elementary school.

It's a good thing our kindergarten teachers didn't believe in force-feeding us academic lessons, because the relaxed atmosphere of *detsky sad* changes dramatically when a child enters first grade. In my generation, the typical elementary school educational experience, beginning at age seven, bore about as much resemblance to loosely structured American schools as military training does to summer camp. I went to school six days a week, Monday through Saturday, from September 1 to June 1. Classes lasted from 8:30 A.M. to 2:30 or 3:00 P.M. Soviet schools had only ten grades before high school graduation, so the curriculum is concentrated and the homework burden heavy.

I received at least two hours of homework each day, beginning in first grade. By fifth grade, four or five hours was the norm. For many years, Soviet parents complained that excessive homework ruined their children's health. During the winter months, there is almost no opportunity for outdoor exercise because a child must begin work

Hilliard Golden, Yelena's paternal great-grandfather, stands at far left in front of his home in Yazoo County, Mississippi, in 1902. At his right are his wife, Catherine, and their youngest daughter, Viola. Hilliard's spread was the largest owned by a black in post–Civil War Yazoo. According to Golden family legend, the house was burned down by the Ku Klux Klan in 1909.

In Warsaw, Poland (c. 1907), Yelena's maternal great-grandparents, Isaac and Bessie Bialek, pose for a family portrait with their children. Bertha Bialek, Yelena's grandmother, is between her parents. Her brothers Jack, Sidney, and Marcus are at left.

Bertha Bialek, age nine, in Warsaw.

Bertha Bialek, age twenty-two, in New York. Bertha told Yelena's mother, Lily, that this was the "look" that Oliver Golden fell in love with.

Aboard the German ship *Deutschland,* Oliver (front row, far right) and Bertha (back row, third from left) leave for the Soviet Union. Other members of the group include George Tynes and Joseph Roane.

Yelena, 1990, interviews Joseph Roane, the only surviving member of the group of black agricultural specialists organized by her grandfather. (Credit: Sergei Petrov)

Oliver Golden (front row, far left) poses with classmates at the KUTV Institute in Moscow (c. 1925). Oliver had joined the Communist Party in Chicago after World War I. He studied in Moscow for several years, before returning to the United States.

Bertha and Oliver (far left) picnicking with Russian friends in the Uzbek countryside in the early 1930s.

Oliver (c. 1933) lecturing to workers and peasants in the countryside.

Bertha (c. 1933) trying to persuade an Uzbek woman to shed her traditional veil. In Yangiyul, the small village where Bertha and Oliver lived when they first came to Uzbekistan, many Uzbek women still wore the veil prescribed by tribal custom.

Oliver (c. 1934) with comrades at a political meeting. In the background is the Russian word *znamya*—"banner"—obviously a part of a political slogan.

Bertha and Oliver vacationing at a spa in the Caucasus in the mid-1930s. In the background is a huge placard featuring Joseph Stalin, whose image was everywhere at the time.

Bertha with her daughter, Lily, in Tashkent (c. 1939). Lily was born in 1934.

Bertha (front row, center) and Lily (right) with Bertha's English students at the Institute of Foreign Languages, Tashkent (c. 1946).

Lily with fellow members of the Uzbek Republic's tennis team at age fifteen. She was the first black woman ever to compete in nationwide tennis matches in the Soviet Union.

Oliver Golden with Yelena's Baba Anya in the mid-1920s. Many years after Oliver's death, Bertha and Anya met and became friends for life.

Baba Anya and her son, Olava Golden, Moscow (c. 1960). The medals Baba Anya wears were awarded by the Soviet government for her military service during World War II, fighting with partisans behind Nazi lines.

Bertha Bialek and Paul Robeson, 1958, Tashkent. Robeson, the great American singer, visited Russia many times. This, however, was his first visit in many years, since Americans suspected of leftist leanings were prevented from traveling abroad by the U.S. government from 1950 to 1958.

immediately upon arriving home in order to finish before bedtime. In 1970, when I was in second grade, the USSR Council of Ministers responded to these parental complaints by passing a decree limiting homework to one hour a day for first graders and four hours a day for tenth graders. Judging from my own experiences in school, most teachers ignored that decree.

I went to School No. 46, a special English school that enrolled children from all over the city. Entrance to these language schools is by competitive examination; I, of course, had a head start because my mother and grandmother spoke English at home. Students in specialized schools work harder than those in ordinary schools, because they receive several extra hours of language instruction each day on top of the regular curriculum.

One of my most vivid memories, from fourth or fifth grade, is of the time my English teacher somehow managed to acquire a tape recording of Martin Luther King's famous "I Have a Dream" speech. It was a rare chance for us to actually hear the English language spoken by a master. We listened to the tape over and over, memorized it, imitated the cadences of Dr. King's speech. I still remember every word, his dream of a nation where men would be judged "not by the color of their skin, but by the content of their character." Thanks to this memorization, there must be dozens of my old schoolmates who still say the words "free at last" with the intonation of a black southern preacher.

For the most part, though, we learned our English from books with British grammar and expressions. Censorship (and the lack of hard currency to buy foreign publications) meant we had little access to contemporary books, magazines, or newspapers. At Moscow newsstands, the only English publications we could buy were communist newspapers from New York and London. This didn't inspire us to read, since the contents were about as exciting as the daily news roundup in *Pravda*. I remember falling asleep when I tried to translate some article from the English *Morning Star* about the perfidy of the Tories, opposition from the Labor Party, and why both Laborites and Tories were enemies of the working class. We would have loved to read some gossip about Queen Elizabeth, Prince Charles, and Princess Anne—like Americans, Russians are fascinated by the British royal family—but that was far too frivolous for our teachers.

I frequently participated in *viktoriny,* local and citywide competitions where we were quizzed on our knowledge of English. I had to retell the same deadly stories from the Communist press (to this day, I can't remember a single political article I used in competition). Then we would display our prowess by reeling off tongue-twisters like, "Peter Piper picked a peck of pickled peppers . . ." and "If a white chalk chalks on a white blackboard, will a black chalk chalk on a black blackboard?" (I think that's how it went, anyway.) Thanks to the conversations I heard at home, I usually won the tongue-twister competition. As far as my grandmother was concerned, there was never any excuse for my not winning an English *viktorina.*

At the end of the school week, the teachers rewarded us for all these rote exercises: We were allowed to listen to recordings of special BBC programs for young people. The children's programs made us realize there was more to English than the polemics of *Morning Star.* I remember my delight at picking up expressions like "it's raining cats and dogs." (Learning English when she was already an adult, my grandmother, and therefore my mother, missed out on many of these sayings.) It's hard for me to avoid using these expressions today, even though they're clichés. To me, they still sound charming and original.

At home, our American visitors would often turn up with livelier books and magazines than the tomes we read in school. Whenever someone left a copy of *Essence,* for instance, I somehow found it much easier to get through the articles than I did when *Morning Star* was in front of me. The first book I read by a black American author was Dick Gregory's autobiography, *Nigger.* With its use of crude, highly specific street slang to describe the experience of growing up in the United States, this autobiography opened my eyes to the range of permissible language in American, as opposed to Soviet, literature. I also began to mull over the difference between life as a member of a large, visible minority—the life of a black American—and my childhood as a member of a minority so small as to be virtually invisible.

As a black Russian, I experienced less overt discrimination but more isolation than African-Americans: I was the only black child in my school. And yet, as I've already said, I didn't dwell on this when I was young. Nor did I discuss my feelings about my color—except, of course, when I was complaining about my hair—with my mother: No excuses. In this respect, I now see that Mama had more in common with certain proud black American parents than I could have realized or understood at the time. Many of my new black American friends remember being told by their parents that they must work twice as hard, and display twice as much talent, as their white counterparts in order not to give the outside world an extra excuse to discriminate against them. My mother didn't put it quite that way, because the white Russian world had never deprived me of anything I wanted, but she did suggest that I was a representative of all blacks to people who had never known anyone else of my color. Any failing on my part might be taken as a universal failing of our race. For a black American child, the parental message was: "You're going to experience prejudice and discrimination. Don't give them a reason to be more prejudiced than they already are." For me, the message was: "You're lucky not to have experienced the kind of prejudice your grandfather knew. Make sure you behave well so that people don't get any different ideas." And I set out from our apartment every day with the neatest uniform my grandmother could clean and press, the best homework I was capable of preparing, the strongest admonitions about working hard.

I usually got good grades in school, but my top marks were all in English. Russian schools have a one-to-five grading system. One is equivalent to an American F and five to an A. Both my mother and grandmother would criticize me sharply if I got anything below a 5 in English; there was no excuse for my not doing better than the other students, they would remind me, because I had heard English spoken all my life. I was expected only to do my best in other subjects; my mother would laughingly recall that Pushkin, our household god, was a dunce in math.

My grandmother was responsible for checking my homework, because Mama sometimes didn't return from her many jobs until nine or ten at night. One of my most vivid images from childhood is of my grandmother poring over my papers, smoking her endless, foul-smelling Russian *papirosy,* and trying to keep the ashes from dropping onto the pages. But she couldn't keep the unmistakeable *papirosy* odor from seeping into the paper. One of my nosy teachers sniffed the pages and said, "Aha, Yelena, you've been keeping secrets from me. You don't only have a mama and grandma, you have a father too. I can smell that he's been checking your homework." (At the time, it wasn't as common for Russian women to smoke as it is now. Today, a large majority of young Russian women, like men, are heavy smokers. Campaigns against smoking, so successful in the United States, have made no headway among Russians. I suspect the only reason I escaped this addiction, since both my mother and grandmother were always puffing away, is that I played competitive tennis during my teens and was aware of the adverse effect of nicotine on lung capacity.)

When my grandmother checked my Russian homework, she needed a dictionary because her command of the language was incomplete. In English, she moved swiftly and easily over the exercises. Part of her insistence that I apply myself to my language studies was attributable to the fact that English truly had been a "piece of bread" for her when she lost her regular job during the campaign against cosmopolitans. The unspoken message was that if trouble came again, I would always have a skill to keep me from starving.

Yet English had a strong emotional as well as practical significance for the aging woman whose most vivid, happy memories were of her youth in left-wing New York. English was her language of intimacy as an adult; she learned to speak it fluently from her beloved husband and passed it on to her daughter and granddaughter.

Although my grandmother would brook no criticism of the Soviet life, she remained deeply attached to America. Most Soviets, expecting a visit from Americans, would hope for stockings and cosmetics, tape recorders and cassettes. My grandmother only asked for newspapers, preferably non–Communist ones, because they had more information about what was really going on. I remember her excitement when some old friend of my grandfather turned up on our doorstep with several editions of the *Washington Post.* When my mother was being courted by Yakovlev, the Russian journalist who became her third husband, he wouldn't try to sway my grandmother with caviar or wine. He knew she wanted American newspapers and magazines, which he was sometimes able to obtain through his journalistic connections.

As she pored over her precious American papers, my grandmother would express indignation at news that was, to both my mother and me, far too removed from our daily lives to arouse or excite us. "Look at what those Republicans are doing. They haven't changed a bit," she would mutter during the years when the Watergate scandal was unfolding. "Let me tell you, it's even worse than the Teapot Dome." Or: "It's terrible, the conditions of those miners in Appalachia." Or: "Aren't those young people in the civil rights marches courageous?" Or (when Jimmy Carter was elected president in 1976): "You know, at least he's better than the Republicans."

I didn't understand my grandmother's interest at all when I was young. As I moved into my self-centered teenage years, I would express my irritation vocally. "Why are you worrying about the miners in . . . where are they, anyway . . . when your life is here? You live in a world of ghosts. Nobody here cares what you think about civil rights in America."

My grandmother wouldn't cry but would straighten her back, purse her lips, and go quietly off to her bedroom to look at my grandfather's picture. The portrait always hung on the wall, and sometimes I would catch her talking to it. He would have understood her. He would have known what she meant by "Teapot Dome." He would have cared about Watergate.

Now I am old enough to understand her émigré's nostalgia. Even though she had come to the Soviet Union voluntarily, out of love for my grandfather and belief in communism, she never abandoned her emotional connection with home, which to her was New York, not the anti-Semitic Warsaw of her girlhood. Her best friends in Moscow were not Russians but other aging "Soviet-Americans." There was so much sadness in the lives of these old people, who believed in the Marxist dream but had never been fully accepted by their adopted country. Once my grandmother visited an old acquaintance in a pensioners' home, and the friend complained bitterly that her fellow octogenarians wouldn't let her into the home's Party cell because of her American past. Who knows, this withered granny might be an American spy! Such was the stupidity and paranoia, unto the grave, of many Soviets shaped by the Stalin era.

How much did my grandmother still care about America? One of the few times I saw her cry was when Leonid Brezhnev made his first visit to the United States in 1973. She would have been overjoyed at the opportunities my mother and I have had to reconnect with America and our American relatives. I now realize that my grandmother was a born activist, that the energy she invested in the Communist Party in her youth would have been directed into the civil rights and anti–Vietnam War movements if she had stayed in America. In the Soviet Union, there was no outlet for her activism, so all of her political energy was directed into arguments with other Soviet-American *babushki* about the respective failings of Republicans and Democrats.

My mother understood my grandmother better than I did and controlled her irritation most of the time. Still, she would occasionally explode when her own problems seemed overwhelming and my grandmother spoke too much about the difficulties of workers and blacks in the United States. Whenever my mother talked about the disappointments she endured in her professional life because of her American background (like being denied the right to travel because of her political "unreliability"), my grandmother would answer, "You're living in the whole world. There are more important things than your own promotion, your own situation at work." I can easily understand my mother's irritation; she, after all, was the one responsible for putting food on our table. She was the one who scraped up the money to pay for my music lessons, my trips to tennis meets, my vacations in the sun. And because she understood more about the true nature of our society than my grandmother did—she, after all, had been born and raised a Soviet—my mother was the one chiefly responsible for bringing me up to function in the world around us without absorbing its official lies and hypocrisy.

In fourth grade, I became a Young Pioneer. Membership in the Pioneers was automatic in elementary school, a universal, more serious form of Boy Scouts and Girl Scouts. The Pioneers played an important role in furthering the Soviet educational system's goal of *vospitaniye* (an almost untranslatable Russian word meaning something like "moral upbringing"). The school version of *vospitaniye* emphasized sharing and conformity. This emphasis has decreased somewhat since the advent of *glasnost;* many schools have even abandoned the once-mandatory brown serge, white-pinafored uniforms, hated by me and my friends but loved by our mothers because they precluded any argument about clothes. On the streets of Moscow today, children head for school in a riot of colorful miniskirts and jeans that would once have earned wearers the epithet *"nevospitaniye"* (lacking in moral upbringing).

My mother was uninterested in my becoming a Pioneer—another difference between the values of my home and school—though she certainly knew I had to belong to the organization to get along with my teachers and the other children. My grandmother, in contrast, was very happy when I came home wearing the Pioneer's red scarf; she was glad I could move through the system in an ordinary way, because she herself had always been outside the structure of Soviet society.

But there were Pioneers and Pioneers, just as, when we were asked to join the Komsomol (Young Communist League) in eighth grade, there were those who enlisted because membership was a prerequisite for university admission and those who were already planning to build Party careers. I was the sort of Pioneer who loved putting on my scarf, belting out the "Internationale" at meetings, and spending a month with my friends at Pioneer camp each summer. Other Pioneers went whole-hog, tattling on their classmates and taking an active part in the student disciplinary councils that enforced school rules.

These disciplinary meetings might be called to discuss such earth-shaking matters as what to do about a boy who had skipped school or used a curse word within earshot of a teacher. School authorities tried to convince everyone that tattling was the duty of a good Pioneer. But most of us despised the children who became miniature informers anyway. Even my grandmother, always a good Communist, disapproved of anything that smacked of informing. Both she and Mama emphasized that if I had a problem with anyone, I should go directly to that person and thrash it out. For the most part, schools in the sixties and seventies had little success in encouraging the development of baby informers; this was a major difference between Stalin's and my Russia.

It was at a Pioneer meeting that I heard the story of Pavlik Morozov for the first time. Beginning in the thirties, this revealing tale was passed on to every Soviet schoolchild; I hope that my generation provides the last audience. Pavlik was a Pioneer during the brutal period (the teacher didn't describe it as brutal, naturally) of enforced collectivization of the land. This wonderful Pavlik listened carefully to everything his parents said at home and denounced them as "kulaks" (peasants who resisted collectivization because they wanted to work their own land) before a Bolshevik court. The villagers (kulaks all, according to the legend) didn't think Pavlik was so wonderful and murdered him in retaliation for his denunciation of his parents. Pavlik Morozov was held up to us as a hero and a martyr. The point was clear: Faced with a choice between the teachings of family and state, we should choose the state.

I came home from school that day—I was about nine years old—and questioned my mother about the story. "The teacher said Pavlik was a hero," I told her, "but I don't see how that can be true if he betrayed his mother and father." My mother looked at me with tears in her eyes and replied, "Thank god, now I know I've done my duty to you as a parent. That you ask me such a question means you understand there is something very wrong about this way of thinking. I would know I hadn't brought you up properly if you accepted this story and thought informers were heroes."

Then my mother delivered her familiar warning: Our low opinion of Pavlik Morozov was another subject we must keep to ourselves.

Americans often ask me why this double standard—one truth for home, another for school—didn't set up an intense conflict within Soviet children. I can't answer for all Soviet youngsters, but I know that the double standard became second nature to me. If you have never experienced any other society, you think everyone in the world lives this way. Only when I began spending time in America at age twenty-five did I realize it might be possible to show the same face to outsiders that you show to people in your intimate world.

Of course, it's not quite that simple: I now understand that Americans have their own set of faces, one for the boss at work, for instance, and one for trusted friends. The difference between the United States and the pre-*glasnost* Soviet Union is you don't risk quite as much here if you speak out against authority. You may lose your job, but you don't (usually) lose your freedom or your life. I'm not forgetting about the McCarthy era, or about the politically inspired vendettas against certain civil rights leaders and antiwar protesters during the sixties and early seventies. And of course I'm not forgetting the American history of violence against blacks. I am simply saying that fear has never been as widespread here, it has never pervaded every level of American society in the way it dominated the Soviet Union for most of its history.

"Don't ever repeat anything our friends say in this house," Mama cautioned me. This was one of the first rules of a Soviet childhood; in fact, I scarcely remember my mother laying down any other laws. Intense involvement with and loyalty to friends is one of the defining characteristics of Russian culture. The material deprivations of Russian society encourage these deep friendships; people cannot distract themselves from the need for human contact by material goods or easily available entertainment.

Mama formed intense, rich friendships with people from every walk of life: musicians, writers, athletes, other historians. From a very young age, I was encouraged to enter into serious discussions to the best of my ability. Russians have a special phrase for the most intense, meaningful conversations between friends—*dusha v dushu* (soul to soul). Such conversations, Mama emphasized, must never be replayed as gossip. The topic didn't matter. It might be something as political as a new novel in samizdat or as personal as a broken love affair. Our business, and our friends' business, was no one else's business.

Svetlana Alliluyeva, Joseph Stalin's daughter and my mother's longtime friend, defected to the West in 1966. Svetlana and my mother had known each other since Mama's earliest days in Moscow. My mother liked her very much and was filled with compassion for her impossible position as Stalin's daughter. "She was a very kind, tender-hearted person," my mother recalls.

> She did everything she could to help people who returned from the camps in the late fifties, yet one thing she could never do was hold her father responsible for these ruined lives. One day I asked her, we were really close, "How do you think your father turned into the kind of man we know he was?" Her reply was, "It wasn't my father's doing; it was Beria."* I understood. This was her father. How can you admit that your own father was a mass murderer?
>
> And I pitied her deeply, because it was impossible for her to escape her terrible heritage. She simply couldn't trust people; how could you if you were Stalin's daughter? I'm sure this desire to escape who she was, no longer to be treated as some kind of a freak, was an important motive for her defection. Of course, she couldn't escape being identified as her father's daughter in the West any more than she could in Russia."

The defection of Stalin's daughter was one of the major news stories of 1966. All of her close Russian friends, including my mother, were suspected by the KGB of having known about her defection in advance. Svetlana made matters worse by calling from New York and babbling on about all the terrible things she was learning in the West about the Soviet government. Sometimes she would begin these phone coversations with the question, "Are you alone, Lily?" as if

---

*Lavrenti Beria replaced Nikolai Yezhov as head of the secret police in 1938. He remained in that post until Stalin's death in 1953, after which he was arrested and executed.

that made any difference. Our phone may or may not have been bugged before Svetlana's defection, but it certainly was afterward. My mother assumed her old friend had become seriously disoriented. It used to be second nature to any Soviet citizen—the daughter of Joseph Stalin or plain Ivan Ivanovich—not to discuss anything sensitive on the phone or in apartments that might be bugged.

In 1968, things got worse for my mother with the publication of Svetlana's second book, *Only One Year*. In one chapter, she discussed her relations with her closest Russian friends, including my mother and their dear mutual friend, Dmitri (Mitya) Tolstoy (a composer and son of the writer Aleksei Tolstoy, as well as a distant relative of the nineteenth-century Tolstoy). Svetlana "disguised" my mother's identity in her book by giving her my grandmother's name, Bertha. Not that it would have helped to give her a less obvious pseudonym. The Soviet Union isn't exactly packed with daughters of white American mothers and black fathers who grew cotton in Uzbekistan in the thirties. Svetlana described my mother as a "strange hybrid"—half Negro and half Jew—who would never be allowed to travel abroad even though she knew more about Africa than any of the Party hacks who represented the Soviet Union at international academic conferences.

She also detailed my mother's difficulties with Soviet censors when she was researching a book on blacks in the Soviet Union. In the republic of Abkhazia near the Black Sea coast, my mother found isolated, impoverished villages of blacks descended from African slaves brought there between the sixteenth and eighteenth centuries, when the area was a part of the Ottoman Empire. She returned to Moscow filled with indignation and hoping to persuade someone to help these forgotten people but got nowhere with the authorities. When her book was finally published—in bowdlerized form in English, by the Novosti Press Agency—the Abkhazian blacks were mentioned but all references to their poverty were deleted.

Finally, Svetlana noted my mother's exasperation when American Communists—some of them old friends of her father—would tell her how lucky she was to be living in the Soviet Union. After only two years in the West, she seemed to have forgotten the watchwords of friendship in Russia: loyalty and discretion. If my mother ever had any chance of being allowed to travel and study abroad in the pre-*glasnost* world, she lost it when *Only One Year* was published. In spite of all the problems the book caused her in the bad old days, my mother did not turn away from her old friend when she returned to the Soviet Union for a visit in 1987. "She was very kind to me when we were young," Mama says today. "What if I were Joseph Stalin's instead of Oliver Golden's daughter? I don't think anyone else could ever really understand what a burden such a childhood must have been." (Svetlana's mother, Nadezhda Alliluyeva, killed herself in 1932 after an agonizing period of personal and political disagreement with her husband. Svetlana only learned the details of the suicide in 1955, when her nurse and one of her mother's close friends returned from Siberian exile and told her the story). Svetlana visited my mother at our Moscow apartment in 1987, but Mama still cautioned me not to tell anyone else about our controversial guest. People were already much less afraid of the KGB than they had been before Gorbachev, but we remained cautious and uncertain about the future and loyal to our friends.

Because my mother was honest with me, I grew up knowing that people in her generation, people she knew personally, had gone to jail simply for telling the wrong jokes, reading the wrong books, revealing their thoughts to the wrong person. On a conscious level, this sounded like ancient history to me: When you're a small child, everything that happened even a few years ago seems a galaxy away. On a deeper level, though, I paid attention to my mother's warnings. When you recognize fear in a parent and see it in her eyes, a sense of unease transmits itself to you by osmosis. Words really aren't even necessary.

Still, encouraging a child to think for herself, even if she is supposed to save her thoughts for home consumption, always opens a Pandora's box. From time to time, I opened my mouth when it would have been smarter to keep it shut. In elementary school, every child had to take a class in military tactics called *voyenka* (literally, "war course"). We would learn how to defend ourselves if someone (the Germans again, or perhaps the Americans?) decided to attack our apartment on Profsoyuznaya Street. I was the best shot in the class— we used mock guns and bullets—but I couldn't see the point of it all. The instructor lectured endlessly about American aggression and the threat of nuclear war, so I asked him what would be the use of knowing how to shoot a rifle in World War III. A nuclear war would be over in just a few minutes, I pointed out. The teacher said, "Yelena, I like you as a marksman, but your political mind isn't prepared."

Our connection with America was something we discussed only among ourselves and with trusted friends. To this day, it's almost impossible for me to separate my race from my "foreignness" when I think about my family's experiences in the Soviet Union. Being descended from Americans, and having American relatives, is an asset now, but that wasn't true for most of my life. If my grandparents had both been white, we certainly would have blended into the society around us by the third generation. But I was always having to explain who I was and how I wound up in Russia. I might have been raised on Tchaikovsky and Pushkin, I might feel Russian in a cultural sense, but my face told another story.

Because I was born at the high-water mark of the Cold War—I was six months old when Khrushchev and Kennedy faced off in the Cuban missile crisis—anti-American propaganda was a constant feature of my education. In school I never told anyone my grandparents came from the United States, even though the teachers always made a distinction between black and white Americans. Whites (except for Communists) were bad; black Americans were oppressed and good. I never had any idea as a child that a great many non-Communist whites had given their energies to the civil rights movement. My teachers also painted a portrait of a United States in which a few were rich and everyone else was poor. My mother knew better. She tried to tell me about the middle class, about millions of ordinary American workers who owned automobiles—something she, a historian with a doctorate, could not dream of owning in the Soviet Union.

Nearly all of the Americans who visited our home during those years had some connection with the U.S. Communist Party. They included, Gus Hall, the general secretary of the Party, and Angela Davis, whose book *Women, Race and Class* my mother translated into Russian. Nevertheless, my mother emphasized that I must not talk about these American guests to anyone outside our home.

In spite of all this caution, my mother was reprimanded for entertaining Americans by one of her bosses at the African Institute. He reminded her that unauthorized visits between Soviet citizens and foreigners were forbidden (this was legally true, though the rule was frequently ignored) and told her she must report prospective contacts with Americans to the "authorities"—meaning the KGB. Mama refused. She told her boss that these were her private guests—most of them were old family friends—and had nothing to do with official business involving the Soviet government.

You would think from the attitude of my mother's boss that we were inviting CIA agents to tea. But any American—even one like Angela Davis, who had no love for the policies of the U.S. government—was suspect. Even American jazz was still slightly suspect. When Mama organized a committee in defense of Davis, she invited Soviet jazz musicians to the first meeting. Someone from the Party Central Committee informed her that jazz was entirely out of place at a gathering devoted to such a serious topic as the imprisonment of a black American. "But I have it on very good authority," Mama said innocently, "that Angela herself loves jazz. How would it look to her if we excluded her musical comrades?"

When Angela visited the Soviet Union, she and my mother became friends, even though Mama strongly sensed, and was angered by, her indifference to political and social injustice in Russia. (They never discussed this sensitive topic. When Mama translated Angela's book for Progress Publishers, the Russian edition was delayed several years by Soviet censorship. One sentence, which described American soldiers "searching Vietnamese women with their phalluses," was deleted because the word "phallus" was considered obscene. The censors were especially vigilant about passages revealing an American feminist consciousness. The official Soviet line maintained that Davis was persecuted only because she was black and a Communist; discrimination against women, and the complicated interaction of race, sex, and class discrimination, was something no Soviet censor wanted to handle. It might have raised questions about the way our own supposedly egalitarian society treated women. It's ironic that Davis's book could be published without censorship in her own "oppressive" country but not in the supposedly liberated Soviet Union.

Another forbidden subject was Soviet anti-Semitism. This topic was not only kept inside our home; it was reserved for my mother and me. My grandmother never wanted to hear any challenges to her youthful belief that communism would eliminate persecution of Jews. Because we were black, many anti-Semitic Russians simply assumed my mother and I would share their views, so we were frequently treated to a inside view of this dirty little secret. When the Jewish emigration movement began in the late sixties, it provided a new rationale for discrimination that already existed in the workplace and in educational institutions. The fact that some Jews wanted to leave our socialist paradise was treated as one more piece of evidence that a *zhid* could never be a loyal Soviet citizen. I didn't really connect any of this with my own or my family's history, because even though I knew my grandmother had been born into a Jewish family, I thought of her simply as an American. But I believed my mother when she told me Soviet Jews were routinely denied jobs and promotions because of their "nationality." To me, this sounded like the discrimination against black Americans that impelled my grandparents to leave their home so many years before my birth.

And I knew about the Holocaust, both from my mother and from carefully phrased school references (in which the sufferings of other nationalities were emphasized and the special fate of the Jews under the Nazis was downplayed to some degree). Yevgeny Yevtushenko's famous poem "Babi Yar," which excoriated Soviet society for failing to build a monument to the 100,000 Jews slaughtered in that ravine, was published the year I was born. My generation knew far more about the Holocaust than Russians had known ten years earlier, yet this didn't stop new forms of anti-Semitism from taking root and flourishing, not only during the Brezhenv era, but during the *glasnost* period as well.

I will never know exactly how much of my grandmother's reticence about her Jewishness had to do with her rejection of "bourgeois nationalism" in favor of communism, how much with the perils of being Jewish under Stalin's rule, and how much with her own complicated, painful relations with her family in America.

I do know that thirty-six years ago, my cousin Eugene Bialek received a hand-embroidered yarmulke from his Aunt Bertha upon the birth of his son, Steve. My grandmother embroidered this yarmulke in secret; my mother never saw it or had any idea that she managed to send it to her family in Los Angeles.

At some point in the mid-Sixties, Jack and his wife, Minnie, came to visit us in Moscow. I don't remember this visit, but my mother recalls it clearly. It would be nice to report that the wounds of the past were healed in a heartwarming, tearful family reunion, but that isn't what happened. Instead, my grandmother finally learned that her brother had never told his family about her marriage and my mother's birth.

After that visit, my grandmother sent no more pictures to America. Correspondence was limited to occasional New Year's cards. I didn't know the whole story when I was a child, but my grandmother's powerful, unarticulated emotions surely contributed to my ambivalence about the American (or at least the white, Jewish-American) side of my heritage. Everything about our link with America was so complicated, so emotionally volatile that it had to be kept private.

CHAPTER SEVEN

MOTHER AND DAUGHTER

Every Sunday—Mama's day off from work—we would set off together on foot for the nearest metro stop, where we would catch an underground train for the Tchaikovsky Conservatory of Music. Mama never wanted me to miss one of the conservatory's weekly classical concerts for children, even though the trip took an hour each way.

I loved the beautiful old neighborhood around the conservatory, set in the midst of pastel stucco nineteenth-century homes (divided into apartments, but retaining their charm), ice-cream cafés, book-stores, and music shops. Unmarred by Stalinesque construction, the whole area still looks much as it did in the 1920s, when Bulgakov used its narrow streets as the setting for *The Master and Margarita*. Walking with Mama along Herzen Street, I felt the pleasant tug of another world—a very different world from *viktorini*, daily tussles with the *Morning Star,* and hours of homework.

What would they play today? Prokofiev's *Peter and the Wolf* or perhaps some passages from a Rachmaninoff piano concerto? These concerts were *fun*—nothing like the dry lessons in school or the scales demanded by my piano teacher. Mama was thrilled that I shared her love of music. She often reminded me that she didn't have the same opportunities growing up in Tashkent. Why, children over twelve didn't even get to go to school in September in Tashkent (this didn't sound so bad to me) because they had to help bring in the cotton harvest from the fields. She, Mama, couldn't even play the piano some days because her fingers bled after picking cotton. Sometimes it annoyed me to be told what a lucky little girl I was. Now I know what it meant for a single mother to give up her free time for such expeditions. How she must have wished, on those cold winter Sundays, to stretch out on the sofa, cover herself with an afghan, and rest!

I heard my first snatches of opera—a lifelong passion—at the conservatory concerts. Then, when I was about eight or nine, Mama took me to a full-length opera, Verdi's *La Traviata*. Entranced, I immediately imagined myself singing the role of Violetta. Thrilled by my interest, Mama bought *La Traviata* recordings in Lithuanian (the stores were out of Russian) and German. I learned to sing the arias in every language. (In Russian, as in the rest of Europe, opera is sung in the language of the country where it is being performed rather than in the original language of the composer. Only in New York have I heard a live performance of *La Traviata* in Italian.) Opera in general, and *La Traviata* in particular, served as an emotional escape for me. Whenever I was angry or upset, when the "no excuses" message got to be too much, I would turn on the record player and become Violetta.

For Mama, there was no such thing as "black" and "white" music, only worthwhile and worthless. Bach, Mozart, Verdi, Puccini, Tchaikovsky, Glinka, Shostakovich: The music of these composers, I was taught from earliest childhood, belonged to the whole world. So too did blues and jazz, the contribution of blacks to everyone's musical heritage. Mama made no secret of her disdain for the music that pervaded the air waves, the kind of schmaltzy Russian pop tunes, with inane words and childish melodies calculated to please the most ignorant commissar of music. Why would anyone bother to listen to lyrics, she asked indignantly, like ". . . You can't make the rose petal blue, some things never change, and so it isn't strange you can't keep me from loving you." Those words, and the tune to an endlessly repeated song called "Moscow Nights," are lodged like a burr in the brain of every Muscovite. (The first five notes of "Moscow Nights" used to announce the evening news and the end of daily television programming.) The new Russia is, mercifully, still too poor to afford Muzak, but that's the closest approximation of the pop songs of my girhood.

When I was about five years old, I invited my friends from the courtyard, including my hero Sasha, to hear some of our American recordings. To my dismay, the other kids hated the singers my mama revered: Sarah Vaughan and Billie Holiday, Ella Fitzgerald and Bessie Smith, Louis Armstrong and Paul Robeson. They'd never heard the blues or black voices. "Why are they shouting?" my friends asked. "That's not music, Lena [the Russian diminutive for Yelena]. That's just noise. We're sorry, we hate it."

I cried bitterly, accusing my mother of lying to me about how good the music was. "You told me this music was wonderful," I said, "but my friends say it's terrible." Mama gently explained—how many times she would make the same point, in different contexts, over the years—that majority opinion doesn't determine good taste. This was one of the first times I remember feeling different from other people. True, the difference had something to do with being black. But it was also about American records and a mother who knew more than most of my playmates' parents.

This changed as I grew up. I felt more comfortable as I realized that our intellectual Russian friends loved jazz and blues as much as we did. When you're small, though, you want to share the tastes of the kids next door. But that wasn't to be. It wasn't long before I realized I literally marched to a different drummer. Even in nursery school, I clapped and moved differently to the simple Russian tunes we learned. The teacher would say, "No, no, Yelena, that isn't the rhythm, this is," demonstrating a very simple, monotonous beat. In my head, I heard something more elaborate and more lively, echoes of the music my race had created on other continents and that I had heard at home. I doubt that all blacks have "rhythm," as the stereotype goes (surely there must be tone-deaf blacks with two left feet), but I do know that I had a very different sense of rhythm than most of the people around me.

So my passion for music always presented me with an emotional paradox: Though music bridged the gap between my black and my Russian identities, it also made me realize that there was, indeed, a gulf.

Clapping out the "wrong" beat in school didn't really bother me, but the all-white casts of Russian operas made me feel like an outsider in a more hurtful way. When I fell in love with *La Traviata,* I began to consider the possibility, for the first time in my life, that being black might prevent me from doing something that really mattered. What roles might be open to a black singer? At the time, I was not aware of black opera singers like Leontyne Price, Grace Bumbry, and Kathleen Battle. This was and is an important difference between growing up black in America and in Russia; in America, I would have taken heart from the fact that some blacks had battled discrimination to make a place for themselves on the opera stage. In Moscow, I only knew the fifty-year-old story of how Paul Robeson's development as a classical singer was stymied by his race. There were no black opera stars in the Soviet Union. The great Bolshoi singer Galina Vishnevskaya wore dark makeup to play the slave girl Aida, and the idea of a black singer putting on white makeup seemed ridiculous to me. But it never occurred to me that a black might take on a traditionally white role without putting on white-face, because there was no precedent for this kind of performance in my country.

I didn't discuss these feelings with my mother, who would have understood them very well, but locked them away until I became an adult. The "no excuses" tone of my home life was part of the reason I kept my sadness and confusion to myself. I think I was also afraid to hear my mother's answer were I to pose the direct question, "Mama, can a black person become an opera singer?" Would she have replied, "You can do anything you want if you work hard enough" (her standard answer to any doubt), or would she have said, "Well, Yelena, you're old enough to know that there are some things you really can't do, some barriers too great to overcome"? Looking back, I see I was protecting my mother and grandmother as well as myself.

To suggest that I was wounded in any way by the color of my skin would wound them even more deeply; leaving the sore spots alone was easier on all of us.

In any case, my love of music turned out to be better suited for listening than performance, though my mother, who thought I was something of a prodigy, didn't see it that way. When I was only three, she hired a music teacher. I was to learn to read music as well as play the piano. These lessons were expensive, so my grandmother paid part of the bill by tutoring the teacher's son in English.

As much as I loved listening to music, I detested taking lessons, even more so because I knew my parents were making financial sacrifices to pay for them. Every day, I would ask my mother to play the pieces the teacher had given me to study, from the usual beginner's scales to *Für Elise*. Then I would memorize the sounds she made and play them by ear, tricking her into believing I had learned to read music. One day she noticed a mistake, pointed to the note and said, "Play it as it's written. I looked at her blankly, since I hadn't learned how to read a single note. Mama was furious at me for using my memory and perfect pitch to deceive her. (I didn't actually learn to read music until nearly twenty years later, when I attended evening classes at the Tchaikovsky Conservatory. I was still under the spell of *La Traviata* and gave up my studies only when I realized I was a mezzo rather than a true soprano and could never hope to sing the role of Violetta in black or white. But my teachers succeeded, at last, in forcing me to learn to read the notes.)

I have nothing but gratitude for my musical education now, because it gave me a bridge between Russian and black culture. The breadth of culture in our home made me understand that everything good belongs to the same world, that there's no need to choose between opera and the blues, between Pushkin and Hughes.

A very different side of my personality emerged when Mama decided it was time for me to begin playing tennis. This, she told me, was yet another advantage of growing up in Moscow rather than Tashkent. My mother thoroughly enjoyed her own tennis-playing days—she'd even been a champion in her native Uzbekistan—but the level of her training (like the entire Soviet tennnis program) was far below international standards. That was beginning to change by the early seventies. Soviet tennis players were making respectable, if not brilliant, showings in international competition. When I was nine, my mother took me to see the tennis star, Anna Vladimirovna Dmitriyeva, who had made a respectable showing at Wimbledon.

The possibility of travel abroad was one of the main reasons my mother wanted me to play competitive tennis. She had abandoned any hope for herself of traveling beyond the borders of fraternal socialist countries in Eastern Europe, but she hadn't given up hope for me. Apart from enlisting in the diplomatic corps or KGB (two possibilities closed to me as a woman and the granddaughter of Americans), athletic success was one of the few routes to foreign travel.

When Mama started inquiring about lessons for me, she was stunned to learn that other potential athletes had started their training at age five or six. She didn't start playing tennis until she was thirteen, so she thought nine was young. Most of the teachers said I was already too old, but Anna Vladimirovna took me on, in part because she had a high opinion of the abilities of the black athletes she had met in international competition.

At first, I made rapid progress in the sport. Two years after I began taking lessons, Anna Vladimirovna took me to the Black Sea, along with her own children, for intensive coaching. The poet Yevgeny Yevtushenko, who was vacationing at a Writers' Union spa, proposed a game with me. He was famous for hating to lose and chose me because I was the smallest person on the court.

He was sure he could beat me. I won. My mother, who had remained at home, was walking down a Moscow Street when a friend, a member of the Writers' Union, told her I had beaten Yevtushenko in a match. "He picked her because he thought she was a pushover," the writer explained, "and now everyone is laughing at him." (Actually, I owe an apology to Yevtushenko for telling this boastful story. There really isn't anything so unusual about a tireless twelve-year-old, coached by an international star, beating an out-of-shape, fortyish weekend tennis player.)

I played for the Soviet Army team, under the old, government-controlled sports system in which many establishments, from the military to factories, sponsored athletes at different levels of competition. Like Virginia Slims, the Red Army got publicity and prestige (though not money) by sponsoring competitions. Individual players earned nothing. (All this has changed. Russian athletes now enter international competitions, and take home prize money, like their competitors in every other country.)

In my early teens, I had considerable success in national competitions. By my mid-teens, though, I realized I lacked the single-minded drive required to be number one (or even two or three). I loved literature and music. I was already thinking about some sort of a career in journalism. Sometimes when officials would come to the court to inspect students, a coach would introduce us by saying: "This girl moves to her right beautifully, and this one has a great backhand. Yelena . . . Yelena reads thick books." Like pubescent American tennis stars, Soviet teenagers were encouraged to neglect their studies and the rest of their lives in order to concentrate on their athletic development.

Most athletes when I was growing up attended special schools for "sportsmen," and the academic programs were a joke. I was the only girl on the army team who didn't attend a sports school, and that meant I had to lug thick books on tour so I wouldn't flunk my exams back at School No. 46. Sometimes I would be away from Moscow for several weeks, playing a dozen matches in as many towns: Minsk one night, Kiev the next. When I came back to school, my teachers made no allowances—quite the contrary—for my tennis-mandated absences. In fact, they were utterly contemputuous of athletes and the sporting life. Every teacher would say, "If you're going to run around the country hitting balls over nets, you'd better not forget what's really important. If you can't keep up with the work, you shouldn't be playing tennis." At night—on the road and at home—I sometimes slumped over my books in exhaustion, waking up in the middle of the night with a jolt to turn off the light.

Part of me enjoyed the spotlight, but another part of me carried on because I didn't want to disappoint my mother. She played tennis at a time when it was more fun and less work; I don't think she fully understood the pressures on me.

My grandmother, who accompanied me to lessons and most competitions, displayed total disdain for Soviet tennis parents who pushed their children. Others would bring presents to the coach, everything from caviar to foreign records, but my grandmother would sit on the bench, ignoring my performance and reading an Agatha Christie novel (purchased at a secondhand bookstore that carried a selection of old English detective stories). All of the other parents loved my grandmother because she would praise each child instead of running down the competition (as most of them did).

At the end of each two-hour coaching session, my grandmother would get up from the bench and order me, in a firm voice, "Baby . . . *home.* You're finished. Here's your apple. Be sure you eat it on the way." (She was convinced that this fruit was essential to restore my energy level.) During competition, she would display no emotion and, win or lose, would ask, "Did you do your best?" My coach, accustomed to hysterical parents who ruined their children's performances by putting them under too much pressure, once asked my grandmother how she could remain so calm. "Don't you want your child to be the best?" she asked. My grandmother admitted she really did want me to be the best and kept her eyes focused on Agatha Christie so I wouldn't know how nervous she was. "I don't want to place the burden of my nervousness on her," she explained. "If she's going to be the best, the desire has to come from inside her, not from anyone else."

Like my mother in her day, I was the only black teenager on the competitive tennis circuit. In this context, I thought of my race not as a liability but as an asset. Sports and opera were entirely different. Although I didn't know there were black opera stars in other parts of the world, I was well aware that black athletes had earned acclaim in many countries. I was deeply moved by the story of Adolph Hitler's fury when the black American track star, Jesse Owens, won gold medals at the 1936 Olympics in Berlin. Anna Vladimirovna, who wrote an introduction to the Russian translation of Althea Gibson's autobiography, spoke admiringly about the many black athletes she had known personally. And she endeared herself to me by caring almost as much as I did about my stubborn black hair. She would work on my head in the locker room, trying to imitate the stylish hairdos of black American women she had seen on her travels. She, too, would look admiringly at copies of *Essence,* only to be defeated, as I was, by the lack of proper hair-care products and instruments. But I loved her for caring, and tennis unquestionably made me feel more positive about being black in a white world.

Soviet sports announcers also spoke respectfully about black athletes, though we heard almost nothing about the achievements of black American politicians, professionals, or businessmen. I remember hearing broadcasters refer to some talented African-American (or plain African) athlete as a *chyornokozhiy gigant* (black giant). Only in America have I come to realize that there is a double edge to this sort of "compliment," that many Soviet sportcasters, like Americans, attribute the success of black athletes to pure brawn. No Soviet announcer ever described a white athlete as a *belokozhiy gigant,* though the white-skinned giants looked every bit as imposing as their black counterparts.

In Soviet terms, succeeding at tennis gave me a psychological boost by enabling me to make black Russians more visible. In cities throughout the country, it was customary for young athletes to take time out from competition to place flowers at war memorials to victims of the Nazis. I was often picked for this task, and it gave me a great feeling of pride that I, a black girl, could represent the whole country, in however small a way.

Still, by the time I was sixteen, both Mama and I understood that I couldn't continue to tour and prepare for my university entrance exams. (My teammates from the special sports schools, if they went to university at all, were planning to major in physical education and become coaches.)

For several years, I had already known, deep down, that I didn't have the makings of a world-class player. I remember exactly when I accepted my limitations. At thirteen, I came in second in the USSR junior women's singles competition. The girl who beat me, Svetlana Cherneva, had already dedicated herself to a life in tennis. Her father was an Olympic biathlon coach, and her mother worked with the Soviet gymnastics team. Svetlana would play through any kind of pain; I wouldn't have been surprised to see her walk onto the court with a broken arm. She simply wanted to be the best; she didn't go on tour because she enjoyed seeing other cities, or placing flowers at war memorials, or smiling at admirers in the crowd. My tennis years forced me to take a realistic measure of my abilities at a young age and to make a choice. Although Mama didn't agree with all my choices, she did prepare me to make them. However hard she pushed me, she never imposed her will once she saw I had made a serious decision. When I explained my feelings about studying journalism versus playing tennis, Mama never even tried to change my mind, in spite of the financial sacrifices she had made on behalf of my halfhearted career in sports. "This is one of the first really important decisions for you," she said, "and you're the one who has to live with it."

Americans often ask what I did for fun during my teenage years, crammed as they were with sports, music, and a demanding school curriculum. "Where did you go on dates?" they ask. "What about boys?"

For me, and for many of my friends, the answer was that we didn't go on dates and didn't have much to do with boys. When I was a teenager, Soviet high schools offered none of the social activities—dances, for instance—that encourage early mingling of the sexes in the United States. Nor did we have interschool athletic rivalries. (Schools did have sports programs, but their only purpose was good health. Competitive sports, as I learned during my tennis days, were strictly professional, even though officials pretended we were all amateurs so they wouldn't have to pay us.)

Moreover, the burden of homework was so great, and the social consequences of not getting into a university so grave, that most fifteen and sixteen year olds spent every spare moment in tutoring sessions for all-important entrance exams. The Soviet educational system was reserved for an elite; only one in five secondary school graduates made it into a university.

When Russian teenagers are bound (they hope) for university life, they don't begin to date, or pair off in couples, until their academic future is settled. Where would they go if they wanted to be alone, anyway? Mama, papa, and *babushka* aren't going to vacate the family apartment so that fifteen year olds can neck on the couch. As for cars, no one under eighteen was permitted to drive. Anyway, hardly anyone owned a car.

The lag in social activity and sexual awareness was not universal, but it was typical for my friends from serious, intellectual families. This delay enabled me to put off all of the painful, volatile emotional issues I would have to face when I began to think about finding a lover or husband in a world where nearly every potential mate belonged to another race. How would my color influence my chances of loving and being loved? Love is colorblind, my grandmother always told me. I wanted to believe her but wasn't sure I did.

CHAPTER EIGHT

COMING OF AGE IN BLACK AND WHITE

I was seventeen when I entered the journalism *fakultyet* (department) of Moscow State University in the fall of 1979. Only one in five of my classmates were girls (in Russia, teenagers do not proudly call themselves "women" as they do in the United States). Journalism is a prestigious profession, one of the few offering a possibility of foreign travel, and it was understood that the best jobs were reserved for men. MGU's journalism department was divided into an international and a domestic section. The international branch, which trained future foreign correspondents and political writers, was for men only, though one girl was admitted each year for the sake of egalitarian appearances. The domestic section, where I studied along with the other girl-women, was known as the "House of Brides" because most of the students were intent not on building careers but on catching a husband with a future.

I knew how lucky I was to have gotten into MGU at all. Most of the other students were children of the Soviet elite, well-connected Party officials, scientists, diplomats, journalists, and writers. This was my first exposure to people from the top of the Soviet pyramid. The girls wore clothes with Western designer labels, the unmistakable stamp of their parents' visits to New York, Paris, and London. Many students drove their own cars (the concept of a two-car family had never entered my head). My classmates chattered about weekend plans at family dachas in places like Peredelkino, the famous writers' colony where Boris Pasternak lived, or Zhukovka, the elite retreat where Svetlana Alliluyeva used to have her country home. Strangely enough, I wasn't envious, but I did sense a profound social gulf between myself and most of my classmates. At the time, I envisioned a future for myself as a sportscaster. I hoped to follow in the footsteps of my old coach, Anna Vladimirovna, who had introduced tennis to Soviet television audiences. I vowed to apply myself to my studies, to take advantage of the training at MGU, because I did not consider myself marriage material for the sons of the Soviet elite. Why would they choose me—dark, full-lipped Yelena, with the kinkiest hair in all of Russia—when they could have a classic Russian beauty with silky hair cascading down her back?

Hair again: It was still on my mind, even while I chided myself for continuing to dwell on such a frivolous matter. I felt like screaming when my Russian girlfriends complained they couldn't do a thing with their hair. *They* couldn't do a thing, they with straight, manageable tresses pulled back into perky pony tails or elegant topknots. I still looked hungrily at copies of *Essence,* at the dazzling array of possibilities open to women in the land of a million hair-care products. Sometimes I would cut out a picture of an especially attractive black hairdo and present it to a stylist in a Moscow beauty parlor. She would ooh and aah and try her best to imitate this vision of black beauty. It never worked out, though; the stylists had no practice on black hair and no products to help them—no chemical straighteners if you wanted your hair smooth, no scissors or conditioners to shape a "natural." At this age, never having had a boyfriend, I simply couldn't imagine that any Russian man would want to stroke my hair.

My black American friends complain, with considerable justification, that white images of beauty continue to dominate their culture. But African-Americans of my age, unless they happened to grow up in a tent with no television set in the middle of nowhere, can't imagine how it feels to walk the streets of a huge city without encountering a black face, to turn on the television set without seeing a black entertainer, to be one of a kind. Once I was visiting a girlfriend in Voronezh, a small city on the Volga River, south of Moscow. Her parents were unsophisticated, poorly educated, but good-hearted souls, and they had never seen a black person in the flesh. My friend's mother walked in on me when I was changing in the bedroom and began to laugh. What, I asked her, was so funny. "You're black all over," she replied, trying unsuccessfully to stifle her giggles. "I feel so foolish. I've only seen black people on TV, and I thought you'd be white in the places underneath your clothes." She thanked me for having corrected her misconception. I wasn't offended—and I would never have encountered such naïveté in Moscow—but such experiences certainly reinforced my sense of myself as an ugly duckling, or an odd duckling at the very least, among white Russian swans.

Walking the streets of New York today, I have an entirely different feeling about my appearance. I delight in the many faces of black beauty, colors ranging from gold to deepest chocolate, hair in corn rows or fluffy naturals or straightened chignons. Black swans, every one: How I love the array of choices! When I was growing up, my mother was my only image of black beauty. And of course the more she told me I was beautiful, the uglier I felt. She was my mama, after all; she had to think I was gorgeous.

It's strange that I assumed no Russian boy would want to marry me, because my mother had two Russian husbands in addition to my African father. There was the first, brief marriage ending in her young husband's death in an auto accident. Then there was her third marriage, to journalist Boris Yakovlev, that has lasted to this day. I didn't think, "Russian men fell in love with Mama—why shouldn't they fall in love with me?" Instead I told myself, "Don't think anyone will fall in love with you just because they fell in love with your mother." It's possible that this reaction, which seems odd to American friends when I tell them about it, flowed from a kind of awe I felt toward my mother. I had seen pictures of her when she was young and considered myself much less attractive. Perhaps this was because she is taller, lighter-skinned, and her features are more Caucasion than mine? I'm not sure.

There's another possibility. Mama's first marriage to a Russian, romantic and star-crossed, ended in tragedy. When I was growing up, we didn't talk about this much, about the way her young husband's family treated her. I wondered sometimes what sort of person I would be had my father been a Russian instead of an African. But Mama pointed out, sensibly, "You wouldn't be you if you were the child of someone else." So we dropped the subject. Here, I sensed, was a wound, though I didn't know how strongly Nikolai's family had objected to the marriage.

But history catches up with you in unexpected ways. A few years ago, I was covering a Japanese-Soviet chess match for *Moscow News* when I ran into an interesting young Russian who was interpreting for the Japanese chess players. Andrei looked vaguely familiar and reminded me that we had seen each other in passing when we were both studying at MGU. We became friends. One evening, he invited me back to his apartment to watch a movie on his VCR and meet his parents. As we were sitting and talking, an older man walked into the room, looked at me, gasped and asked, "Lily, is it you?" He turned out to be the brother of Mama's dead husband, and he hadn't seen her for years. Of course, he knew my mother couldn't still be in her twenties, but for a moment he reacted as if he had seen a ghost. The young man I met at the chess match was his son. Andrei, it turned out, had some idea that we were vaguely connected because his grandmother had asked about me when he told her there was a pretty black girl studying journalism—family secrets, again.

When I told Mama I had met some members of her first husband's family, she seemed almost angry. She had liked Andrei's grandmother, she told me, because she was was one of the few family members who hadn't made her feel like an outsider. "Some of them are fine people, . . ." she said, and I could hear the "but" coming, *but* if I weren't a reporter and a minor celebrity, I would be treated as an outsider too.

My family gave me a confusing double message about sex. On the one hand, I was raised with a very positive view of interracial love, sex, and marriage. How could it be otherwise, when both my mother and I were the products of my grandparents' taboo-defying love? On the other hand, I was told over and over to beware of the kind of white boys who would only want me because I was exotic, who would sleep with me but reject me when it came time for marriage. And I was in a very different position from American blacks, who can choose to limit their romantic and sexual attachments to members of their own race, if that is what they want to do. Living in Moscow— and assuming I would never be able to travel abroad—I knew that if I found love, the man would probably be white.

And my mother had been quite blunt about warning me against the sort of white men who believed myths about the superheated sexuality of black women. Stereotypes about the sexual performance of blacks, men as well as women, are every bit as prevalent in Russia as in the United States. Given the small number of blacks in my country, I don't have any idea how this belief made its way into the mind of the average Russian. It's hard to place the blame on popular Western culture, because we were isolated for so long from celluloid images of black men as superstuds and black women as hot mamas. I suppose every culture is saturated with sexual stereotypes of various "others". The supersexiness of Georgians and Armenians is also a feature of many Russian jokes.

How could I distinguish between "good" whites who would love me for myself and "bad" whites obsessed with notions of exotic black sexuality? I couldn't begin to answer these questions at age seventeen, so I decided to turn myself into the most industrious future journalist in the House of Brides.

In spite of this resolution, I promptly fell in love for the first time. Misha★ was the dreamy-eyed captain of the chess team, I was still

---

★His name has been changed to protect privacy.

playing in a few tennis matches, and both Misha and I were considered athletes in the Soviet system. We met for the first time in a lounge where all of the journalism department's half-hearted jocks were discussing the MGU sports program. Soon we were seeing each other every day, studying together, going to movies together. At first, remembering my mother's warnings, I was on guard for any sign that Misha was ashamed of our relationship. But he was always looking for ways to spend time with me, in public and private, and our friends soon began to treat us as a couple. He had a sweet, head–in–the–clouds aura that helped win my trust, and he never pressured me sexually.

Most important of all, Misha took me home to meet his parents, which proved to me that he didn't regard me as an exotic piece of "dark meat." They couldn't have given me a warmer welcome, sitting me down at the kitchen table and feeding me a meal of *shchi* (cabbage soup) and homemade *pelmeni* (small, meat-filled dumplings). Misha's father asked me point-blank, in a nosy manner typical of Soviet parents, how I was doing in school and whether I intended to start a career before I got married and had children. The American notion that adult children have a right to privacy, and that you don't ask personal questions five minutes after you meet your son's girlfriend, seems ridiculous to Russians. If your children get married, they're going to live with you or your in-laws: It can take years for a young couple to be assigned a separate apartment by housing authorities. So you might as well ask the girl (or boy) about her intentions and make your own position clear.

When I told Misha's father I intended to establish a career before I married, and described my own mother's emphatic advice on the same subject, he nodded approvingly and said, "You have a head on your shoulders." Just before we left—Misha always saw me home in the evening—his father reminded us once more, "All we want is for both of you kids to graduate with good grades, so you'll have every possibility open to you. After that, your lives are your own."

Among friends our own age, the reaction to us as a couple was mixed. Some people didn't see any problem at all and thought that our reserved temperaments made us a perfect match. Others leaped ahead to the time when we might marry and have children and took it upon themselves to warn us of the difficulties we would face raising a mixed-race family. One of Misha's closest male friends reminded him, as if he didn't know, that our children would surely be colored.

"Of course I know the children will be colored," he told the friend, "but remember what happens when you put a black together with a Russian. Greatness! Genius! Beauty! You get Pushkin! So what's your problem with me and Yelena?"

For the most part, my Russian friends liked Misha and approved of our relationship, but my friends among the African students were not so pleased. Christina, a Nigerian, insisted I was wasting my time with white men in general and Misha in particular. "What do you see in him?" she would ask. "Look at his lips. There's nothing to kiss. You need a black guy, and then you'll see what a real man is. White guys are just lousy in bed."

Christina, of course, was looking at my situation from the perspective of an African woman who would one day return to Nigeria to marry. But her comments had little relevance to my life. What was I supposed to do, confine my romantic experience to African students passing through the Soviet Union, men raised in a very different culture from my own? And there's no point in arguing with people who truly believe that the color of a man's or woman's skin is what makes a good or a lousy lover.

My Russian gym teacher's concern was the exact opposite of Christina's: She saw Misha as a sexual exploiter who might get me pregnant and dump me. "They use you and leave you," she warned me. "Misha's a good guy, but in the end they're all the same." This, by the way, is typical Russian women's wisdom. Russian women are accustomed to men, of all ages, who refuse to take any responsibility for contraception. Abortion is free and legal, though the actual procedure, performed with ineffective anesthetic (or no painkillers at all) in state clinics, is painful and humiliating. Young men simply assume an unmarried woman will get an abortion if she becomes pregnant. You never see a man accompanying his wife or girlfriend to an abortion clinic, either, as many men do in the United States. Contraception, pregnancy, and childbirth are considered strictly a woman's business;

as a result, most Russian women have an extremely suspicious attitude toward men.

The irony was that Misha and I were not sleeping together—although most couples our age were having sex. I was, as I've said, a very serious young woman; the struggles of my grandmother and mother in raising children alone made me determined not to get pregnant before I established myself in life.

And Misha and I were both romantics: We believed we should be married, or at least have a firm commitment to marry, before we made love. I realize now that our relationship was a kind of puppy love; neither of us was ready for a fully committed, fully sexual involvement at that point in our lives. And Misha was less mature than I, because he allowed his romantic fantasies about me (in spite of what he had promised his parents) to interfere with his studies.

I doubt that Misha and I would have stayed together even if our relationship hadn't been complicated by race—or, to put it more accurately, by everyone else's concern with our respective races. The sad thing is I can't be sure; as time went on, it became more and more difficult for us to separate color-blind emotional issues from racial ones. Misha was more in love with me than I was with him. Or perhaps he found it more difficult to be in love and concentrate on other tasks. He began neglecting classwork in order to spend more time with me. I continued to earn excellent marks while his grades fell. As his performance dropped off noticeably, several teachers told him he should start spending more time with his books and less time with me. He was convinced that his professors were trying to break us up because they were racists and responded by spending even less time with his books. He actually started skipping his own lectures and following me around to my classes to show the teachers they couldn't push him around. This behavior worried and embarrassed me, because I knew what it could mean to both of our futures to run afoul of the university authorities. Russian universities didn't take a casual attitude toward class attendance: If you didn't want to bother, twenty other young people were eager to take your place.

Then my busybody gym teacher made her contribution to the painful situation. She called Misha's mother and took it upon herself to relay the information that his academic performance was deteriorating while mine was improving. Misha's mother then telephoned my mother and accused me of ruining her son's future. My mama wasn't having any of that and told off Misha's mama in no uncertain terms. Misha certainly wasn't the right boy for her daughter, Mama said, if he couldn't keep up a romance and his grades at the same time. Then my mother turned around and asked me to break off the relationship. "I don't need any more phone calls like that" was her line.

None of this interference was unusual in the Russian scheme of family relations. It would never occur to a Russian parent or teacher that she ought not to treat a twenty year old—or a forty year old for that matter—like a child. An American friend recently expressed indignation with her mother for having read one of her letters. I just laughed. Any Russian would be astonished at a mother who didn't pry into her daughter's affairs. My mother, in fact, interfered less frequently than most of the other mothers I knew: She took a firm stand only when Misha's own doting mama entered the picture.

In fact, Misha and I went on seeing each other for some time, but the end was inevitable when his grades continued to fall. Finally, he failed an important examination and flunked out of the university, which in the Soviet Union meant you were immediately drafted into the army. He asked me to come to the train station to see him off to training camp but I refused. For the next few years, he—an educated city boy—would have to get along with men from every conceivable social class. I didn't think it would do him any good to begin his new life by kissing a black woman good-bye in front of his fellow draftees.

The chief outcome of my involvement with Misha was a growing realization that I would need a very strong man to survive the extra pressures surrounding an interracial couple in my society. This experience reinforced the lesson I had already learned from my grandmother, who said the bond between lovers of different races must be especially strong to survive whatever disapproval and outright hatred they might encounter. I would have to be tough enough to tell the rest of the world to go to hell in defense of my love (though I would rather live in a world where people mind their own business). My man would have to be just as strong.

I'm grateful that the bittersweet experience of first love didn't prevent me from taking advantage of everything the best university in the Soviet Union had to offer. For both students and faculty, the political atmosphere at MGU was less charged than it had been thirty years earlier, when my mother was a student. "Informers" were more apt to turn up in the guise of busybody gym teachers mixing into student romances than in the form of KGB *stukachi* (stool pigeons) trying to get someone arrested. The kind of gung-ho Komsomol types planning to build Party careers were regarded by other students with contempt rather than fear. Everyone knew these budding Party hacks were too stupid to succeed in a real profession; they were preparing for a lifetime of shuffling papers. Not that you couldn't get into trouble at the university for doing something really out of line—say, writing "Marx and Lenin were idiots" on a political science exam—but as long as you didn't go out of your way to flout the official pieties, you'd be fine.

How terrible life must be now for people of my generation who planned on Party careers! They bet on the wrong horse. What will they do with the rest of their lives?

In high school, I had already read many of the great Russian classics by Pushkin, Tolstoy, Gogol, and Dostoyevsky. (I've enjoyed being exposed to different American interpretations of some of these classics. I especially liked an American feminist's critique of *Anna Karenina*. Why, she asked, does Anna have to pay for her sins by throwing herself under a train while Vronsky simply goes on to a new affair? This question occurred to me long ago, but Soviet students were never permitted to make even slightly irreverent comments about our classics.)

In the university's journalism program, students were expected to complete a survey of European literature, beginning with Virgil and ending with French and German writers of the early twentieth century. Some of my favorites were Bocaccio's *Decameron* (Soviet censorship had the least impact on translations of old works); Stendahl's *The Red and the Black,* and Erich Maria Remarque's *All Quiet on the*

Western Front. I continued my English-language studies, which meant I was also expected to take additional courses in literature by American and British authors (though we studied most of these books in Russian translation). We read a great deal of Shakespeare in high school and college. His works are revered in my country, in part because they were translated by the great poet Boris Pasternak. Pasternak knew English well. Although verse inevitably loses something even in a fine translation, a great poet who knows both languages is uniquely suited to the task of interpreting a master from another culture.

The university's selection of American authors was eclectic and, in some cases, downright bizarre. Works in my curriculum included Theodore Dreiser's *An American Tragedy,* Upton Sinclair's *The Jungle,* F. Scott Fitzgerald's *The Great Gatsby,* Sinclair Lewis's *Main Street,* Mark Twain's *Huckleberry Finn,* William Faulkner's *Intruder in the Dust,* and Margaret Mitchell's *Gone with the Wind.* Arthur Hailey's *Airport,* which everyone liked, was on the optional reading list; American writers of great literary stature, like Nathaniel Hawthorne and Henry James, never appeared on our reading lists at all.★

The ideological rationale behind some of these selections is obvious. Many are works of social criticism pointing out the deficiencies of unrestrained capitalism or the emptiness of bourgeois life. Our professors explained *Gatsby* as an indictment of America's ruling class, but most of the students liked Fitzgerald because he portrayed a glamorous, romantic world we knew nothing about.

The approved list of books for university courses was determined by the stuffiest brand of Soviet academic bureaucrat. All are white and nearly all are men. They take their cue from ideological superiors and from whatever their American counterparts regard as important. Unless a novel was anointed "great" in standard works of American literary criticism, it wouldn't be included on a Soviet list.

★Although these authors were not included in the journalism department's curriculum, they would have been read by students majoring in American literature in the philological *fakultyet.*

Gone with the Wind could have made its way into the curriculum because some powerful Soviet diplomat, stationed in America during World War II, read it, liked it, and used political clout to order a translation. It's exactly the kind of broad historical saga that Russians love. (When the movie version of it opened in Moscow in 1990— Ted Turner and Jane Fonda showed up in person to celebrate the historic occasion—a month-long box office stampede ensued.) Forty years later, no Russian doubts that this is one of the greatest American novels ever written. I learned only in the United States that *Gone with the Wind* is not considered a literary masterpiece by American critics: My professors had equated it with *War and Peace*. And only a minority of Russian readers realize that this novel represents a one-sided, white southern view of the American Civil War. I was aware of the work's historical deficiencies, but I must confess this didn't make me love Scarlett and Rhett any less.

Not a single black writer was represented in my university courses on American literature. Excerpts from the works of Richard Wright, Ralph Ellison, and Langston Hughes had been translated into Russian—by my mother, among others—but they usually appeared in specialized magazines, like *Mezhdunarodnaya Literatura* (International Literature), that were not widely circulated, and they did not make their way into a standard university curriculum. If *Invisible Man* wasn't included on a standard American syllabus for a survey course in the novel (and it wouldn't have occurred to a Soviet specialist in American literature to consult a black studies syllabus), it wouldn't have found its way to my classes. Furthermore, works by contemporary authors were rarely considered appropriate for study in a university. The wheels of ideological censorship ground very, very slowly: Soviet authorities used to take years to make up their minds about the suitability of new literary and cultural trends. Our professors took no note of the explosion of writing by American blacks and feminists during the decade before I entered MGU. I had never heard of Alice Walker and Toni Morrison, for example, before my first trip to the United States.

One of the most enlightening parts of my education was a course in the journalism of prerevolutionary Russia. It was easy for us to see that Tsarist censorship had been much less restrictive than Soviet censorship. Consider just one example: Dostoyevsky's famous account of his years (1849–53) of penal servitude, *Memoirs from The House of The Dead*. This scathing description of the treatment of prisoners in Siberia was first published in Leningrad in 1861 in the review *Vremya* (Time), founded by the novelist and his older brother, Mikhail. It was widely quoted not only in the nineteenth century Russian press but also in samizdat of the sixties and seventies. My teachers would never have made any explicit comparisons between Tsarist and Soviet press controls; the entire system, as well as the very word *tsenzura* (censorship) was off-limits (though nothing was of greater concern to future journalists). Nevertheless, we students drew our own conclusions from the raw information in this course. Cracks were developing just beneath the opaque surface of the Brezhnev years.

At the end of the first year in journalism school, every student had to spend the summer gaining *praktika* (practical experience) on a real newspaper. None of the *prakitka* internships were available in Moscow or Leningrad; big-city papers weren't interested in saddling themselves with inexperienced students. Many of my classmates, whose parents had summer homes in resort areas, decided to combine their *praktika* with getting a tan by the Black Sea. Newspapers in vacation spots like Sochi were inundated with MGU interns; because there were too many of them, the students didn't get a chance to write many articles or see them published. I decided to take a job on a tiny village newspaper, about an hour from Moscow by train, because I knew no one else would want to work in a backwater offering no possibility of fun in the sun. (Also, I didn't need a tan.) I hoped for a chance to write lots of stories and learn my craft. The newspaper I worked for was called *Prizyv* (Appeal) and served all of the hamlets within a thirty-mile radius.

Only on the poorest backroads of Yazoo County have I encountered the kind of poverty in America that I saw every day when I took the train from Moscow to the end of the suburban line. Unlike Yazoo, these Russian villages lost even their history. Most of them didn't have real names: They were called by some all-purpose Soviet label like "October Station" or "Pioneer Point." (By now, perhaps they've recovered some prerevolutionary identity, the name of a noble's estate or a homely monicker like "Cherry Grove.")

In these villages, people lived much as they did centuries ago. Most roads were unpaved; many of the houses had no hot water or indoor toilets. The small wooden homes, clustered in groups of ten or twenty, would have been charming if someone had painted them, provided them with modern conveniences, and put in sidewalks so people wouldn't have to sink in ankle-deep mud during the spring and autumn rains. Some day, if Russia ever develops a normal economy, these houses will be snapped up and renovated. They could be someone's summer cottage or suburban dream house, if Russians lived like Europeans or Americans.

The editor of *Prizyv,* a kindly, harrassed man named Pavel Pavlovich, was delighted to have, as he put it, "a warm body" to send on assignments throughout his circulation area.

What I saw during that summer was a revelation: I realized, for the first time, how privileged my life was by Soviet standards. Most of the people I interviewed were old. The young did their best to run away to the city in spite of the *propiska* requirements that made it difficult to move about legally. It was easy to see why the young wanted to leave; the only real work to be found was on nearby collective farms. The unemployed, who supposedly didn't exist back then, wandered about the muddy lanes. From the windows of the passing train, you could see men with dead, sad eyes sitting near the tracks, sharing a liter of vodka in Russian fashion.

How the old women touched my heart! I thought of my own grandmother, poring over her dozens of newspapers in our well-heated Moscow apartment. These grannies in the countryside weren't warm; they sat near traditional Russian wood-burning stoves to avoid freezing in winter. Each conversation with a *babushka* would go something like this: *"Dochenka, dorogoya* [daughter, my dear] the pump in my kitchen is broken and I have to melt ice to get water in winter. Could you write something so that they [the authorities] will fix it?"

I was shocked by the poverty, but the sight of so many people in misery didn't lead me to question the system as a whole. (All sorts of people now claim they always knew how rotten the system was, but they're erasing the memory of their own naïveté.) If you had asked me then, having no standard of comparison, I would have assumed that people an hour outside of Chicago, New York, and Paris lived exactly the same way.

Since I was writing human interest stories rather than political articles, I didn't have to worry about censorship. You could talk about a granny's broken pump or a late pension payment as long as you made it clear that her problem was an exception in an otherwise benevolent system. (This wasn't true, of course, but all Soviet journalism in the pre-*glasnost* era operated on the exception-to-the-rule principle.) For the first time, I began to feel my work could make a difference, however small, in people's hard lives. Pavel Pavlovich, who let me ramble on at great length because he needed copy to fill his paper, bolstered my self-confidence. "It's not a small thing," he would say, "to get something fixed in the home of an old woman who has nothing. It's not a small thing to make a person feel she counts for something."

And I was deeply moved by the kindness of the villagers. Regardless of how poor they were, they always sat me down in front of their samovars and served me tea and cookies. Sometimes there would only be bread; I felt guilty about eating because I knew this must be the only food in the house, but to refuse food would have been a terrible insult. These people never complained in any general way about their hard lives; they would talk only about the broken pump or the lost check I had come to investigate. They all possessed the centuries-old fatalism of Russian peasants. Sometimes they would reminisce about the war and express gratitude for more than three decades of peace. These days, they would say, no one starved. And no soldiers would come to take away their pitiful homes. Their modest expectations were formed by a lifetime of hardship; hot running water and white bread were their not-always-attainable dreams.

I was the first black person most of these villagers had ever seen. They were openly curious; old women would pick up my palm and turn it over. Like my friend's mother in Voronezh, they weren't sure if I was the same color all over. I often used the phrase "we Russians" in discussing some aspect of our society. This expression seemed natural at the time, but it was also a subconscious way of saying, "I'm like you, in spite of my black skin. We speak the same language, we come from the same place." The villagers laughed when I said "we Russians"; even though my language convinced them I was a Soviet citizen, they suspected me of having some connection with America. One woman told me a convoluted joke about a black American spy, one who spoke not only perfect Russian but perfect village dialect, who parachuted into the countryside during the war. The minute he asked for a cup of water, the peasants responded, "So, how are things in America?" The astonished spy asked, "How did you know I was an American; is there something wrong with my Russian?" All of the grannies in the village were dying to ask me about my origins but were too polite to put the question directly; the joke was their way of encouraging me to spill the beans.

I didn't open up, though; I never talked about our American connection with strangers. The villagers didn't hold my reticence against me. After my stories produced repairmen to fix a few of their broken pumps and windows, they considered me *odna iz nashikh* ("one of us"). I was genuinely sorry when the summer ended; I finished up with a thick book of my clippings and returned to the university with new insights into the way many of my countrymen really lived.

Looking back on my university days, I realize that none of us could have predicted the massive changes in store for our society in only a few years. We were preparing for lives in a system that seemed unshakable: There might be a little more or a little less food, a little more or a little less opportunity to travel, a 20 percent instead of a 15 percent chance of seeing our ideas in print. But nothing fundamental would change. Our jobs would be a way to support ourselves, not a source of personal pride or identity. Our real lives would center around our families and intimate friends. Friendship was as important to us as it was to our parents; at this age, we were forming a circle of like-minded people who would be our trusted confidantes for life.

My best friend Nina★ was a student in the MGU psychology *fakultyet*. We were tennis partners for many years and won the Moscow

---

★Her name has been changed.

women's mixed doubles championship in high school. Sport originally drew us together but our friendship deepened as we discovered
we had many other, more important interests and values in common.
One trait we shared was a profound hatred of any form of bigotry.
Nina was disgusted by people who cared about what color Misha's
and my children would turn out to be. Her only concern was
whether the men I dated were good enough for me.

We both loathed anti-Semitism and refused to tolerate remarks
about the "greediness" and "disloyalty" of Jews. Anti-Semitism in-
tensified and became more socially respectable as Soviet Jews continued to leave for Israel and the United States during the seventies
and eighties. Old prejudices against Jews fused with a new envy of
those who had a choice about whether or not to stay in the Soviet
Union. I never got over my shock at hearing ostensibly cultured,
college-educated people use the epithet *zhid*. When my grandmother
slapped me for picking up the word from my five-year-old playmates,
she explained that anti-Semitism, like racism, was the result of ignorance. It's as hard for me to understand how anti-Semites can revere
Pushkin and Tolstoy as it was for the world to figure out how Nazism
could be spawned by the nation that produced Bach and Goethe.

In Russia, many people who are not anti-Semites themselves nevertheless remain silent in the face of hostility toward Jews. Nina never
held back. Whenever we encountered anyone who told anti-Semitic
jokes or made casual anti-Semitic comments, she would immediately
say, "Excuse me, but I don't want to hear that kind of garbage." We
agreed that we didn't want to keep the kind of friends who passed on
this poison. If they said these kinds of things about Jews, Georgians,
or Armenians, what did they say about blacks when I wasn't in the
room?

Unprejudiced talk is cheap, but I loved Nina because she always
put her beliefs into action. Many of my Russian friends felt uncomfortable around my African friends and vice-versa. But everyone was
comfortable with Nina.

Before our final year at the university, we took a vacation together
in the Black Sea port of Odessa, where many Africans study. At the
time I was learning Portuguese (my mother, still dreaming of foreign

travel for me if not for herself, suggested that this language might one day earn me an assignment in Angola or Mozambique or Brazil). While Nina and I were sunning ourselves on the beach, two Angolan students approached us and started talking. We made a congenial foursome (I got a chance to practice my woeful Portuguese), and they invited us to dinner in a foreign-currency restaurant the night before we were supposed to return to Moscow.

Should we go? The restaurant was reserved mainly for Western tourists. Most of the Russian women there, with or without escorts, were prostitutes. In every Soviet establishment where payment is allowed in foreign currency, guards monitor the comings and goings of Soviet citizens. Sometimes they simply bar Russians, especially women, from entering. It wasn't risky for me to go to the restaurant, because the guard would assume that I was a foreigner. But Nina was in another position altogether. If a guard stopped her and demanded her identity papers, the authorities might send a negative report on her to the university. The young Angolans said, "Don't worry, we'll protect you," thinking we were worried about violence directed at racially mixed couples. They didn't understand Nina's concern about being caught with foreigners, and we felt too humiliated to explain everything to them. I was to feel this shame in the presence of foreigners many times before *glasnost;* it's degrading to tell strangers you are afraid to be seen with them simply because they come from another country.

I told Nina I would go to the restaurant with the two men by myself. "It's too risky for you. I understand," I assured her. She replied, "Yelena, there's no price on my sense of justice and honesty." So we went together and had a wonderful time—once we got past the door without being stopped. To any Westerner, this must sound like a small matter; to a Russian, Nina's act conveyed courage and solidarity.

With someone like Nina to share my hopes and fears, I was never conscious of the color of my skin. I didn't have to conceal our family's American background or anything else from her. We were true friends of the soul.

Although Nina and I were not political dissidents, we considered ourselves cultural dissenters. One aspect of Soviet life that troubled us more and more as we grew older was the position of women. We had no real intellectual framework for our inchoate discontent; at that point, we were not even aware of the existence of a feminist movement in America and Europe. But we realized something was wrong when we began to think about finding jobs at the end of our university years. So many more jobs were open to our male classmates than to us. Just as I couldn't dream of becoming a foreign correspondent, a girl at the prestigious Institute of Foreign Languages couldn't dream of applying for a diplomatic job. What would happen to a young woman who passed through the House of Brides without catching a husband?

Still, neither Nina nor I wanted to focus too narrowly on preparation for a career. We shared our contempt for the sort of students who were only interested in grades, who cared about pleasing their professors but not about genuine learning, who refused to read books or take an interest in any cultural activities that weren't required for their courses.

Moscow is a city of concerts, theater, and ballet, and Nina and I made a point of taking time out from our books to attend as many performances as we could. Tickets were cheap—three or four rubles, at most—and we tirelessly ran around Moscow. We might take in a song recital at the conservatory one week, a performance of *The Cherry Orchard* at the Sovremmenik (Contemporary) Theater the next, even a production of *Evgeny Onegin* at the Bolshoi. During our university years, 1979 to 1984, few Muscovites owned VCRs. Today, I'm afraid we might be sitting at home watching a tape of a movie instead of actively trying to "broaden" ourselves (as we put it in the self-conscious fashion of the young).

And I still hadn't given up on my old dream of singing opera in spite of my preparations for a career in journalism. At the time, the conservatory offered an evening program for aspiring musicians and singers who couldn't study full-time during the day. It was tough to get into the program—apparently there were lots of aspiring Violettas walking the streets of Moscow—but I was determined to try (even though, at age twenty-one, it was a bit late in the game).

When I walked into the building, a *dezhurnaya* (one of the ubiquitous old women who guard the entrances to every institution) told me the director of the program wasn't available because he was already conducting auditions. "Well, and where are the auditions?" I asked. She pointed to a small auditorium. When I walked into the room, the director told me I was already too late. He expected me to leave—Soviets simply didn't burst in on officials unannounced—but I figured this was my last chance. Before the director could throw me out, I began singing "We Shall Overcome" at the top of my lungs, verse after verse after verse: "We'll walk hand in hand" . . . "we are not afraid" . . . "the whole wide world around." Astonishingly, the director agreed to let me into the classes. Did he really like my voice or did he just want to shut me up so he could go on with the rest of the audition? Perhaps he simply thought I was a madwoman who would never return.

But I did return and studied conscientiously, far more seriously than I had when I was a child. During that year, my only formal voice training, my teachers convinced me that I was a mezzo and being a mezzo, no Violetta. In spite of my disappointment, the time at the conservatory was well-spent. Having matured enough to apply myself to the lessons scorned as a child, I learned at last to read music.

Thus, my mother did succeed in her aim of raising a Russian intellectual. I'm the antithesis of American yuppies of my generation, who seem to have pounced on a single career goal by age twenty and pursued it relentlessly. To a Russian, there's something strange about the kind of young American who settles in at Columbia University's law or journalism school and never takes the time to go to the theater or a concert at Carnegie Hall.

I've noticed that this single-minded, practical orientation carries over into the lives of young American adults, black and white. When I meet friends for dinner in New York, they'll usually talk about what they did in the office that day. In Russia, you don't go to a friend's home and discuss what you've accomplished on your computer. You may talk about politics or a novel, and not necessarily a new book but one from the last century. I was astonished the first time I met a successful American who proudly declared that he "never has any time to read books." In Russia, a scientist would be ashamed to say such a thing (even if it were true). I don't know whether Russian intellectuals will ever make good businessmen, but I do know that nothing would have changed during the past few years without these "impractically" educated humanists. Cultural and political dissent are closely linked; people who know nothing outside their specialty are rarely able to question the received opinion of their society.

But I would by lying if I portrayed myself as a former student rebel on behalf of my private form of cultural dissent. As fear has receded in Russian society, it's been truly amazing to find out how many of my contemporaries were dissidents all along. They were only pretending to enjoy the dachas and other privileges—the vacations abroad or in the Crimea, designer clothes—acquired by their parents through a lifetime of service to the state! They were really members of a secret underground dedicated to overthrowing a rotten system! Why, the KGB was about to arrest them on the very day Gorbachev came to power! It's amazing the system didn't crumble long ago, since the country was populated by so many brave people. Why didn't I know any of them then?

In fact, Nina and I were rather typical of our generation. Our dissent was fragile. We saw the hypocrisy around us and didn't want to be contaminated by it, but we also didn't want to do anything to jeopardize our futures in the only system we knew. Our sense of adventure and curiosity were constantly at war with what our society expected of us. Usually we tried to compromise.

At MGU, I had almost nothing to do with foreign students unless they were Africans (my racial brothers and sisters) or eastern Europeans (our political comrades). The few American exchange students, especially if they spoke good Russian, were suspected of being spies. Why wouldn't we have assumed this? Most Soviets sent abroad for any length of time did in fact have KGB connections. Even if you didn't believe all Americans and Western Europeans were working for the CIA, you had to worry about how it looked if you hung out with students who weren't from the Soviet bloc. Women who dated foreigners were often considered little better than prostitutes; what reason other than material gain would our fair Ludmillas have for spurning glorious Soviet manhood?

Even so, Nina and I didn't want to be the sort of conformists who avoided all contact with those dangerous, glamorous foreigners. One day, Nina received a phone call from a Russian friend who said he'd met a nice American student and wanted to introduce him to some real Russian girls. The only Soviet girls who had been willing to go out with him so far were prostitutes. It was our patriotic duty to entertain the American. Did we want to send such a nice fellow back to his own country thinking that all Soviet women were only out for what they could get? Of course we didn't, and that was how I met Alex,★ my first American friend who didn't connections with the Communist Party.

Nina and I agreed to keep our real names from Alex, so he wouldn't be able to identify us if anyone should ask. I decided to introduce myself as "Anne." First, though, we had to figure out a way to get rid of our parents so they wouldn't give us away. Since my grandmother never went anywhere at night, my apartment was out. Nina's parents had a dacha near Moscow, and she convinced them to go away for the weekend alone by expressing great concern about the fact that they so seldom had any time to themselves. Once we knew we would have a parent-free apartment, we began looking for food to impress the American with our Russian hospitality. We spent our entire month's student stipend on caviar and beef from the farmer's market (beef cost the equivalent of ten dollars a pound at that time) to make *pirozhki,* the classic Russian meat-filled pastries. Then we pre-pared a program of Russian and American songs—good girls putting on a performance—to make everyone feel at home. Our presentation was to include my old standbye, "We Shall Overcome," and the romantic Pushkin lyrics I had learned as a child from my mother. If

★His name has been changed.

either of us had taken ballet lessons, we probably would have put on feathery costumes and performed the second act of *Swan Lake*. Our excessive preparations betrayed our nervousness: What would interest our American?

On the long-awaited night, Alex arrived, bearing flowers, wine, and vodka, accompanied by Nina's Russian friend, Dima. The American's stock soared in our estimation when we saw the flowers; he was obviously a *kulturnyy* young man who knew how to treat women with attentiveness and courtesy. And Alex was spectacularly handsome; a tall, broad-shouldered blond, he looked exactly like the cowboy I had seen in Marlboro ads in American magazines. To me, he was the embodiment of America (white America, that is). I was still slightly suspicious because he spoke Russian so well. He had been an exchange student in both Leningrad and Moscow, but I wondered whether he might have received earlier language training from an American intelligence agency. But why worry, I happily told myself. I didn't possess any state secrets and felt free to indulge the most sudden, intense crush of my young life.

My reservations melted further when I saw how much Alex loved Russian poetry and music. Nina and I soon began calling him by the Russian diminutive Alyosha, after the pure and gentle character in *The Brothers Karamazov*. Alyosha glowed as we sang and recited poetry for hours. I can't even remember the verses; alcohol and infatuation made me see only Alyosha's blue eyes. Alyosha's smile grew broader, while Dima's scowl deepened with every toast to the glories of peace, international friendship, and Russian literature. Alyosha was thrilled to sit, Russian-style, around the kitchen table, gobbling all of the *pirozhki* and caviar slathered on black bread. (Then caviar was still relatively cheap—about ten dollars an an ounce. Now you can't buy it at all unless you pay in foreign currency). Our Russian comrade, however, was interested in quite another kind of cultural exchange. Every toast and soulful song meant there was less time to coax Nina into the bedroom. Not that his clumsy attempts at seduction would have worked; Nina and I were determined to show the American what *nice* Russian girls were like. And Alyosha made it clear that he respected us as real Russian ladies and would never confuse us with the kind of trollops who entertained foreigners only because they wanted to finish the encounter by taking home American cosmetics or jeans.

Alyosha and I were simply entranced by each other; he was as intrigued by meeting a black Russian as I was by my first encounter with a Marlboro man. Our hands touched lightly and we exchanged shy glances in the manner of two very young, potential lovers who aren't quite sure what to do or what the other expects. By the end of the evening, I wanted desperately to confess that my real name wasn't Anne but Yelena. I had already given Alyosha a wrong number when he asked if he might phone me. I wanted so much to explain that my Soviet upbringing made me fear the consequences of friendship with an American, but I didn't know how to begin because I had never spoken honestly or intimately with a foreigner before that night.

I felt ashamed and humiliated: What would he think of me for having lied to him in the first place? Still, I knew there was no way to avoid telling the truth if I wanted to see him again. I decided to explain everything on the way home, since Alyosha had already offered to accompany me on the subway. Even in New York, there's nothing remotely resembling the crush on Moscow's metro. As we were trying to enter the car around ten o'clock at night—our party began early in the afternoon—we were separated and Alyosha was swept outside by a relentless human wave. Tears rolled down my face as I saw him mouthing through the window, "Don't worry, I'll call you later." Of course he would call, but he would only reach the phony number I'd given him. With no phone information service and no directory, it would be impossible for him to reach me. (Nina's friend, who could have been a link, left town on vacation the next day, and Nina, too, had given out a false name.) For years afterward on the Moscow streets, my heart would pound when I saw a tall, blond man dressed in Western clothes. I wondered whether Alyosha had tried to find me; I dreamed of meeting him again. Six years later in America, I did run into my American Dream. In post-*glasnost* Washington, I was talking with a Russian friend in a hall that serves as a meeting place for Soviet and American journalists, students, and businessmen. A tall, bearded man approached me and said, "I think we've met somewhere." I brushed him off, since I was in something of a hurry and in no mood for a pickup. Just as I was about to walk out the door he touched my hand and said, "Don't you remember me? It's me, Alyosha. I've never forgotten you." Then I recognized him, an older, more distinguished version of the youthful fantasy I carried in my heart since the night the metro doors separated us.

Alyosha had searched for me many times in Moscow. Since I told him I was studying at the conservatory of music, he stopped by the main office and asked if anyone knew a black student named Anne. No one had heard of this mysterious black Anne. Someone undoubtedly could have figured out that I was the girl he was trying to find, but no one on duty during the daytime had ever seen me, because I only attended classes in the separate evening program.

It would be lovely to report that we were able to pick up the threads of our attraction when we met again in America but it didn't happen that way. Alyosha, Alex, had been living with a woman for many years, and I had been involved in a long relationship with a Russian in Moscow. We were different people; we lost our precious moment in time and moved on. Even today, I think of the love that might have flowered between the two of us if we had not been trapped in the dying days of the Cold War. I see the whole episode— my life, the doors closing between us—as a metaphor for mistrust between nations and people. I regret all of the sweet moments lost to bigotry and suspicion.

As I entered my twenties and developed more confidence in myself as a woman, I still found it difficult to separate color from foreignness as an obstacle to love in my own culture. In many ways, I consider myself fortunate to have been a late bloomer; I'm not sure I could have handled the complications of being a "black beauty" as a teenager. When I met Tanya Tomas,★ the daughter of a Ukranian mother and a black Cuban father, I was disabused of any idea that extraordinary beauty was the solution to the problem of how to fashion a

---

★Her name has been changed.

satisfying romantic life as a black woman in a white country. Tanya is one of the loveliest women—of any color—I have ever known. Her combination of white, black, and Latino ancestry produced the kind of looks that would attract stares in any country; her glowing eyes remind me of Diana Ross, and her perfectly proportioned body is a magnet for men and a source of envy for women.

But Tanya's beauty was almost a curse. She grew up in a small town in the Ukraine, where prejudice against all minorities is much stronger than it is in Moscow. From her early teens, women hated her because of her looks and men made constant, unwanted sexual advances. When she grew up and became a singer—working mainly in restaurants—Tanya always had to contend with the powerful stereotype of black sexuality. Men called her a bitch if she spurned their advances; restaurant owners fired her when they found she wouldn't sleep with them. "Yelena," she told me, "It's as though I have no right to say no to these men. The attitude is, 'Honey, we know you black girls love it, so what's the matter with you.'" Tanya had a devoted husband, but even that didn't ease the pain of her situation. Men would reach out and touch Tanya on the street, stroking her hair and trying to press against her. Her husband had to pick her up after work every night, because so many men waited outside the restaurant doors that it wouldn't have been safe for her to go home alone. "It's humiliating," she said. "I used to wonder what I was doing wrong, that these men picked me. It's a torment. Sometimes I long to be very old so it will finally stop."

I rarely discussed such matters with another black; unlike African-Americans, blacks in the Soviet Union seldom open up to one another on issues connected with their color. There are so few of us, not enough blacks to make up a "community." Beyond that, many of us are reluctant to blame problems on race (or the combination of race and gender). Tanya and I could both have benefited from an American-style consciousness-raising session or the intersection of racial and sexual stereotypes; we lacked a larger framework that would have enabled us to view her (or my) experiences as something other than individual troubles. In a collectivist society, I was raised to think of my problems, and try to solve them, in purely individual terms—no excuses.

CHAPTER NINE

BLACK BEAUTY

"Black is beautiful." The first person who spoke these words to me was a white Russian man. The statement had long been a cliché in America, but it resonated inside me with life-transforming power because it came from a man I loved. Volodya,★ a Soviet naval officer, would bring me greater joy and pain than I had ever known. I was twenty-two when we met. Our relationship marked the end of my youth.

Volodya and I met through a mutual friend, an actor from Leningrad. In his crisp white naval uniform, Volodya was beautiful to me. A tall, muscular man with jet-black hair and slightly tilted eyes that

---

★His name has been changed.

displayed a trace of a Kazakh ancestor, Volodya looked like my idea of Rhett Butler. His father was a high-level Soviet intelligence officer; he had been a deep undercover agent in Nazi Germany during World War II. Knowing about his background, I should have sensed trouble ahead—our family's pasts were on a collision course—but I was impressed by Volodya's openness. For a Soviet citizen, his revelation about what his father did for a living was an extraordinary act of trust.

He could quote Pasternak endlessly. Imagine how exciting it was to hear him recite, in his deep voice, the poems Pasternak wrote at the end of the novel *Dr. Zhivago:*

> Distorted shadows fell
> Upon the lighted ceiling:
> Shadows of crossed arms, of crossed legs—
> Of crossed destiny . . .
>
> A corner draft fluttered the flame
> And the white fever of temptation
> Upswept its angel wings that cast
> A cruciform shadow.★

On his guitar, Voldoya played prerevolutionary songs of the Russian Navy. Although he was a member of the Party, his heroes were Tsarist naval officers who fought the Bolsheviks to the bitter end during the civil war.

Most of all, Volodya made me feel beautiful. What touched me most deeply was that for him, my blackness was the source of beauty. No one else had ever instilled this pride in me—not Mama or my grandmother, not the inexperienced Misha, not my American Alyo-

---

★It's hard to convey the erotic flavor of this poem in translation. It's known now that Pasternak was referring to his long love affair with his mistress, Olga Ivinskaya.

sha. (To Alyosha, my "Russianness" had been far more important than my blackness.)

On the day we met, Volodya followed my walk with admiring eyes. "Yelena," he said, "you are like a black puma, a black princess. I love the way you move. But I don't think you see your own beauty. You want to look like everyone else, but everyone else should be looking at you." My swaying gait, and a curvy behind that my gym teachers were always telling me to "tuck in" like the other girls, had long been a source of embarrassment to me. For whatever reason, I moved differently than Russian girls. No matter how hard I tried, my behind wouldn't tuck in the way the teachers thought it should. In 1991, when I visited my father's family in Zanzibar, I saw many East African women who moved like me, whose shapes resembled mine. Lysenko was wrong; a Soviet upbringing couldn't flatten out the genes that gave me a full, curved bottom.

So Volodya was right when he sensed my embarrassment about my body. I was still hiding out in the typical student costume of jeans and baggy shirts; in that uniform, no one could criticize my body or notice me. For Volodya, I began to wear dresses. It was midsummer, and we walked up and down Gorky Street—he in his white naval uniform with gold buttons, I in a skirt and high heels. I was so unaccustomed to dressing up that I would look down at the pavement. "Why do you do that?" Volodya asked. "When you hold your head up high, people look at you and are drawn to you. We're going to walk up and down the street until you understand and feel in your soul just how beautiful you really are."

We became very serious very fast. We saw each other every day (Volodya was on shore leave from his ship that summer). He introduced me to his best friend—something a Russian never does unless he expects a woman to become a permanent part of his life. While Volodya was away at sea, he told me earnestly, I must call on his friend for anything I needed.

I soon decided that Volodya was far more important than any of my other plans. Even though I hadn't finished my diploma dissertation, I planned to leave the university and wait for Voldoya in his home port. The location didn't matter—Arkhangelsk in the far north, Vladivostok on the Pacific—it was all the same to me as long as Volodya and I were together. My happiness was marred only by my grandmother's obvious dislike of my dream man. He was too old, she told me; he had "been around"; he might not be sincere. I pointed out that people said the same things about my grandfather. He was forty when they married, I reminded her, and she was only twenty-four. They had been happy together, and so would Volodya and I. What my grandmother might have told me, if she had been so inclined, was that she and my grandfather shared the same values and wanted the same things out of life. But she saw it was useless to argue with a young woman truly in love for the first time.

Volodya and I had already talked about our future together, and I expected him to propose formally the night before he was due to return to his ship. I put my lipstick on with shaking hands as I waited for him to pick me up at our apartment. I remember wondering whether we would be married in Moscow or whether the legal formalities would take place in some port city where his ship was docked. The bell rang. As soon as I opened the door, I knew something was wrong. Volodya came straight to the point, even before we sat down to talk. "Yelena, I have to tell you something. I love you very much, and I can't begin to say how sorry I am, but I won't be able to see you again. We can't be married." He was a Party member, he emphasized (as if I needed reminding) and a military officer. His career would be ruined—he would never be allowed to do intelligence work or travel abroad—if he married someone like me.

"What do you mean, someone like me?" I asked. "I have a Soviet passport, I am absolutely Russian. My mother is too."

His reply was straightforward and shocking: "It's written on your face that you're connected with America." There it was: I may have been his black puma, black pearl, black princess, but my genes ruled me out as a wife.

Mama wasn't home, but my grandmother was typing away, as usual, in her bedroom. The phone rang, and I went to answer it. By the time I got rid of the caller, Volodya had left. Tears running down my cheeks, I ran into the street and called his name. He was already out of sight and out of my life. When I came back to the apartment, my grandmother told me she had thrown Volodya out of the house. She had seen the tears on my cheeks when I rushed past her room to answer the phone; perhaps she even overheard part of our conversation (though she didn't ask me to explain). "Baby," was all she said.

Americans often see this story as evidence of pure racism, but the truth is more complicated. In the end, I don't think Volodya could have married me and stayed in the navy even if my American grandparents had been white. The KGB and his military superiors would have found out about my American background, even if the connection hadn't been, as Volodya so aptly put it, written on my face.

Strangely enough, I never doubted that Volodya had truly loved me. Like me, he was living in a fantasy world during that beautiful Moscow summer. Before he left, he must have had a talk with either his father or his military superiors. He told them about me, and they informed him he would have to choose between love and his career. "I could stay in the navy, sure," he said that night, "but I'd never have any real work to do. I'd just be a clerk, pushing papers around. You'd grow to hate me; I'd hate myself." I remember saying, plaintively, "But I'm just like everyone else—I'm a loyal citizen like everyone else." He replied, "You're *not* like everyone else. Your phone is tapped, for one thing. Your apartment is bugged." How do you know, I wondered silently. Outwardly, I dismissed his comment. "So what, half of the intelligent people in Russia have bugs in their apartments. Who cares if they listen? They don't hear my family plotting to overthrow the government. We're talking about music, or what we're having for dinner."

Volodya returned to his ship the next day and left me to my lost innocence. He permanently altered my sense of where I belonged— and didn't belong—in my own country. I might consider myself absolutely Russian in a cultural sense, but other people didn't necessarily see me the same way. I was like many of my Jewish friends, who also considered themselves absolutely Russian—until it came time to apply for certain kinds of politically sensitive jobs.

I now knew—absolutely—that I would be a liability as a wife to anyone whose job demanded political reliability. What Soviet journalist, for instance, would want to marry me if he had ambitions of becoming a foreign correspondent? A black wife with American relatives would probably prevent him from being allowed to travel abroad.

Voldoya's rejection dealt me a personal shock as a woman and a social shock as a citizen of my country. Embarrassed by the realization of my own naïveté, I vowed to become less trusting and less open. There would be no more love at first sight for me. I would erect barriers at every stage of a relationship in an effort to protect both myself and the other person. I would be the first to explain, "My family is not like every family; you must understand, we must be careful." This was the pain behind my mother's double messages about Russian men.

During the first two weeks after Volodya left—he wouldn't even give me his address, because he said there would be no point in our writing each other with marriage out of the question—I stopped eating and lost fifteen pounds. My mother and grandmother were frantic with worry, but I liked my newly svelte body: It gave me back some sense of control. If I were an American, I suppose this grief might have produced some sort of chronic eating disorder. (Anorexia and bulimia aren't unheard of in Russia but they are much rarer than in the United States. These disorders are diseases of affluence; for Russians, all food is expensive and good food is hard to find. We have our full share of emotional disorders, but rejecting food isn't one of them.)

Eventually, I started eating again and turned to my standard solution—activity—for any pain or disappointment. I was finishing my diploma dissertation, but I didn't want one free hour to think about Volodya. I decided to start private Portuguese lessons—the university wasn't offering any courses at my level that term—and take on a second job to pay for the tutoring.

Moscow's Cosmos Hotel, which caters to foreign tourists and offers entertainment in its restaurant every night, was looking for a female singer. I introduced myself to the bandleader, Sergei Davidovich, and his eyes lit up. I was black. I spoke English. His customers would surely think I was an American, and this would draw more people into the restaurant. What tips I would pull in! Here was a place where my black skin and American aura would be a distinct advantage. Was I a good singer? A short, enthusiastic man from Siberia, Sergei couldn't have cared less. I was perfect for his act. He would bill me as . . . "Lolita from America."

Sergei reinforced Volodya's "black is beautiful" lessons, and it was wonderful for me, at this painful juncture in my life, to hear the same words from a man whose only interest in me was professional. Sergei had a VCR, an extremely rare possession in Moscow in the early 1980s, and invited me home to watch his tapes of Diana Ross and Donna Summer. I had heard them on records but never seen them perform. "Look at the way Diana Ross walks," he would instruct me, swiveling his hips and throwing a scarf around his neck. "She walks like a queen. You must walk like a queen. Don't clump around trying to make yourself look like some girl from a peasant village. Move proudly, move like a black goddess." When the customers offered me tips, Sergei instructed me not to accept the money with my own hands but to tell the men to leave the bills on the table. "Think of Diana, think proudly. Would she touch those dirty old bills with her fingers? Does a goddess allow mortals to get too close?" Sergei's tapes gave me my first taste of the varied black beauty in America. I truly began to believe that there might be more than one kind of beauty, that blonder and whiter weren't necessarily better.

The customers at the Cosmos loved me as Lolita. It must have been my appearance that attracted them, because I was a mediocre (to put it charitably) pop singer. Sergei and the members of his band were good musicians, who loved jazz and played it for their own enjoyment, but our restaurant programs featured American pop hits from the fifties and sixties. "Stormy Weather" and "Baby, Won't You Please Come Home" were out. "Rock Around the Clock" (which I belted out in English) and "Lara's Theme" from the movie *Dr. Zhivago* were in. (The American movie of Pasternak's novel hadn't been shown in the Soviet Union, but the soupy theme song became a staple of Soviet restaurant entertainment. It was said that Leonid Brezhnev's eyes teared over at the sentimental lyrics: "You'll come to me, out of the long ago. . . .") There's a wonderful word in Russian—*poshlost*—for this combination of sentimentality, banality, and philistinism. (In English three words are needed to express the concept.) There was a good deal of *poshlost* in our performances at the Cosmos. I have to admit that I enjoyed the whole experience. Sergei decked me out in a slinky white dress that revealed more than it concealed, and I managed to do a pretty fair imitation of Diana Ross when I danced. On stage I felt like another person and that was exactly what I wanted at a time when my own life was miserable.

The job made it possible for me to accomplish my aim of filling every minute. I would rehearse with the band in the morning, work on my dissertation, play tennis, and take Portuguese lessons in the afternoon, and begin singing at 10:00 P.M. By the time I got home at 2:00 or 3:00 A.M., I was too tired to think about Volodya.

There was only one fly in the ointment: I was having trouble explaining my late hours to my mother. She didn't pry as often as many Russian mothers do, but she could hardly be expected to ignore the fact that her only daughter was out on the streets until all hours in a city where there is absolutely nothing to do after midnight (unless you're staying in a hotel). After a few weeks of making up stories about overnight stays with girlfriends, I came clean with Mama. Sergei, not wanting to lose his star Lolita, agreed to come to our apartment and explain the details of my job.

Mama was surprisingly receptive—she, after all, had sung in a jazz band when she was young—and was reassured by the bandleader's fatherly attitude toward me. She simply told him she didn't want me involved in the dirty extracurricular activities—drugs, heavy drinking, prostitution—that surround show business everywhere in the world.

Sergei, in fact, took my mother a bit too literally; he tried to get the hotel management to discourage prostitutes from attending my shows along with their clients. My protector had decided it would besmirch my reputation even to talk with hookers. I did talk to them, though, and I got an eye-opening look into a side of Soviet life, and women's lives, that I had never encountered in my sheltered upbringing. Many of these young women had children to support; they couldn't find any other jobs that paid a living wage. One woman helped me out by urging her clients to give me tips, and I felt a sense of shame at all the advantages I had always taken for granted. I was able to use some of these insights several years later, when *glasnost* made it possible to talk honestly about prostitution in the Soviet press. In the old days, the entire subject, and the desperate situation of the women themselves, was off-limits: Prostitution was a vile product of capitalism; of course we didn't have women who were forced to sell their bodies.

I sang at the Cosmos for about a year, until the scar tissue began to form over my heart and I no longer needed to fill every waking minute to avoid thinking about Volodya. By then, I was working full-time at *Moscow News* and trying to figure out a way of fitting myself into the Soviet system as an adult.

Like most women who have been deeply hurt by a man, I used to fantasize about Volodya returning and saying, "I made a terrible mistake." In 1988, I got a chance to see how the fantasy played out in reality. By then, *glasnost* had made everything American, and everyone connected with America, extremely fashionable. I was appearing on a new Soviet television show after my first trip to the United States, and Volodya looked me up. He was wrong all those years ago, he told me. He truly loved me and had never found anyone to take my place in his heart. Could we start over again?

By then, I was beyond either vindictive satisfaction or compassion. All I felt was a sense of relief that Volodya hadn't summoned up the courage to propose to me when I was twenty-two. What would I have done with myself, waiting on some godforsaken Soviet naval base for my husband's ship to come in, my only distinction being my status as the one black woman who managed to snag a promising officer in the Russian fleet? Had I married Voldoya, I would never have become a reporter. I would have missed out on all the difficult, rewarding, exciting experiences of the *glasnost* years.

During those years, I grew to love another man, one who wasn't fazed by the foreign connections "written on my skin." Yuri, a freelance photographer, didn't belong to the Party. He wasn't planning a political career in the military or the diplomatic corps. He was free to love whomever he wished. Unlike my involvement with Volodya, which began with passion and ended with despair, my feelings for Yura began with friendship and deepened into a long-term romance.

We met in the spring of 1984, when I was about to graduate from MGU. Giddy with relief at having passed my final exams, I was celebrating with Marina, a classmate from the journalism *fakultyet*. We drank toasts to the future, so many toasts, in fact, that we wound up dancing atop the kitchen table in Marina's apartment. A photographer-friend recorded the occasion for posterity.

As it happened, Yura developed his pictures in the same photographic studio as our friend. He was intrigued as the images of two dancing girls—one dark, the other almost black—emerged from the developing tray. "You made a mistake," Yura said. "The girls are too dark." After the negatives were processed once again, Marina's image emerged in her proper light shade, but the bewildered Yura saw that my picture was still black. His colleague laughingly explained that this was my real color. "Oh, she's so pretty," Yura said, "I'd love to meet her." He begged to deliver the photos to me in person, and that's how we laid eyes on each other the first time.

I liked Yura immediately, not because I saw him as a prospective lover but because he listened to me as no man (including Volodya) ever had. American women bemoan the failure of men to listen—I do it myself now—but no Russian woman expects to find a man who listens to her as another woman does. I found myself confiding in Yura, telling him about Volodya (the wound was still raw during that first year after our breakup), revealing details about my family that I'd never discussed with anyone outside our home. Blond, blue-eyed, at least six feet two, Yura towered over me, but I thought of him as a friend rather than a boyfriend.

We continued as "just friends" for nearly a year, until my grandmother died in the spring of 1985. That was when I realized he was more than a friend. He was, along with Nina, the best friend I ever had. "Don't you worry," he said. "I'll do anything you want me to. I'll call your boss, friends you want to invite to the funeral. Here . . . sit down, dry your eyes, I'll make you a cup of tea."

My grandmother was the last to die in her circle of American friends, Communists, white and black, who had come to Russia during the twenties and thirties. Their children came to our apartment to pay their respects. Mama called old friends in Tashkent—most had taken English lessons from my grandmother—and they flew to Moscow for the wake.

I realized I didn't want to show my grief to colleagues at the newspaper—much as I liked some of them. I only wanted people who really knew me to comfort me, to lay my *babushka* to rest. Mama felt as I did: She didn't want a business funeral attended by colleagues who hadn't really known my grandmother. Russians typically stage elaborate, open-casket funerals, but my grandmother—true to the end to her spartan, rationalist, nonreligious principles—asked to be cremated. That's what we did, and her ashes were interred in the Vagankovskoye Cemetery, where many artists, writers, and scholars are buried.

Obtaining space in a cemetery, by the way, involves as much wheeling and dealing as moving into a new apartment. Without a connection to some official organization, it's tough to gain access to the grave. My grandmother didn't have any such connection, so Mama first had to obtain a letter of recommendation from the African Institute and request a space for her own burial at some future date. Then Mama spent hours at the offices of the Moscow City Soviet, waving the letter of recommendation and detailing my grandparents' contributions to the building of communism. Finally Mama won: She got a space in the cemetery. We didn't have a formal ceremony there, but my grandmother's ashes were interred in a wall, with her name inscribed on a stone. (It's even more difficult to secure a grave in Moscow today than it was in 1985. People say it's impossible to bury a loved one in Vagankovskoye unless you pay in dollars.)

Back at our apartment, Mama cooked huge batches of *plov*, the traditional Uzbek dumplings my grandmother always made. One of her former students recalled my grandmother's insistence on English lessons during the war years. "You don't for one minute think the Germans are going to win?" Bertha told her pupil. "Soon the Nazis will be done, finished, and you'll be so happy you learned English." Yura hovered quietly, inconspicuously in the background, patting me on the shoulder, refilling glasses, running out to the store for extra bread. I saw how dear he was to me, this man I had taken for granted as a friend.

Soon afterward, we asked Mama if Yura could move in with me. My mother had always told me that if I were serious about a man, he should move in with us. Since we would have to live with either my parents or his, she wanted me to stay with her—"the devil you know. . . ."

Mama had no objection to my living with a man without being married. I'm sure she would have argued strenuously had I told her I planned to have children (the only reason, as far as I could see then, to marry) at age twenty-three. Because I had my own bedroom, adding a man to our household was much easier for us than for most Russian families. Whole books could be written (indeed, have been written by Russians) about the sexual and emotional problems of several generations obliged to cram their lives into one or two rooms.

Yura cooked for us. That fact—far more astounding in Russia than in America—symbolized the difference between my fantasy love affair with Volodya and my real life with Yura.

For most of my life, I was helpless in a kitchen. My grandmother and Mama didn't care whether I learned the "feminine" art of cooking, so I was happy to let them take charge. But when I fell for Volodya, I immediately imagined myself as the mistress of a household. I would serve tasty dishes to his fellow officers and their wives. So I took myself off to a cooking school where, for a few rubles a lesson, I expected to find the way to a man's heart through his stomach. I would learn how to make beef stroganoff! (Exactly where I would find beef, the cooking teacher didn't say.) I would produce blini and elaborate chocolate tortes. Well, at the very least I might learn how to boil an egg and fry potatoes. I never told anyone about these cooking lessons; my friends would have hooted at this ludicrous effort to turn myself into a *khoroshaya khozyayka* (good little housewife). In any event, Volodya left before I learned anything about the mysteries of the kitchen, and I never returned to class after our breakup.

Yura, bunking with various friends in Moscow, had to learn how to cook for himself, and he did. When he moved in with us, he took over in our kitchen. His freelance schedule gave him greater flexibility than my schedule at *Moscow News,* and he never expected me to cook because I was a woman and he was a man. In this, he was unlike any Russian man I'd ever known. (And though American men don't consider it shameful to cook, I don't notice too many of them taking over the job on a daily basis.) I remember walking through the door of our Moscow apartment, my nose twitching at the aroma of Yura's borshch or roasted potatoes. I even learned how to cook a bit myself by watching him chop garlic, add parsley, and deftly whisk pots and pans off our small stove.

Yura simply accepted me as I was. With his photographer's aesthetic sense, he even managed to help me with my eternal hair problem. By then, I was able to subscribe to *Essence,* but I was all thumbs when I tried to coax my hair into a shape resembling the look of the models. Yura saw I was hopeless and figured out how to place pins in my hair, twist a rubber band to produce a proper ponytail or chignon. I nearly forgot the years when I thought no man would ever want to touch my nappy black hair.

Race didn't enter into our private relations at all—you really *do* forget the color of someone else's skin when you live together every day. Occasionally, someone on the street would remind us of the racial difference by commenting—as people did when Misha and I were dating at the university—on the beautiful children we would have.

Our quiet, domestic life contrasted sharply with the political turmoil in the world outside. *Glasnost* would one day present us with incompatible career possibilities, and work would pull us apart. But we didn't know that at the beginning of our private life together.

CHAPTER TEN

A NEW WORLD

November 22, 1987—Dawn is breaking somewhere over the Atlantic, and my stomach tightens with apprehension and excitement as I watch the first streaks of light outside the windows of the Aeroflot plane bound for New York. In just a few hours, I will land in the country my grandparents left more than fifty-six years ago. I clutch my Soviet passport, looking for the hundredth time at the American visa inside. I still can't believe that I am the first reporter selected for a Soviet-American exchange of journalists. I will work at the *Christian Science Monitor* and observe the operations of an uncensored newspaper.

I have no idea what to expect. Will Americans be as friendly toward me as they always seem in Moscow? What will it feel like to be black in the country where my grandparents suffered the pain of racial discrimination? Enough, Yelena—no excuses. You are one lucky girl to have this chance. Only two years ago, you had about as much chance of flying to America as you did of taking off for the moon. I hear the voices of my mother and grandmother inside my head. I fasten my seatbelt.

My journey to America really began in March of 1985, when Mikhail Gorbachev became the leader of the Soviet Union. It was my good fortune to be working as a reporter for *Moscow News*, a Soviet paper that would play a critical role in the battle for social change. I was just two months short of my twenty-third birthday when I first heard the words *glasnost* and *perestroika*. Like my friends, I had high hopes for my country under this new leader, who seemed far more intelligent and vigorous than the senile old men who had been in charge for most of my life.

But I had no idea that the process of *glasnost* would irreversibly alter my own view of my past, present, and future. I also had no inkling that the press in general, and stodgy old *Moscow News* in particular, would help transform the political consciousness of an entire generation.

Change announced itself in the person of our new editor, Yegor Vladimirovich Yakovlev. A respected journalist who had always been considered a liberal in Soviet terms, he left his job as a foreign correspondent for *Izvestia* in Prague to take over the editorship of *Moscow News* in August 1985. On his first day, he called a staff meeting to tell us he wanted his reporters to write with the passion, insight, and truthfulness we had formerly reserved for *dusha v dushu* conversations. "Write the way you talk at home," he insisted.

This admonition stunned us. To be honest, I simply didn't believe the man meant what he said. Who was he kidding? Write the way you talk at home—ha-ha. What was I supposed to do, forget about everything I had been taught all my life? In fact, that was exactly what my new boss expected of his staff.

I spent five years at Moscow State University preparing myself to be a housebroken, pre-*glasnost* Soviet journalist, which meant always remembering what was and was not permitted. The last thing I expected was that my bosses would ever want me to report what I really saw.

Even the way I landed my first job was typically Soviet. Gennadi Gerasimov, then the editor of *Moscow News*, agreed to interview me as a favor to a friend of my family. Everything in Russia is accomplished through personal contacts. Sending off a resumé to a stranger, something I've learned to do in America, is unheard of. No Soviet boss would bother to look at a stranger's credentials; he'd simply toss the piece of paper in the wastebasket.

Problem number one: I had nothing to wear to a job interview. My best item of clothing was a prized pair of jeans; I didn't own a suit or a pair of black leather shoes with respectable heels (standard business garb for Russian as well as American women). Instead of looking around in stores where any decent article of apparel sells out within a half-hour of arrival, I enlisted the help of my girlfriends. One had a jacket in my size, the other a blouse. The only suitable pair of pumps didn't fit, so I stuffed the toes with paper to keep them from falling off. Hoping I could keep the shoes on my feet long enough to get through the interview, I wobbled into Gerasimov's office.

I had written my MGU diploma dissertation on the black American press, and this interested Gerasimov because he had spent so much time in the United States. For once, I had the feeling that my American background might be a help instead of a hindrance. If Gerasimov already had reason to hope for Gorbachev's rise to power—and I'm sure he did—he must have known there would be enormous changes in the press. At that time, though, he had to stick his neck out to hire someone like me—and I'll always be grateful to him for giving me my first chance.

Gerasimov offered me a job not as a reporter but as a glorified secretary in the letters to the editor department. I would answer letters from Auntie Masha in the village of *Lozhka* (Spoon), where a neighbor had stolen her prize goat. I would explain apologetically that our newspaper couldn't do much about her goat. But I would thank her for reading *Moscow News* and tell her how much we appreciated hearing from our readers. Occasionally a letter, like one from a couple living in one room with two children, on an apartment waiting list for fifteen years, would provide material for an indignant article. In typical pre-*glasnost* fashion, the article would focus on the couple as an exception to the rule; the paper wouldn't talk about millions of other families in exactly the same situation. It wasn't a waste of time for me to read these letters, because they gave me a broad view of the everyday problems of Soviet citizens.

In 1984, when citizen exchange programs with America were just beginning, I got the chance to interview Americans visiting our newspaper. (True to my grandmother's prediction, I was chosen for this "piece of bread" because I spoke English.) Since this was still the pre-*glasnost* era, I knew I was supposed to confine my interviews to thoroughly satisfied tourists. My article wouldn't be printed if I interviewed a man who was furious because he tried to sit down at a table with Russians in a restaurant and was quickly shunted aside into a section reserved for foreigners. (In crowded restaurants, customers are seated with strangers, but management used to be under orders to keep Soviets and foreigners strictly separate.) Instead of wasting my time writing about malcontents, I asked the Intourist guides to point out the "right sort of people" to interview. They knew exactly what I needed: men who praised the quality of Soviet ice cream, women who visited nursery schools and were impressed by the cuteness and cheerfulness of Soviet children. Small wonder that our readership was confined mainly to tourists who received the English-language version of the paper in their hotel rooms and were desperate for something, anything, written in their own language. I'm not sure any Russians, except for my mother and grandmother, read the paper at all.

I understand now what it means to be a real reporter, and I can't imagine going back to the old style of Soviet journalism. But if anyone had asked me how I saw my job then, I wouldn't have expressed (or felt) any genuine complaint. It would have been like asking someone blind from birth about her perception of colors.

At that first staff meeting after Yakovlev took over as editor, he told us a joke.

Question: *What do a fly and a government minister have in common?*
Answer: *They can both be killed by a newspaper.*

We laughed dutifully—he was the boss, after all—but none of us could imagine a newspaper really changing anything about our government.

How could I please my new boss? Perhaps, I thought cynically, I should write a column about turning down dinner invitations from friendly American tourists because I was afraid, even with my press card, of being turned back at the entrance to their hotel? Or maybe Yegor Vladimirovich would like to read that I was still afraid to let any Americans have my home phone number. When they asked how to get in touch with me, I gave them my office number, knowing full well that they probably wouldn't reach me because I was rarely at my desk. (Russian offices don't have message centers or answering machines; if you can't catch people at their desks, you won't get through.)

I always used to look down at the ground whenever an American asked for my number; I was too ashamed of my own cowardice—and of the system of spying in my country—to explain my fears. Maybe Yegor Vladimirovich wanted me to write an entire article about how the system prevented honest, person-to-person contacts between Russians and foreigners. Maybe he wanted me to jump off a bridge.

Today I feel a deep sense of pride in my capacity for change. This is not my story alone, of course, but the story of an entire generation transformed by the introduction of democratic ideas and institutions.

After that first, unsettling staff conference, our new boss met with each of us privately. This was unusual; bosses never conferred with underlings in the past. Yegor Vladimirovich made it clear he didn't want to force anyone to practice the "new journalism"; he found other jobs, on more conservative publications, for those uninterested in becoming investigative reporters after years of accepting government handouts.

I wanted to stay, to become an investigative reporter, but I couldn't figure out what there was to investigate about Intourist.

"What do you mean?" my new boss asked sharply. "Is it your opinion, Yelena, that Intourist is a wonderful and efficient organization?"

"Of course not," I said, "It's awful." But I didn't really have any idea how to dig up dirt on an established Soviet agency.

Yegor Vladimirovich shook his head in exasperation. "I can see this is all going to be harder than I thought," he muttered. "Well then, I'm going to give you your first assignment: Find out why foreign tourists are treated so badly at the National Hotel." Not long before an American businessman had walked into the offices of *Moscow News*—he'd gotten the address from the free copy in his hotel room—to complain that he had waited an hour in the dining room of the National without being served. Accustomed to being served attentively in hotels throughout the world, he was first astounded, then enraged, when waiters repeatedly ignored him. He finally told one of the white-coated slugs that he was famished. "So what?" the waiter replied. The man said, "But I don't understand? I give good tips for good service." The waiter's unbelievable reply was, "Fuck your tips."

Even by the low standards of Soviet service, it was considered extreme to tell a tourist to "fuck off." My editor advised me to spend at least a week, eating and drinking and observing the National's dining room. Here was an interesting contrast between the old and the new regime. My previous boss (a senior editor under Gerasimov) became outraged whenever a reporter left the office for any length of time. On one occasion, after dumping one of my manuscripts in the wastebasket, he said, *"Anyone* can go out on the streets and write a story about what he sees. It takes real talent to stay here at your desk and make it up out of your head." And no, he wasn't being sarcastic.

Armed with a press card, I was still apprehensive about trying to enter the National. As usual, I was afraid of being turned away—and accused of being a prostitute into the bargain. The hotel and restaurant guards' concern for Soviet morality was pure sham. They really wanted to keep out any Russian, male or female, who hadn't paid a bribe to get in. (A man would be accused of black marketeering.) Without my press card, I would certainly have been turned back at the entrance to the restaurant, its windows shielded from public view by opaque curtains.

I sat down timidly, surrounded by at least a dozen bored-looking waiters who made no move to take my order. A quarter-hour of glaring produced no results, and I finally started saying *Pozhaluysta* . . . *POZHALUYSTA* (Please) in a voice that grew louder and changed from a polite request to a demand. After another half-hour wait, the waiter slammed a warm glass of apple juice on the table in front of me. (Yegor Vladimirovich hadn't said anything about expense money to pay for my trips to the National, so I ordered the cheapest drink on the menu.)

As a Russian, I found nothing unusual about this experience. Warm juice, stale bread, filthy glasses and silverware were standard. But I knew foreigners were used to something better and they, too, were unable to coax the surly waiters to take their orders. Why on earth didn't the staff want to serve them?

Studying the waiters day after day, I noticed they were much more eager to serve groups than couples or solitary diners. There was a very good reason for this, as I learned from sources who explained the business to me. Diners in Russia order caviar by the gram and alcohol by the milliliter. When a group orders a large quantity of vodka and caviar, it's easy for a waiter to short the serving, charge the higher price, and pocket the difference. At a table for one or two, it's much harder to cheat on the portions.

On the last day of my assignment, when I planned to demand an interview with the restaurant's director, I brought along two women friends from the newspaper because I was apprehensive. In spite of the management's ostensible concern with the problem of prostitution, the dining room was filled with working girls. One young girl, with her blouse literally unbuttoned to her waist, sat down at a table of foreigners and the waiter acted as if he didn't see her. After she left with a customer in tow, the *maitre d'hotel* (if that's the right word for the head of such a sleazy operation) walked up to me and my friends and accused us of being prostitutes. "You're all going to be in trouble; I'm going to call the *militsiya*," (police), he said. I flashed my press card and told him the other women were my witnesses, but he said, "Ha, you're probably all hookers." I loudly demanded a meeting with the director and the man grudgingly said, "All right, just to get you out of here and avoid a scandal."

When I questioned the restaurant director about the corruption in her operation, she explained: "You don't understand. It's not the waiters, it's not me who wants to pocket the money: It's the whole system. I can't get the tablecloths washed unless I pay bribes to the laundry. I suppose the laundry has to pay bribes to someone else to get the soap. Who knows?"

I was proud of my enterprise when I returned to the newspaper office. I hadn't gotten myself in trouble with the police, and I now knew why the service was so bad at the National Hotel. My exposé was published and the director was eventually fired. A few months later, I returned to the National to check up on the operation and was told by an angry waiter, "You have no right to be proud of what you wrote. That was the best director we ever had. She took money not because she wanted to get rich but only because she needed it to run the restaurant. Our new director steals five times as much, because she wants it for herself. A lot of good you did—why didn't you go after some big shot?"

I was chastened and deeply depressed to hear this story. I had followed the usual Soviet tradition of pinning the blame on a low-level scapegoat instead of going to the top. That was when I began to understand the connection between the small, everyday miseries of life in Soviet society and a larger system in which no one has any incentive to do a job properly.

I began to learn how to go after the big shots; I requested and got an interview with the head of Intourist, who wouldn't even have spoken to a reporter in the old days. When I brought up the corruption I found in various tourist enterprises, he cheerfully told me these were isolated problems. The basic Intourist operation was sound, he maintained, "known all over the world for its high quality." When I told my boss what the Intourist head said, Yegor Vladimirovich bellowed, "He lies. You can see with your own two eyes that he's lying." "But how can I prove it?" I asked timidly. "That's what I pay you for," my boss shot back. "That's not my problem, it's yours. Don't come to me with bullshit from lying officials. Talk to waitresses. Talk to people who sell tickets to the Bolshoi. Talk to doormen when they're off duty. Get the proof, or you can go work for some nice little Party house organ."

In truth, I didn't mind Yegor Vladimirovich's bullying. Those were the early days of *glasnost,* when all of us were struggling to develop the courage and initiative the system had tried to stamp out of us. It helped to have a strong, determined leader. He was like the head of a moutain-climbing team, the man who must keep his grip to prevent the weaker links in the chain from sending others tumbling to their deaths.

Some weak links—people who couldn't bring themselves to ask hard questions—did tumble off the mountain. Today's tough-minded Soviet journalists are the result of a winnowing-out process that began at papers like *Moscow News*. The day after the abortive 1991 coup, the world saw Russian reporters stand up and bluntly ask Gorbachev why he had the poor judgment to surround himself with traitors. Now our press is second to none in its investigative zeal.

In 1985, we were just beginning to learn what to do with freedom to write. Before *glasnost,* many writers used to talk about the wonderful articles they would produce, if only the censor would let them. "So where are these great stories now?" my editor would berate us. "You're like a dog who barks fiercely as long as he's chained to a tree. Let the dog loose and he just folds his paws over his head and sits in the sun, because he's never learned how to bite. You've got to learn how to bite."

Moscow News was one of the papers that sank its teeth deeply into the old system of repression. Along with the journal *Ogonyok* (Flame), edited by the equally courageous Vitaly Korotich, our paper was dubbed one of the "flagships of *glasnost.*" The newspaper kept pushing into forbidden zones. It started with investigations of relatively unimportant agencies like Intourist and ended with the KGB and the Red Army, the pillars of state power. My mother used to say, only half-jokingly, that she was afraid to pick up the newspaper each morning because we were printing articles on topics we had always gone outdoors—away from any possible bugs—to discuss.

During those transitional years, two jokes made the rounds among journalists. One concerns the *anketa,* a detailed questionnaire Soviets had to fill out before taking any "sensitive" step, such as applying for permission to travel abroad. The *anketa* is designed to ascertain political reliability; my *anketa,* for instance, revealed the unsavory fact that I had an African father and a Negro mother. In the year 2000, so the joke went, one vital question on the *anketa* would be: "Did you ever work for *Moscow News* or *Ogonyok?*"

Another joke involves a roll call of prisoners in a concentration camp in the year 2000. The guard calls off several names: "Ivanov." "Here." "Pavlov." "Here." "Korotich"—No Answer. "Korotich, Korotich." The angry guard screams, "Back then when you were publishing that trash at *Ogonyok,* back *then* was when you should have kept your mouth shut. *Now* you have to open your mouth."

The jokes aren't as funny to Americans as they are to Russians, but they convey the real fear we felt at a time when we were far from certain that democratic forces would prevail in our country. My first, tentative articles on the incompetence of Intourist were followed by investigative reports on a wide variety of once-forbidden topics: organized crime, government corruption (a topic so broad that it meant writing about everything from sports to airports), religious freedom, the rise of right-wing neofascism (late in the *glasnost* era), the limbo of would-be emigrants who had applied, but hadn't received permission, to leave the country. Reports on emigration weren't concerned only with Soviet Jews, as some Americans mistakenly think, but with Armenians, ethnic Germans, and people of many "nationalities" with relatives abroad. I interviewed Armenians who had received Soviet exit permits, but not U.S. entry visas. At the American Embassy, I found U.S. diplomats could stonewall as effectively as our Soviet bureaucrats.

My mother took great pride in my work, but she occasionally had an attack of nerves. "Can't someone else do some of these articles?" she would ask, usually when I had touched on some subject that could interest the KGB. "Why does it have to be your name over these stories?" Even my contemporaries would sometimes advise me to be careful about what I wrote. "We don't know how long this is going to last," one friend reminded me. "You know what happened after Khrushchev—wham, they shut the lid again."

I knew what they were talking about; I still shared their fears. But freedom is a powerful narcotic. In spite of being scared, I didn't want to give up the rush of satisfaction I got from performing as a real reporter. And you didn't have to be a hero to write the truth anymore. That was the great achievement of men like Yegor Yakovlev, Vitaly Korotich, and their newspapers: They made honest journalism—once so heroic and dangerous—a reality of daily life.

During those years, though I still grieved for my grandmother, I often reflected that she was fortunate to have died at the beginning of *glasnost*. In the early eighties, elderly visitors from New York—her former colleagues in the Party—would occasionally stop by our apartment when they were passing through Moscow. One day, not long before her death, two of these old men rang our bell. Mama tried to get rid of them. By then, my grandmother, who had congestive heart failure, was so weak she slept most of the time. Hearing voices in the other room, she cried out to Mama, "Baby, I want to see them." When the old comrades appeared in the doorway of her room, she propped herself up on the pillows and said in a firm voice, "Tell people back in America that I did the right thing. I was never sorry I came here, to the land of socialism." Then she sank back, exhausted, into the pillows. She was still a believer.

My grandmother had taken great pride in my old puff pieces on Soviet tourism, articles that never would have seen print in the new era of honest reporting. It would have been agonizing for her to read the new Yelena, a member of a press corps that was exposing one failing after another of the society she revered in her youth. She might have been able to stand reading critical articles about the Stalin era but could never have tolerated doubts about communism itself, about the legitimacy of the Bolshevik Revolution, about the sacred mummy in his mausoleum. I know many old people like my grandmother, and everything that has happened in the Soviet Union during the past seven years has been a source of immense pain and confusion for them. They've been told that they dedicated their lives to an ideal perverted into a system that murdered millions. My grandmother would have died with a broken heart if she had lived into the *glasnost* era. She would no longer have been able to rationalize the sufferings of the Russian people (and her own sufferings) as having been necessary "for the good of the cause."

It wasn't just the old or the true believers who were shaken and angered by *glasnost*. After my newspaper received numerous complaints from foreign and Soviet tourists, I went to the central customs office to question officials about their actions regarding books and magazines from abroad. Officers at Sheremetyevo Airport frequently took it upon themselves to confiscate reading materials ranging from the Bible to *Playboy* magazine. Sometimes they would seize a newspaper if they thought it contained an anti-Soviet cartoon. This time, I didn't bother with the underlings but went straight to their boss. Looking at me with utter contempt, the man explained, "It's my job to see what's anti-Soviet and what isn't. When someone is carrying a cartoon of a bear and the bear is named 'Misha,' it's perfectly obvious that's a mockery of our government and its leader, Mikhail Sergeyevich Gorbachev. Why, the very image of the bear is anti-Soviet."

This middle-aged man couldn't believe he was now expected to answer a reporter's questions about his operation. He treated me as an enemy intent on ruining his life, and his attitude was entirely understandable: My newspaper *could* ruin him.

If our country abolished censorship, he would be out of work. To him, taking away people's books and magazines was just another job; he didn't think of it any differently than a sanitation worker thinks about hauling away trash. Censorship was his living; the system fed and clothed his children. No wonder he hated me!

Millions of these men and women, whose only task was to impose control from the center, are now out of a job. Not all of them were bad people, but all of them made a living through the exercise of petty power.

As an investigative reporter on a newspaper known for digging up dirt, my color helped and hurt me. It helped because I was easily recognizeable: People knew I was the one to approach with tips. It hurt for the same reason: As the only black writing for a major Moscow newspaper, I couldn't go undercover. A few months after my first exposé of the National, I stopped by another hotel to visit a friend. The doorman immediately recognized me. "Aha, you're looking for something filthy going on here too," he said. "Well, you won't find it. We don't need nosy girl reporters here."

Several years later, when I was trying to gather information about Russian *mafiosi* who run rackets at the airport—everything from massive, well-organized theft of electronic equipment brought back by Soviet tourists to quick muggings of foreigners—my editor received a phone call from a high official. "We know you had that reporter asking questions out at the airport," the man said. "We want to tell you that this could be a very dangerous story for everyone and for your newspaper." If I'd been white, the racketeers wouldn't have spotted me. Still, the phone call did give us the useful information that airport *mafiosi* had high-level protection from "the organs."

On another occasion, I stopped by an ordinary (as distinct from a KGB) police station to arrange cooperation for a story on currency speculators. The officer did a double take when I introduced myself and said, "Don't I know you? Weren't you in jail here just about a week ago?" I bridled, informed the man I had never been in jail in my life, and produced the always-mandatory press card. He inspected the document, eyed me closely, and apologized, explaining that a black prostitute had used my name to identify herself when she was arrested. "I guess she'd read your articles and thought using your name would get her out of the lockup," the officer explained. Of course, the cop had confused the two of us because we all look alike to him.

My mixed heritage gave me a special interest in stories about ethnic minorities, another forbidden zone in the pre-*glasnost* years. I interviewed Armenians and Jews about the difficulties they had encountered (sometimes from American as well as Soviet authorities) in trying to emigrate. Some of these articles gave me unwelcome insights into the prejudices of people I considered my friends. I wrote one story about Moscow's small community of Hasidic Jews, who, like believers of many faiths, had come out into the open and begun to proselytize as controls on religion were eased.

After the article appeared in print, a man I had known for years asked me why I wanted to "spoil my reputation" by writing about Jews. "You don't have any connection with these people," he said. "Why do you want to be identified with them?" That's how I learned the man was an anti-Semite; that's how I lost a friend. My story, by the way, wasn't "pro-Jewish" or "pro-Hasidic"; it simply described the religious rituals observed by the Hasidim, as many other articles during the same period described long-suppressed Russian Orthodox or Roman Catholic customs. With religion a forbidden zone for so many years, Russians wanted to read about religious observance and belief, how Hasidim celebrate marriages beneath a *chuppah,* how Muslims fast during Ramadan, the difference between Orthodox and Roman Catholic attitudes toward married clergy.

Only a few years have passed, but I already feel a strong sense of nostalgia for the early, heady days of *glasnost,* when Russians wanted to learn anything and everything, when articles about religious and ethnic minorities excited people more than the opening of a new Terminator movie.

In the early eighties, it hadn't yet occurred to me that *glasnost* would alter my family's relations with America. Then came a flood of information, and visitors, from America and Europe. Americans were no longer creatures from another planet, to me or anyone else in Moscow.

At the beginning of 1987, a reporter from the *Christian Science Monitor* spent several months at *Moscow News.* I showed her the ropes, for she was as baffled about where to go and whom to call for news as I would have been if I'd suddenly parachuted into the city room of an American newspaper. Take the simple matter of phone books. In Moscow, the reporter from the *Monitor* had to learn how to find sources without the help of a directory. (I, in turn, had to learn how to use the phone book when I came to America.) Suppose I want to write on article on New York's Metropolitan Museum of Art. All I do is call the number listed in the phone book, ask for the public relations office, and give the P.R. person an idea of what I want to know. She, in turn, passes me on to the museum staff member best suited to answer my questions. If a reporter in Moscow wants to write an article on the Pushkin Museum, she must find a friend or colleague who knows someone on the museum staff. The friend introduces the reporter to the staff member, who may or may not pass her on to the person who can really help her at the Pushkin. To get anyone's office number (remember, no switchboards) you have to make a connection inside the building. I had to explain all this to our exchange reporter from the *Monitor,* just as she had to educate me when I wound up in their Boston office.

Not long after the departure of our American guests, my editor's secretary called and said the boss wanted to see me at eleven on the dot. I assumed I'd done something wrong. Soviet editors didn't ordinarily meet with junior reporters except to bawl them out for making a mistake. "Don't worry," the secretary reassured me. "I think you're going to be happy." Soon afterward, I learned I had been selected for the Soviet half of this new journalistic exchange program. I would represent my country and my newspaper by working at the *Monitor* for three months. Having spent the last two years learning how to behave like a real reporter in Soviet terms, I would now find out what it meant to be an investigative reporter in America.

My heart was pounding as I rushed home to tell my mother the news. *This* was something I wished my grandmother had lived to see. In spite of the pain she and my grandfather experienced in America, I know deep down that she would have given anything for another glimpse of the streets of New York. And I know she would have wanted me to understand the American part of my heritage.

I never did get to see New York on that first trip to America. I touched down at Kennedy Airport just long enough to change planes for Boston, the *Monitor*'s headquarters. By then I had a horrible cold and stomach ache, no doubt induced by an overwhelming combination of excitement and anxiety. My hosts, however, couldn't offer me so much as an aspirin, for, like every member of the newspaper staff, they were Christian Scientists who didn't believe in artificial drugs or medical treatment. This began my education in the many varieties of religious belief in the United States; my introduction to the many varieties of over-the-counter medicine would have to wait until I visited my first American drugstore.

Throughout my initial stay, I constantly reminded myself not to draw quick conclusions about this vast, complicated country. I had met many foreigners in Moscow who thought they knew everything about us after spending a week in our country and was determined not to make the same mistake. Still, it was much easier for me to get to know Americans than it was at that time for Americans to get to know Russians.

At first, everything was strange as well as fascinating. As I stood at a bus stop in Boston one morning, an elderly black man, who obviously couldn't see very well, asked me for help. "Tell me, sister," he asked, "is this the bus to Fenway Park?" I told him this was indeed the right bus but assumed his poor eyesight had led him to mistake me for his sister. "You know, I think you've made a mistake," I replied gently. "I'm not your sister."

Hearing my foreign accent, the man explained, "Wherever you come from, if you're black, that makes you my soul sister and me your soul brother."

I was suffused with an unfamiliar warmth: Here I had many sisters. In Moscow, I might stand at a bus stop for a month without ever encountering another person with a brown skin.

I wouldn't learn what it really means to be a black American until I returned to the United States to live on my own for a year in New York. I knew only that here in America, I was no longer one of a kind.

Two people, a white woman, the other a black man, exerted the strongest influence on me and helped me sort out the bewildering new impressions I acquired during my first American journey.

Kay Fanning, the *Monitor*'s distinguished editor (now retired), transformed my Soviet-bred image of what is possible for women. In Russia, I had never encountered a woman in a position of unquestioned professional authority. All of the top newspaper and magazine editors, and their seconds and thirds in command, were men. (The one exception was the editor of the magazine *Rabotnitsa* [Working Woman].) The rare women who do achieve positions of power are considered highly unfeminine; the Russian image of a female boss is that of a gimlet-eyed Party *apparatchik,* hair pulled back into a tight bun, throwing her weight around. We call this kind of woman a *muzhik v yubke* (a lout in a skirt). A perfect example of the type was Yetakerina Furtseva, Nikita Khrushchev's heavy-handed minister of culture (and the only woman in Soviet history to achieve such a powerful position in the Party hierarchy).

Kay—it took me months to feel comfortable calling her by her first name—combined a sympathetic, feminine demeanor with ease in exercising authority. I saw how much respect she commanded, that she didn't have to threaten people to get something done. Once I saw a graying senior editor—I didn't know his name, but I judged his eminence by the distance between his large desk and the desks of cub reporters—walk out of Kay's office and look closely at her comments on a sheet of copy. "You know," he muttered to himself, "she's got a point here. I'd better run it through the typewriter again." Nothing dramatic about this, except I'd never heard a man commenting on a woman's professional judgment as if she were his equal, much less his superior.

She never yelled at subordinates, never called them nitwits or lazy bums—standard invective in Soviet offices. She asked people about their children, their vacations, the health of a parent who had been ill. Again, this was a completely different executive style for me. In Russian offices, there's an absolute barrier between professional and personal life. Russians don't even keep family pictures on their desks. And a Russian boss would never invite a subordinate home for dinner.

So I was astonished when she invited me to her apartment for dinner. I couldn't believe that the boss—I considered her that for the duration of my stay in America—was going to cook for me.

Actually, Kay's husband, Mo, did the cooking. He whipped up chicken curry—this was my first taste of the spicy Indian food—and waited on us. True, Yura cooked for me, but he's the only Russian man I've ever seen in a kitchen. The last thing I expected was to be served dinner by a distinguished, silver-haired man who turned out to be a retired engineer and who took obvious pride in his wife's success.

To me, Kay's life and career were an adventure story: I was mesmerized by her tale of running a small newspaper in Alaska and working her way up to become the editor of one of the most respected papers in the United States at the same time that she raised a family by herself after she and her first husband were divorced.

Thanks to my editor at *Moscow News*, I had begun to develop a new sense of initiative as a reporter. Thanks to Kay, I developed a new sense of strength as a woman who wanted to be both feminine *and* professional. I had been injected with the virus of American feminism. This germ would cause me a fair number of problems when I returned to Moscow, where the word *feministka* was still pejorative.

My internship at the *Monitor* gave me access to an assortment of Americans I never would have met on my own. During the 1988 presidential primaries, all of the candidates spoke before the newspaper's editorial board; I was invited to sit in on the meeting. General Alexander Haig, then a Republican candidate, made an anti-Soviet speech loaded with Cold War rhetoric. His basic message: Americans musn't trust Gorbachev (this was before the Berlin Wall came down) or be led into arms control agreements that would give the Soviets a permanent military advantage. Someone on the *Monitor* staff said, "By the say, sir, we have a Soviet journalist here on an exchange program." As soon as the general heard this, he changed his tune and his tone completely. "Of course we must work together," he cooed when we were introduced. The future, Haig told me solemnly, was in the hands of both our countries. Then a photographer snapped our picture. For the first time in my life, I understood how a politican behaves when he's running for office. (Free elections, which are now becoming a normal feature of Russian life, were still in the future in 1988.) A politican doesn't like to offend anyone in his audience, even if she's a citizen of another country. If I hadn't heard the first part of Haig's speech, I would have believed he was the Soviet Union's best buddy.

I had an interesting experience of a different kind when a prisoner wrote me a fan letter after reading an article about me. I answered the letter and decided to visit the man in prison; I was surprised at the fact that American prison inmates could correspond with anyone they wanted. (In the Soviet Union, the right of correspondence is limited to immediate relatives.) At the time, "20/20" was doing a feature on my family and the producer asked if the camera crew could accompany me to the jail.

On the appointed day, a well-groomed man came to greet me. He was so nicely dressed that none of us realized he was the prisoner. When the guards sorted out the confusion, the prisoner came out and embraced me. "Yelena Khanga," he said, "on behalf of all inmates, welcome to our prison. I hope you'll stay with us a long time." The

ABC crew didn't like his entrance; they thought the embrace was too much. On hearing that, the prisoner said to the cameraman—with great dignity, I thought—"You're in my home. Please have some respect."

My fan, who had committed a great many serious, drug-related crimes, had a horrifying background. His mother was only thirteen when he was born, and his father was killed in a street shooting. He was a career criminal until he finally realized he would end up like his father if he didn't change his life. He decided to take advantage of a prison study program leading to a college degree. He had even learned French.

I was stunned by the fact that American prisoners can take high school and college classes if they want to seize the opportunity. We have no such programs in Russian prisons (though that may change in the future). Convicted criminals—I'm talking about ordinary, not political, offenses—were long considered to have no rights at all. Many Americans have told me about the brutal, inhuman conditions in U.S. jails, and I'm sure the conditions are terrible from an American's point of view. In Russia, though, prisoners are fed on thirty kopecks (worth about thirty cents) a day, far less than what is spent to feed an American convict. Of course, these kinds of comparisons can be dangerous; I don't usually make them because I think every country should be judged in terms of its own state of development.

Throughout my stint at the *Monitor,* I was extremely (most Americans would say overly) conscious of my sensitive position as a representative of my newspaper and my country. *Glasnost* was still in its relatively early stages and *Moscow News* was under attack from conservative forces wanting to turn back the clock. I was afraid to say anything about Soviet politics that might be used as an excuse to criticize my newspaper or to prevent other Russian journalists from visiting the United States on exchange programs. As American reporters began to discover the presence of a black Russian in their midst, they were naturally curious and wanted to interview me. I agreed, but always on the condition that they not ask me any questions about my opinion of such political topics as the struggle between reformers and conservatives.

I became more visible as a black Russian when I traveled to Washington in December to witness the signing of an arms control agreement during Gorbachev's first visit to the United States. There, in the press room of the Marriott Hotel on Pennsylvania Avenue, I was "discovered" by an American reporter as we waited for news of progress on the final stages of the treaty to cut back strategic nuclear weapons.

Worrying about his deadline, the American grumbled to me, "Why don't the Russians just give it up?" I decided to give him something to think about. "Why do you Americans always think we should be the ones to give in?"

The reporter's eyes widened. "What do you mean, 'we'? You're an American, aren't you?"

"Sorry to disappoint you," I replied. "I'm absolutely Russian. I'm a reporter for *Moscow News.*"

Now came the familiar response: "I didn't have any idea there were blacks in Russia." This was a scoop, a bigger scoop, in his eyes, than the tedious progress toward arms control. A Japanese photographer caught the word "scoop" and started taking pictures. Dots were still flashing before my eyes when my first boss, Gennadi Gerasimov, approached the podium with his opposite number from the White House, press secretary Marlin Fitzwater.

That was the beginning of my modest fame, which led to interviews everywhere I went. Some questions were perceptive, while others were astoundingly naive.

"Did you live in an all-black neighborhood? Did you go to a segregated school? (No, there weren't enough blacks in Moscow to make up a segregated anything.) "What did you hear about the way blacks are treated in America? Are all blacks in the Soviet Union poor? Can blacks and whites marry each other in Russia?" (I usually resisted the temptation to turn the last question back on my interrogator and ask how Americans regard marriage between blacks and whites.)

One thing was certain: As a black Russian in America, I felt like more of a curiosity than I ever did as a black Russian in Russia.

One of these interviews was printed in *Jet* magazine. That's how I met Lee Young, a black businessman from Los Angeles whom I now think of as my American father. Lee would become one of the most important people in my life. He had a special, potent reason for caring about person-to-person contacts between Russians and Americans, but I didn't know that when this unknown man phoned me at the *Monitor*.

"I read about you in *Jet,*" he explained, "and I was astonished to learn that there are any blacks in the Soviet Union. I would love to meet you and have you meet some of my friends in the black business community here. Would you like to come out to Los Angeles for the weekend?"

Why would a complete stranger want to meet me? Given my cautious nature, I'm amazed that Lee managed to make me listen to him. I was still thinking in Soviet terms. My visa listed Boston as my only destination, and I was afraid the American police would pick me up and throw me in jail if they found me in Los Angeles. Lee patiently explained that Americans don't need permission to travel from one city to another. (In fact, Soviet journalists permanently based in the United States did need permission to travel outside certain areas. But those restrictions didn't apply to me as a special exchange visitor and most of them have since been lifted for everyone.) How would I get a ticket, anyway? In Russia, you have to buy a ticket weeks in advance to get one of the scarce seats on domestic planes. Lee assured me that buying plane tickets was no problem in the United States; he would simply charge a round-trip ticket to his credit card and send it to me. Finally, I said the trip was impossible because I didn't know him. Again, he reassured me, explaining that he was a black businessman dedicated to the idea of fostering person-to-person contacts between Russians and Americans. How better to do this than by meeting a black Russian? My colleagues assured me that the trip to Los Angeles would give me a look into a whole new world. If I wanted to go, I should.

Reassured by their approval, I boarded a plane for Los Angeles. I was still scared enough to leave my Soviet passport in my apartment, so that the police—which police, I wasn't sure—couldn't identify me as a Russian if anything went wrong. The flight was uneventful,

except for an announcement from a pilot who fancied himself a co-
median. "Ladies and gentlemen," he announced as we encountered
turbulence over the Rocky Mountains, "I'm very sorry, about this,
but we can always take a detour to Honduras." The news that week
had been filled with reports of guerrilla fighting in Central America. I
had difficulty understanding humorous inflections in English and my
stomach clutched. Why were the other passengers laughing? Honduras? What would the police do to me in Honduras without a passport? (I still hadn't gotten it through my head that no American
carries a passport on a domestic flight.) I jumped out of my seat and
headed toward the pilot's cabin. "What's wrong?" asked the steward-
ess. I explained that I was a Soviet journalist who couldn't possibly
land in Honduras, since I wasn't even supposed to be in Los Angeles.
The woman had never heard of black Russians and obviously
thought I was crazy. In the soothing tones a hospital attendant might
use when trying to talk a patient into a straitjacket, she said, "Don't
worry dear, it was just a joke. Sit down and finish your ice cream.
We're not really going to Honduras." (Sometimes people have trouble believing a pilot would make such a dumb remark, but it really
did happen.)

Relieved to get off the plane in Los Angeles (not Honduras), I felt a
new kind of anxiety as I walked toward the gate at the airport. What
would these strangers be like? I saw two people smiling and waving—
Lee and his beautiful wife, Maureen—and the knot in my stomach
started to dissolve. By the time we found Lee's car in the airport
parking lot, I felt comfortable enough to ask him, "Do you have any
soul food in Los Angeles?" Although I'd been in America for more
than a month, I still hadn't tasted any of the soul food my grandmother remembered so longingly. Lee informed me there were more
than a million blacks in Los Angeles and said we'd drive straight to the
best soul food restaurant he knew. (I hadn't realized there were so
many African-Americans and Hispanics in Los Angeles. I'd imagined
L.A. as a land of blonds and beaches.)

We stopped by Roscoe's Chicken and Waffles in Hollywood,
where, for the first time, I tasted real southern fried chicken (crispy on
the outside, juicy on the inside), yams, collard greens, and black-eyed

peas. My grandmother had always talked about the incomparable chicken my grandfather made, but she couldn't produce the same results with the scrawny fowl available in Moscow. After polishing off the food, we went on to Memory Lane, a nightclub, owned by the actress Marla Gibbs, on Martin Luther King Boulevard in the center of Los Angeles. Lee asked if I'd ever drunk a "black Russian," and my reply was, "Whatever are you talking about?" For the first time, I sipped the drink consisting of vodka and Kaluha. I thought the concoction was invented just for me, until Lee explained it was a standard American cocktail. Finally, around 3:00 A.M., Lee told me I'd have to continue my night life with his daughters. He needed some sleep. I realized that I, too, was tired; I'd been running on pure adrenaline. It was already six in the morning by my East Coast body clock.

The next day, Lee saw to it that I visited all of the usual tourist spots from Hollywood to Disneyland. Miniature trains transport visitors around the park, and I took a front seat. Just as we were emerging from a tunnel, I heard shrieks behind me. Michael Jackson was sitting in back, and some of his fans had recognized him.

Ever the alert reporter, I was determined to ask a few profound questions for my readers back at *Moscow News*. The star's bodyguards tried to push me away but finally agreed to three questions when they understood I was from the Soviet Union. "Michael, what do you know about Soviet pop music?" I asked. "Not much" was his scintillating reply. "Would you like to visit the Soviet Union?" "Maybe." "When?" "Well, not this year." Then the guard brought the "interview" to an end with the firm statement, "Your three questions are over."

I managed a better interview with Stevie Wonder on Los Angeles radio station KJLH, which he owns. When I told Eleanor Williams, the station's public affairs manager, that Stevie was one of my favorite American performers, she said, "Well, why don't we call him up for you." I began by telling Stevie how much Soviet audiences liked his song, "I Just Called to Say I Love You." There was a long silence and then he said, "Yelena, you say Russians listen to my tapes all the time. Why don't I get paid any royalties for this?" I explained that Russian movie studios, television, and radio had long made a practice of pirating American music without permission from the performer. He playfully suggested that I become his Soviet agent and try to collect the money. I told Stevie he not only wouldn't get any dollars, he wouldn't get any Soviet rubles either. But I promised to play his tape and discuss the whole subject of pirated music on a television program when I returned to Moscow.

The glamorous, fantasy-filled aspects of my trip to Los Angeles were exhilarating, but they were much less important than the opportunity to meet Lee and his family. Although I had made some black friends my own age in Boston, I hadn't really gotten to know any Americans, black or white, on an intimate, *dusha v dushu* level. My emotional response to Lee and Maureen was strong and immediate, in part because their open-hearted embrace reminded me of home. Russians, so closed-off in public, behave very differently in private. If we feel empathy toward a stranger, we don't hesitate to take that person into our homes.

Maureen is white, and I'm sure I felt especially comfortable with the Youngs because they are a mixed couple. I understand that many black and white Americans disapprove of interracial marriage, but my own background predisposes me in the opposite direction. When I see a loving interracial couple, I relax. For me, the subliminal message is, "You won't find racism here. We're like your grandparents; we believe love is colorblind." I try not to argue with Americans about this subject, because I know their feelings run deep and are ingrained in them from childhood. But I make no apologies for my own very different beliefs. Being with the Youngs makes me think about the life my grandparents might have enjoyed if they had fallen in love during a less bigoted era of American history.

During that weekend, Lee explained why he wanted so badly to promote personal contacts between Russians and Americans. To my astonishment, I learned he had spent fifteen years of his life working as an engineer on the missiles that had long maintained a balance of nuclear terror between the U.S. and USSR. Born in 1933 in the small town of Mt. Pleasant, Tennessee, he graduated with an engineering degree from Tennessee State University in Nashville and went on to become a specialist in rocket propulsion. He worked on the Titan I and II and MIRV missiles; I could remember our teachers telling us in school that these very nuclear warheads meant we had to go on spending money to defend the Soviet Union.

All my life, I had wondered about the feelings of technicians and scientists who helped build the weapons of destruction for both governments. I asked Lee a question that always troubled me: "Don't any of these specialists ever think about the human beings who might die because of what they do for a living?"

Lee answered honestly. "As a young man," he told me, "I just didn't think much about the individuals who might be on the receiving end. They had no faces, no families. Applying my technical skills was more a math problem than a human problem. And it was a way of supporting my family." Lee told me about stocking a shelter with canned food in the basement of his apartment building during the Cuban missile crisis, when I was a five-month-old baby in Moscow. "I prayed a great deal during those days," he remembers, "prayed that the unthinkable wouldn't happen." When the crisis passed, Lee pushed the fear to the back of his mind, returned to his job, and continued building the next generation of weapons. "At the time," he explained, "I thought it was an honor to be involved in the design of weapons systems to be used in the defense of my country."

I've never spoken (knowingly) to anyone in the Soviet Union who worked on our nuclear weapons. But I'm sure these men shared Lee's feelings. Somewhere in one of our weapons factories, a Russian engineer also took pride in creating nuclear warheads to defend our way of life. That Russian, too, would have been brought up on propaganda, focused on the American government rather than on Americans as people who want only to grow up, fall in love, have children, and die in bed of old age.

In the late sixties, after the racial violence that devastated so many black American ghettoes, Lee wanted to use his talents in more socially productive ways. He left the government and started a program to train young blacks as printers. Now Lee owns his own business, manufacturing many kinds of thermal equipment.

Although Lee had been thinking for years about the need for person-to-person contacts with Russians, I was the first Russian he'd ever met. "When you came into my life," he told me, "my change in attitude was completed. Targets became people, buildings became homes, roads leading to missile silos became freeways. While I had understood the theoretical consequences of war, meeting one of my 'targets' in flesh and blood placed an indelible mark on my mind and heart. Bingo: the people-to-people mission was accomplished."

Lee had arranged a reception for about one hundred black businessmen, and I agreed to speak about my life as a black Russian. By introducing me to his friends in the black business community, Lee hoped to accomplish his mission on a larger scale. When I walked into the hotel for the reception, my knees shook. I had never made a public speech in either Russia or the United States. Looking out into the sea of dark faces—journalists, bankers, contractors of all sorts—I realized I had never seen so many black people in one room.

I told the story of my grandparents and talked a bit about what it felt like to grow up black in a virtually all-white country. I described the first jazz club in Moscow, opened only a year earlier. Musicians played for free, and white and black Russians gathered to celebrate the birthdays of Ella Fitzgerald, Oscar Peterson, and Count Basie. I called this "a small world of people who understand one another and share one culture."

For the most part, I confined my remarks to the positive side of growing up as a black Russian. (My struggles with my hair drew a big laugh from the women.) But I wasn't about to share any of my secret hurts—my rejection by Volodya, for instance—with a roomful of people who were essentially strangers, even if I did think of them as "brothers" and "sisters." In those early, fragile years of *glasnost,* I didn't want to say anything that could be interpreted as criticism of my own country. I loved Russia in spite of her shortcomings, in the same way, I was beginning to understand, that most blacks love America in spite of its failings.

In the spring of 1988, just before returning to Moscow, I taped an interview about my family for ABC's "20/20." The program didn't appear on the air until I was back in Moscow, and that's when I finally found out I had living black American relatives. My Golden relations were able to find me only because I showed my grandfather's picture on camera. Without the television show, I might never have learned that I have dozens of black American cousins, aunts, and uncles. But their surprising phone call to our Moscow apartment was still in the future when I boarded my Aeroflot flight for the trip home. I was prouder of being black, of being Russian, of being a woman than I had ever been in my life. I now believed my country, and the world, could change for the better. I wanted to help.

CHAPTER ELEVEN

THE MOSCOW–NEW YORK SHUTTLE

Before I recovered from jet lag after my first American trip, the producers of a new television show, "Vzglyad" (View), invited me to prepare a series of commentaries on my impressions of the United States. No black Russian had ever appeared as a commentator or reporter on Moscow television. In fact, it was extremely rare to see any minority faces—whether Asian, Georgian, Armenian, or Jewish—on national TV. Members of national minorities—Georgians, for instance—would appear on camera in their own republics. Many Russian Jews worked behind the scenes as writers and technicians, but it was exceptional for a Jew—Vladimir Pozner was one of the few—to attain a position in front of the camera.* Soviets always inferred a political meaning whenever a non-Slav appeared on a na-

---

*In his memoir *Parting with Illusions* (New York: Atlantic Monthly Press, 1990), Pozner touches on anti-Semitism in state radio, where he worked for many years, and television, where he came to prominence after *glasnost*.

tional broadcast. No one would hire an Armenian to read the evening news broadcast throughout the nation, for example, because viewers would assume television was taking the Armenians' side in their bitter conflict with neighboring Azerbaijanis.

Soviets also assumed that everyone receiving national exposure must speak for a large constituency. That left me out, since there were too few blacks to deserve a representative by Soviet standards. But "View," which soon became one of the most popular television shows in the country with its combination of lively commentary and investigative reporting, didn't care whether I represented anyone but myself.

The two-year period after my first stay in America, from the spring of 1988 to early 1990, represented the high-water mark of *glasnost* under the old central government. In early 1990, growing economic chaos began to dampen the ardor of even the strongest supporters of Gorbachev's *glasnost*. Thus began a period of political and social instability that led inexorably to the August 1991 coup and the breakup of the Soviet Union as we knew it. But in the 1988–89 "Moscow springs," everything still seemed possible to Russians of my generation.

In its weekly broadcasts, "View" offered an alternative to the more cautious, established news programs on state television. The show presented hard-hitting documentaries on a wide variety of topics: pollution, the appalling quality of Soviet medical care, suppression of national minority and religious movements, the plight of mental patients. It also offered uncensored commentary from people like me, back from trips abroad, who would never have been allowed to speak so freely a few years earlier. As controls on information withered away, Russians were especially hungry for every morsel of news about America.

I was proud to be the first (and I think still the only) black commentator on Soviet television. Soon I acquired another distinction that held even greater interest for my contemporaries. I became the first woman—probably the first person—to talk about condoms on Russian TV. "View" had already tackled the once-taboo topic of AIDS in Russia, and the producers asked me to discuss America's approach to the epidemic.

When I packed my suitcase to return home to Moscow, I made

sure to leave space for some American educational pamphlets aimed at young people on the subject of AIDS. One was titled, "Looking for Mr. Condom." I knew this booklet would interest my friends, not only becaue of its un-Soviet frankness but also because the condom shortage has always posed an infuriating problem for young Russians—the minority of men who were willing to take responsibility for contraception and women who wanted them to do so. Russian-made condoms were hard to find then; today, foreign-made condoms are readily available—but they cost 900 rubles (three times an average monthly salary) for a packet of three. Even men who aren't terribly concerned about contraception are concerned about AIDS, so the search for a *perservativ* (the polite word for condom) is unending.

"View" wanted me to display "Looking for Mr. Condom" on camera to demonstrate the kind of educational materials needed in Russia. This request ran counter to my good-girl Russian upbringing, in which a woman (or, for that matter, a man) would never actually say the word *preservativ* in mixed company. I told the host it would be easier for me to undress on camera than to sputter out the word *preservativ* in front of millions. Not to worry, he promised. When the moment came, he would read the headline and pronounce "the word."

On the air, I chattered brightly about AIDS education and about the fact that Americans understand that the virus isn't only a threat to gays but to the rest of the population as well. Then I picked up the booklet and said, "Now, I've brought along a pamphlet to show you. It's meant for kids between the ages of ten and fifteen." The host said cheerfully, "Oh, we could really use something like that here. Yelena, could you please translate the headline for us." I looked at him and gulped, furious at his betrayal. In a barely audible voice, I whispered, "Looking for *Gospodin Preservativ* [Mr. Condom]."

"Please speak up, Yelena, so that our audience can hear you."

"PRESERVATIV," I shouted, feeling the blood rise to my face and wondering whether the blush was visible even under my dark skin. Whatever the deficiencies of sex education in America, Russia is in the Dark Ages by comparison. The very fact that I, a grown

Yelena at one year old, 1963, Moscow.

Lily and Yelena, 1963, Moscow. Lily wears an African dress adorned with a portrait of Kwame Nkrumah, president of Ghana—the first state to be freed from colonialism in Africa.

Yelena with her grandmother, Bertha.

Yelena's nursery school class, 1968, with a portrait of Lenin in the background.

Yelena and her next-door neighbor Sasha Panin, both age three. She and Sasha were both nursed by Sasha's mother when Lily's milk dried up.

Yelena as a
snowdrop in
a nursery school
pageant.

Yelena celebrating the new year at a pageant in *detsky sad* (kindergarten). In the background is a *novogodnaya yolka* (New Year's tree). At the time, New Year's was the main Soviet holiday, promoted by the state to replace traditional religious feasts like Christmas.

Yelena playing the fox in a traditional folk tale at a kindergarten pageant in celebration of her fifth birthday.

A kindergarten children's concert, 1967, with Yelena in the center.

Yelena, age six, practicing the piano.

Bertha, Yelena, and Lily (c. 1970). In the background is a contemporary painting (in a style called "poto-poto") of an African village near Brazzaville, from Lily's extensive collection of African art.

Yelena, age thirteen, practicing tennis in Moscow.

Yelena, age eight, ice skating in Gorky Park in Moscow.

Yelena, age fourteen, at a nationwide tennis tournament in Kiev, Ukraine. She played for the team sponsored by the Soviet Army.

Yelena in the press room at the Reagan-Gorbachev summit in December 1987, Washington, D.C. This was Gorbachev's first visit to the United States.

Yelena with her colleagues, the "three Natashas," in front of the offices of *Moscow News,* 1987—from left to right, Natasha Izumova, Natasha Davidova, Natasha Paroyatnikova. In the background, Muscovites are reading the day's edition of the newspaper on a public bulletin board.

Yelena with
Dick Gregory
in Boston,
1988.

Yelena with presidential can-
didate Jesse Jackson at the
Christian Science Monitor in
Boston, 1988.

Yelena in her *Moscow News* office, 1988, after returning from her first trip to America as an exchange journalist with the *Christian Science Monitor*. Her *perestroika* T-shirt is a reminder of the Gorbachev era.

Lily placing flowers on her father's grave in Tashkent. The grave site disappeared during World War II, when so many refugees overwhelmed Tashkent that even the cemeteries were reorganized to make room for new corpses. Archeology students rediscovered Oliver Golden's grave in the 1980s.

In 1990, representatives of the committee Thirty-three Plus One—thirty-three women and one man—met with officials to discuss the underrepresentation of women in serious journalistic jobs. This meeting took place with Vladimir Kryuchkov, former head of the KGB. Yelena is at his right and well-known Soviet television anchorwoman Tatyana Mitkova is at his left.

Yelena's father's family poses for a portrait, Zanzibar, c. 1955. Seated are Yelena's grandmother and grandfather. Her father Abdullah Khanga (standing, left), a school-teacher then, was assassinated by political opponents in Zanzibar in 1964. Beside him is his brother.

Yelena and her grandmother, Mashavu Hassan Hanga, meet in 1991 for the first time.

Yelena with her family in Tanzania.

Yelena, Lee Young, whom she calls her "American father," and his wife Maureen. (Credit: Griffith Photography)

Yelena with her cousin Mamie Golden, Oliver's niece, in Chicago, 1990.

The Golden family reunion dinner in Chicago, 1990, attended by more than seventy descendants of Hilliard Golden. Yelena (center) is holding a picture of her mother. She is flanked by her cousins Ollie Morris and Mamie Golden.

Yelena at the Golden family reunion with cousins Gerald Robinson (left), Ennis Morris (right), and Jacqui Robinson (far right).

Yelena and Lily meet some of the Bialek cousins for the first time on Thanksgiving, 1991, in Sagaponack, New York. Back row (left to right): Mark Bialek (Irv's son), Sheila Hoffman (Al's wife), Lily, Irving and Al Bialek (Lily's first cousins). Front row (left to right): Melody Weschsler, Cindy Bialek, Yelena.

Lily on the day she received her passport, with proud Chicago cousins Irving Bialek and Delores Harris.

woman, could hardly bring myself to utter the correct word for a common contraceptive attests to the level of inhibition.

On the streets of Moscow the next day, a few older people scolded me for my "vulgarity." One middle-aged man waved his finger at me and said, "You are a lady. How could you possibly say that word in public?" But I found I had become a heroine to the young. My contemporaries applauded my courage. Still, one teenager pointed out, quite rightly, that it wasn't enough just to say the word *preservativ* on TV. The press should broadcast reports on the near-impossibility of finding condoms or any other contraceptives in Soviet stores. What good does it do to know a condom can help protect you from AIDS if you can't buy one?

Unfortunately, anyone appearing on TV in Russia, as in the U.S., runs the risk of attracting attention from genuine loonies. Outside the *Moscow News* building, an innocuous-looking man approached and said, "It's great that you had the courage to talk about condoms. So many people have kids who shouldn't reproduce, like cripples and Jews and the blacks and retards." I began to back away, but he persisted, proudly introducing himself as "the leader of the neo-Nazis in all of Moscow." *All ten of you,* I thought silently, intent on getting away without any further conversation. But then my reporter's curiosity got the better of me. "Don't you understand," I asked, "that I'm one of those people you think shouldn't have children? Look at me. Can't you see that when I have children, those children will be brown? They certainly won't be what you consider "pure." His answer was, "Well, for you it's okay to have kids. You're obviously a nice person, very cultured, very educated. You're not like those other blacks, and you're certainly not a Jew." I decided not to give the man a heart attack by enlightening him about the skeletons in my family closet. He offered me his telephone number and told me if the Nazis could ever help me in any way, he was at my service.

Through my appearances on television, I hoped I could begin to change Russian stereotypes of blacks everywhere, not just within the Soviet Union. I wanted to expand Russians' image of my race beyond *chyornokozhiye giganty,* the black-skinned giants lionized by Soviet sportscasters.

I took special pride in one segment, filmed with a hand-held mini-camera during my first trip to Los Angeles, of a Sunday service at the West Angeles Church of God in Christ. Located at Crenshaw and Adams Boulevards, in the heart of black Los Angeles, the congregation typifies the kind of church that has bound African-Americans together since slavery. Clapping and singing gospel songs, the congregation and its minister gave the Russian audience an entirely new picture of African-Americans in particular, and of church services in general.

After the show, viewers phoned to ask the same questions: "Why are those people laughing? Why do they look so happy when they're in a church?" Russians aren't used to seeing religious fervor expressed in a physically joyful way. Orthodox services (the only kind most Russians have ever seen) are outwardly somber affairs, with worshippers bowing low before God.

Before my first visit to America, I myself knew almost nothing about the importance of religion in African-American history. My grandparents were both atheists, and my grandmother could tell me only that Oliver's father was a preacher. By the time she met my grandfather, he had, of course, moved far beyond the church-centered world of his childhood. But I learned what I told my audience: Black American churches served not only as sources of spiritual inspiration but as centers for education and leadership.

When I first began appearing on TV, many viewers assumed I was an American. They called to ask how I happened to speak such perfect Russian. To answer the questions, I delivered a short version of my family's story, just as I had told it to Americans on "20/20." Not surprisingly, my audience knew little of the American blacks who came to the Soviet Union during the thirties. The involvement of foreigners, white or black, in the development of the Soviet state was just another submerged chapter in our history.

In Russia—startlingly unlike America—viewers displayed no special interest in my family's story. The standard reaction (some put it politely, others rudely) boiled down to, "How could your American grandparents have been so stupid as to come here?" Russians now look at everything American through rose-colored glasses. They can't imagine why anyone, even during the Depression, would leave the land of plenty for the hardships of life in Russia.

As a result of my television appearances, I did, however, begin to receive touching letters from blacks across the country. They told me how proud they were to see one of their own on television. "I never, ever, thought I'd see a black face on TV here," wrote one Nigerian student from Moscow State University. "I thought, it'll be seven years until I go home and see someone who looks like me doing a normal job."

Black Russians described their sense of isolation. Lusya,* a young woman from Leningrad, asked if I could possibly help her locate her African father. She didn't even know what country he came from, and I had to explain that it was impossible to find one man on a vast continent without at least knowing his citizenship. This woman, the daughter of an uneducated factory worker, hated her life in Russia and fantasized about her father in Africa. "I just want to live in a place where people won't call me a monkey," Lusya said. I had *never* encountered such prejudice in Russia. My mother brought me up to take pride in my African and black American origins, but Lusya was raised by a mother who didn't know anything about blacks. She didn't attend a special English school, play tennis, or spend Sunday afternoons at conservatory concerts. In her early twenties, Lusya foresaw a bleak future, surrounded by uneducated people who called her "monkey." Unprotected by my educational and social advantages, she viewed her black skin as a curse rather than a mark of separateness. As I heard from blacks with harsher experiences of Soviet life than mine, I realized more and more that I couldn't speak for *all* black Russians. Like much larger black America, black Russia, too, has many faces.

During this time, Mama and I reestablished black American family connections severed since 1931. My interview on "20/20" aired in October of 1988, and my Chicago cousins took only a few days to

*Her name has been changed.

track us down through ABC. Mamie Golden, my grandfather's niece, and Delores Harris, his grandniece, were the first to call. Mama knew these were our true relatives (we'd already received a few crank calls) when Delores identified herself as the granddaughter of Oliver's oldest sister, Rebecca. "I knew right away these were real relations," Mama says, "because my mother always told me the first child in my father's family was named Rebecca." After a lifetime of seeing ourselves as an isolated unit (which also included Baba Anya and Uncle Olava), we suddenly learned we were members of a large family.

A flurry of letters and phone calls followed the first contact. We wept when Mamie passed along a letter my grandmother sent from Tashkent in 1956. In that year, Bertha had received a letter from Viola, Oliver's youngest sister (the one in the turn-of-the-century portrait of the Golden "big house" in Yazoo). It was the first communication from the Chicago Goldens in more than twenty years. (From my grandparents' arrival in 1931 until 1936, letters from America got through with some regularity. After that, nothing arrived until the thaw after Stalin's death.)

When Viola finally got a letter through, my grandmother faced the sad task of telling her that Oliver had been dead for sixteen years.

"He was the best husband and father in the world," she wrote. "In 1939, he started ailing. . . . His sickness and death were so sudden, so unexpected. During the twelve years we were married, he was never sick. A big, strong, healthy man, and suddenly such a serious, fatal disease. Oliver thought that his kidney had been injured in New York during a demonstration, when a policeman hit him hard on the hip with his club. I remember him complaining about it in N.Y. Sixteen years have passed since his death. I devoted all my love and life to bringing up Lily, our only child. She took after her daddy in looks and character."

Since my grandmother didn't hear from Viola again, she assumed that Oliver's sister had died. But who knows how many letters vanished into the censor's memory hole during the Cold War? Perhaps Viola wrote again but the letter never reached my grandmother. When she died in the early 1960s, Viola passed on my grandmother's letter to her niece, Mamie, along with the precious portrait of my great-grandparents and their house.

In 1989, my mother finally met our Golden relatives when she lectured around the United States on a tour organized by the Center for U.S.-USSR Initiatives. A San Francisco–based citizens' exchange group, the center arranges for Americans and Russians to stay in one another's homes. This group opened up entirely new travel possibilities for "unofficial" Russians, who couldn't possibly afford American hotels.

And in 1990, I met several of my relatives—all of them descended from Hilliard Golden—when they came to visit us in Russia. The group included Delores Harris (the cousin who first phoned us in Moscow), and Gerald and Jacqui Robinson, all three from Chicago. Jarvis (Jay) Green, executive director of the American Heart Association, came all the way from San Francisco. Like Delores, Jay is the grandson of Rebecca, my grandfather's oldest sister. (Jay's family moved to Omaha after leaving Mississippi, while most of the other Goldens wound up in Chicago.)

Because I grew up without much family, I didn't know how to behave. I started to shake hands and was startled when my relatives began to hug and kiss me. Should I love these people just because they were family, when they were complete strangers to me?

I gradually came to understand what it means to belong to a large, African-American family with a proud history. We were of the same blood; we shared a past even though we had been separated by time, language, and culture. When my relatives flew to Moscow, they did so not because they had any special interest in the Soviet Union but because we were kin and they wanted to understand our lives.

Mama organized a trip to Tashkent to visit her father's newly rediscovered grave. "I knelt down to place flowers on the grave, Mama recalls, "and there was something truly special about being there with Papa's blood relatives from America. A connection, long broken, was being repaired. This was a unique feeling in my life." A year later, in 1991, when old census documents led me to my great-grandfather's land in Mississippi, I somehow felt I was repaying my Golden relatives for their visit to us in Russia. They had given us back a piece of our past; I wanted to do the same for them.

・　・　・

My friendship with Lee Young, which began with his out-of-the-blue phone call to the *Christian Science Monitor* in 1988, deepened in spite of the ten thousand miles separating Moscow and Los Angeles. In the summer of 1990, Lee and Maureen flew to Moscow to visit Mama and me. I wanted to give them a taste of life outside Moscow, so we took a short trip to the Caucasus.

Everywhere we went, from the capital of Tbilisi to small mountain villages, Georgians extended their fabled hospitality. We enjoyed one feast after another, with spicy local specialties like chicken *tabaka*, home-fermented yoghurt (a source of exceptionally long life, according to American television commercials), and endless bottles of Georgian wine.

Lee and I vividly remember one banquet, because he suddenly began to weep amid the toasts and joke-telling. He told me his mind flashed back to 1966, when he was a young engineer engaged in multiple-warhead missile design. He remembered target maps that included Georgia and had an image of his friendly hosts standing on those old charts. He realized that the weapons he helped design, had they ever been used, would have killed all of the people in the room.

In my view, this kind of moment—in which the Russian or American "other" suddenly takes on a human face—represents the most important, glorious change in both of our countries during the past few years.

On a personal level, my relationship with Lee, whose three daughters are my contemporaries, filled a barely acknowledged paternal void. My mother's husband, Boris Yakovlev, has always been a loving and generous stepfather to me, but I was already sixteen when he and my mother married. At that ornery age, having grown up without a man in the house, I was still too young to admit (even to myself) that I might need a father figure in my life. By the time I met Lee, though, I was old enough to acknowledge my need for a father's love and concern. "Would you mind if I called you "Dad" sometimes?" I asked hesitantly as he and Maureen were about to walk through airport customs. I find it hard to display my emotions, so this request was highly uncharacteristic. "I'd be honored," Lee replied instantly. "Nothing would make me happier."

. . .

Even as I forged new ties to America, I was taking a more active role in the birth pangs of a new Russia. My American experience meshed in a great many ways (not only those involving family) with the changing consciousness of my Russian world. I finally grasped the connection between problems I used to consider personal and the larger structure of society. The personal is political, as American feminists say.

I was no longer willing, for instance, to let men dismiss issues like contraception and abortion as trivial "women's problems." Certainly, the fact that abortion is the only generally available means of contraception in is one more manifestation of an underdeveloped economy. (A country that can't supply meat and eggs to grocery stores naturally can't manufacture birth control pills either.) But the lack of attention to specific women's needs must also be connected with the fact that men run nearly every institution. These are serious subjects, deserving of serious reporting.

As I contemplate America's wealth, I don't think about big cars or swimming pools or skyscrapers. I think about tampons. When I packed for my first trip to America in 1987, I filled my suitcase with rolls of cotton gauze. This turn-of-the-century way of coping with menstrual periods is the only choice for Russian women; we feel lucky if we can manage to find enough cotton in the stores to avoid using rags. I didn't want to spend my precious time in America searching for cotton, so I brought everything I needed.

In Los Angeles, I was sitting next to Lee's daughter, Lore, at a concert when my period started unexpectedly. I whispered to her and she said, "Don't worry, there's an all-night drugstore near here." When we walked into the store, I asked Lore where I could find the cotton. "What do you mean, cotton?" she asked. She walked me over to a long counter stacked with boxes of tampons, but I didn't know what a tampon was. With my formal, still-shaky English, I understood only that she was talking about something that goes inside a woman's body—probably making a joke about intercourse, I assumed. "Do you like them long or short?" she asked. "Scented or unscented?" she asked. "Lore," I said in a shocked tone, "Who cares? It's never occurred to me." Finally, Lore recognized my hopeless confusion and explained, in the way I assume an American mother explains to her twelve-year-old daughter, exactly what a tampon is and how it works. My eyes widened as I looked at the array of sanitary products for women in different stages of their period, at the choice of medication for cramps and bloating. Then I understood: Western women don't have to plan ahead like generals, wasting time and energy to satisfy their most basic needs.

Trivial? I don't judge the success or failure of an economic system by its nuclear weapons or its expensive cars. I judge the system by its aspirin, its bandages, its condoms, its tampons. This endless waste of energy is no small matter to our Yelenas and Ninas and Olgas. How can we work our way up to editor-in-chief? We're always out shopping, battling for items the rest of the industrialized world takes for granted.

Everything is connected.

In the Moscow of 1990, it was hard for my mother and me to remember the fear that kept us isolated from Americans for so long. Foreign visitors seemed to turn up on our doorstep every day. I never knew who might be sitting around the kitchen table when I came home; my mother made so many friends through the Center for U.S.-USSR Initiatives that our living room floor was frequently covered with overnight campers.

Moscow News was in the forefront of *glasnost,* and American reporters and camera crews constantly invaded our newsroom to discuss the latest controversy. Because of the black-Russian-American connection, they often wanted to take pictures of me; I posed outside our offices so many times that I began to feel like a substitute for St. Basil's Cathedral in my own Red Square.

Russian and American reporters now talked to one another constantly, and a colleague of mine at the Novosti Press Agency came up with an enterprising idea to enlist the aid of women journalists from abroad in calling attention to the fact that Soviet women were seldom allowed to cover politics or foreign affairs. The women correspondents based in Moscow immediately agreed to help, and we called our committee "33 plus 1," the one being a man.

We sent a letter to high government officials, and many of them agreed to meet with us. Through these meetings, we were trying to make a point: Russian women journalists, like their Western counterparts, are capable of writing about traditionally "masculine" subjects like defense and foreign policy, not just "soft" domestic issues. (Still, if the demand for these meetings had come only from Russian journalists, the government ministers would surely have ignored us.)

Our most memorable meeting took place with Vladimir Kryuchkov, the unlamented former head of the KGB. Kryuchkov was one of the "Gang of Eight" who tried and failed to seize control of the government in August of 1991. At the time of our meeting, the KGB head and his organization still inspired great fear.

In a picture of this session, Kryuchkov, surrounded by smiling women, is smiling broadly himself. I am seated at his right, and I'm grinning too. Pictures *can* lie. On the inside, I was quaking and anxious to leave the KGB headquarters, where so many people were interrogated and tortured during the preceding decades. It was hard for me to walk through the door of the ominous-looking building on what used to be called Dzherzhinsky Square. (The statue of Felix Dzherzhinsky, the founder of the secret police, was pulled off its pedestal in the wake of the abortive coup.)

The meeting with Kryuchkov started awkwardly. Our genial host made a joke about how much easier it was to open the door to his office from the outside than from the inside. Get it, ladies? He greeted us with champagne, chocolates, and carnations to demonstrate the KGB's respect for "our valiant Soviet women." (I was most interested in the chocolates, of a quality never seen in ordinary Soviet stores.) The candy, the crystal champagne glasses, even the plush carpet on the floor and the richly textured drapes shielding the windows: All evinced a luxury unknown to most Soviets. The KGB certainly didn't live the way it told everyone else to live. One American correspondent asked Kryuchkov how many women held high positions in the KGB, and he mentioned a few names. I wasn't terribly distressed to hear that women were underrepresented in the ranks of the KGB; it seems to me that there were better ways for women to improve their status in Soviet society than by advancing themselves through such a hated and feared organization.

The KGB demonstrated its real attitude toward women on a rainy

day in October of 1990. Thousands of Moscovites had gathered outside its headquarters to dedicate a memorial to all victims of secret
police terror throuhout Soviet history. To distract public attention
from this moving and important event, the secret police announced
that they had held a beauty contest and selected a "Miss KGB." After
presenting a buxom secretary (said also to be a crack shot) holding a
huge bouquet of roses, the witty KGB spokesman fielded questions
about how the beauty queen was chosen. "That's a state secret," he
replied.

On the one hand, this was a period of excitement and hope, on the
other, a time of worsening ethnic unrest, street crime, and consumer
shortages. Because of these problems, every democratically inclined
Russian feared a military-KGB coup. As a reporter, I grew frustrated.
Yes, I had the freedom to write about everything, but my stories
didn't have the power to change anything. I could write about contraception and say *preservativ* on television, but the teenager who
accosted me outside *Moscow News* was right. These articles didn't put
the means of birth control into Moscow pharmacies or bedrooms.

In Moscow, I was careful not to flaunt the few items of clothing I
bought in America. Any sign of affluence had become an invitation to
a robbery. One afternoon, I climbed into a taxi outside the newspaper
office, and the driver asked me, in perfectly straightforward fashion, if
I would like to buy an Uzi machine gun for my own protection. "A
woman really isn't safe these days," he added. I politely declined.
"No thank you, I'm fine." I wanted to ask how he acquired his guns
but was afraid he might guess I was a reporter. I didn't want to be
known to the kind of Muscovite who peddled Uzis.

I was most impressed, and scared, by the casual way in which the
man proferred his wares. He wasn't the least bit worried about offering a gun to someone he didn't know. Did this mean he had police
protection at a high level? I wasn't sure.

I never used to be afraid to walk the streets of Moscow at all hours
of the night, but I soon became as cautious as American women. One
night I was about to enter the door of my apartment building when I
saw a man loitering outside. Something about him made me nervous,
but I didn't want to challenge him. Who was I, a meddling *babushka,*

to ask a stranger, "What are you doing here?" He followed me in the door and at the last minute, I decided not to get into the elevator with him. He tried to push me into the lift and I struggled, yelling and trying to push him away. (If any of the neighbors heard me, they didn't come to my rescue.) "You won't get away so easily," he warned me, and suddenly he took out a razor and started slashing my blouse. Fortunately, I was wearing a Soviet-made brassiere. Compared to American lingerie, Soviet bras are thick as army flak jackets. Both my blouse and bra were slashed to ribbons before the man finally gave up and ran away, but I was intact. If I'd been wearing one of my new, prized American bras, I would have been bleeding.

I realized I must change the habits of a lifetime. After that night, I always made a point of calling Yura before I left the office, and he always met me at the metro stop. Before then, it never occurred to either of us that I might be mugged or raped on the five-minute walk home, much less in the foyer of our apartment building.

Such incidents are now common in Moscow, where ordinary police authority has broken down and deprived people envy anyone who appears to have something worth stealing. One neighbor was mugged when he made the mistake of hauling his groceries home in a plastic shopping bag. Plastic bags are used only in foreign-currency stores, so they're a tipoff that the bearer has traveled abroad (or at least knows someone who's been overseas).

The day after the man slashed my blouse in the apartment lobby, I went to the police station to report the crime of attempted rape. "So? What do you expect me to do about it?" was the response of a bored police officer. I showed him my slashed clothing and he said, "So what. It's not a new shirt." Gesturing toward a stack of files, he told me he already had so many backed-up cases that he didn't have enough men to investigate murders, much less an assault that didn't even end in robbery. "Really, what happened to you?" he said. "You lost your blouse, but you didn't even lose one drop of blood. You're fine. I'm sure the man wasn't a rapist, because if that's what he really wanted he wouldn't have run away." How reassuring!

Given the indifferent attitude of an overworked, understaffed police force, the underreporting of crime in cities like Moscow must be staggering. We've become like urban Americans, exchanging battle stories about our encounters with ordinary street criminals and the organized criminal underground. We're no longer amused by American gangster movies. In 1990, just before leaving Moscow to begin my Rockefeller Foundation fellowship, I researched an article about the Hotel Savoy, a new, luxurious establishment built by Finns and supposedly reserved for foreign tourists. In the hotel's hard-currency gambling casino, I encountered dozens of hard-eyed young men, speaking perfect Russian and spending thousands of dollars on chips. Here was our new class of *mafiosi,* spending the proceeds from a wide variety of illegal enterprises—drugs, prostitution, protection rackets. Owners of new, private restaurants springing up around Moscow complained that they had to pay protection money to *mafiosi* in order to ensure the safety of their customers. Many restaurant patrons were robbed at gunpoint during this period, sometimes as they sat eating their meals. Judging from the rolls of bills flashed by the young men in the Savoy casino, business was booming.

When I interviewed the hotel director, he assured me there were no *mafiosi* in his establishment. I told him what I had seen in the casino, and he suggested that the ominous-looking men were really Soviet diplomats or journalists who'd brought back a few dollars from a tour of duty abroad. Then the director's eyes turned hard, and he said in tones that conveyed an unmistakable warning: "Remember— you didn't see anything."

The rise of ethnic hatred or, I should say, *openly expressed* ethnic hatred was another disturbing phenomenon associated with the late *glasnost* era. Fear and loathing of minorities, or between minorities, has always festered like a boil beneath the repressive surface of Soviet society. When fear of the center began to ease, all of the pus poured out, whether in armed conflict between Armenians and Azerbaijanis in the Caucasus or anti-Semitic demonstrations in Moscow. I've been genuinely frightened by the rise of anti-Semitism in Moscow during the past few years. As a very visible black Russian, how could I feel otherwise? I'm reminded of the wartime rhyme, recounted by Anatoly Kuznetsov in his novel *Babi Yar:* "First the Jews, Gypsies too, then Ukranians, then comes you."

In the late eighties self-appointed vigilantes began to study the newspapers for evidence of "undue" Jewish influence. At one raucous meeting in the House of Cinematographers, my editor, Yakovlev, was taken to task by an anti-Semite who wanted to know why there were so many Jewish bylines in *Moscow News*.

"Are they really all Jews?" Yegor Vladimirovich replied. "You know, that's very interesting. I forgot to ask these job applicants to unzip their pants when I hired them."★

Because black Russians are such a tiny minority, the new prejudice has focused not on us but on the larger, better-known ethnic groups inside Russia. Africans however, are an exception: They bear the brunt of an ugly mood fueled by the public's association of Africa with the dreaded AIDS virus. All Africans students, but no Europeans or Americans, were required to take a test for the HIV antibody before entering the country. Soviet medical authorities single out Africans on grounds that AIDS is much more prevalent on their continent than in any other part of the world. In a country without condoms and safe-sex education programs, it's understandable that poorly educated bureaucrats think the best way to control the spread of AIDS is to try to bar carriers from the country. But there's also a strong undercurrent of racism in this policy, however insistently officials may deny any such motives. Everyone knows, for instance, that large American cities have more AIDS carriers than small towns, yet the Soviet Union doesn't require New Yorkers to be tested. Furthermore, I know Russians who will walk out of a dental clinic if they see an African in the waiting room; they don't want to be treated by anyone who has worked on an African's mouth. Again, this behavior is partly attributable to poor medical practices in Russia, where there are no disposable plastic gloves or syringes. But why single out Afri-

---

★Circumcision in Russia is still a reliable way to tell a Jewish from a non-Jewish male. In Russian hospitals, baby boys aren't routinely circumcised. People who go to the trouble of having a boy circumcised are nearly always Jews (or in Asia, Muslims).

cans? Since they must be tested before entering the country, they're far less likely to be AIDS carriers than the average, untested Ivan Ivanovich waiting to have his tooth pulled.

There's no question that Russians today hold more negative attitudes toward blacks than they did when I was a child, not to mention fifty years ago. When an American tourist called Joe Roane a nigger in 1931, the Russian barber threw the racist out of his shop. I don't think this would happen now; almost anything goes in public discourse today.

It pains me to report that some of the new, negative images of blacks are a byproduct of more contact with America. Our newspapers pick up the biases of the American press, and we read a disproportionate number of articles about black crime and poverty. So we're predisposed to believe that all American criminals are also members of minorities.

And influenced by movies like *The Godfather,* some Russians now view all Italian-Americans as gangsters. Since we're free to gorge ourselves on junk entertainment—lines for American gangster movies stretch around the block—we're adding Western racial and ethnic stereotypes to our native prejudices.

The answer of antidemocratic reactionaries, the kind of men who staged last year's coup, was to clamp down from the top and try to push poisonous hatreds back beneath the surface of society. I, and millions like me, believe that the way to deal with the infection is to fight the poison openly while the sore drains. In Moscow, a newly established Jewish civil rights organization, patterning itself after the B'nai B'rith–Anti-Defamation League, is trying to combat anti-Semitic ravings with information of its own. In a democratic political culture, many more of these organizations will spring up. Before *glasnost,* there was no possibility of Soviet society producing organizations like America's NAACP or its Anti-Defamation League. The old system never acknowledged the existence of prejudice or discrimination in our "advanced" society, so what need would there have been for organizations to fight for the rights of ethnic and racial minorities? I regard the building of a truly democratic political culture, characterized not only by freedom of speech but respect for people of differing colors and beliefs, as the most urgent task for both Russian and American society.

Habits of intolerance die hard. As new political movements emerged in the late eighties, Russian families sometimes split along ideological lines, just as they did in the years after the Bolshevik revolution. My mother and Yura, for instance, battled over Boris Yeltsin's candidacy for the presidency of the Russian republic in 1990. Mama and I had always supported Yeltsin. But Yura didn't agree. He said Yeltsin had been a Party leader most of his life, and he wasn't voting for anyone with a Communist past. (A year later, though, Yura joined the young people who surrounded the Russian republic building—we call it our White House—to defend Yeltsin and his government against the military-KGB plotters.) At the time of the election, I wasn't at all disturbed by Yura's position. Everyone, it seemed to me, has a right to his own opinion. But Mama was furious. She even threatened to throw Yura out of the house where we had lived amicably for six years. I asked Yura not to flaunt his opinions in order to keep peace in our home. "Look, it's ridiculous," I argued. "It's like Mensheviks and Bolsheviks cutting each other dead in 1917. Mama's not going to be the one to give in, so let's not talk about it at home."

I know that this little scene was repeated in thousands of Moscow apartments. I even heard of people refusing to speak to a friends who subscribed to the "wrong" newspaper. If you read the opposition press, you were considered not simply someone who wanted to know what was going on in society but a traitor. I hate the kind of thinking that insists, "He who is not with us is against us." For too many generations, my own family has suffered from intolerance on several continents, dressed up in a variety of ideological wrappings.

In many ways, the story of my family is a history of shifting tolerance and intolerance. Tracing this history was the formidable goal I set myself when I received the astonishing news that I had been selected by the Rockefeller Foundation as a Warren Weaver fellow for 1990–91.

The foundation circulates applications for these fellowships in countries throughout the world. I had filled out the form at *Moscow*

News in the winter of 1990, but I never expected to hear another word from the Rockefellers (what wicked capitalist fantasies the very name conjures up to a Russian!) So I was stunned when my phone rang in April and the voice at the other end invited me to come to New York for a personal interview. That great city—my grandparents' city—would be my home base for a year.

I realized this fellowship would offer a very different experience from my brief exchange visit three years earlier. This time I would represent no one but myself, a woman in search of her family's lost past. As far as many Americans were concerned, I wouldn't be "Yelena, that interesting black Russian." I would be just another black woman with a slightly foreign accent. In New York, people sometimes assume I'm from the Caribbean.

Unanswered questions about my racial identity, as well as my family history, drove me to accept the fellowship. I knew this meant separation from Yura—who knew for how long?—but neither of us ever considered the possibility of my turning down the opportunity. We both knew that no Russian of our generation could afford to pass up such a chance.

When I returned to America in September of 1990, friends were waiting for me at Kennedy Airport. This time, I didn't clutch my Soviet passport quite so tightly.

CHAPTER TWELVE

O MY AMERICA!

It's the first real day of spring, the first day you feel secure enough about the weather to leave your coat at home. In Moscow, the longed-for change never comes until late May; in New York, it's already here in March. As usual, I'm walking to work at the Rockefeller Foundation. This is New York at its best; the air seems unpolluted in spite of the cars clogging the narrow streets of midtown Manhattan (so different from the broad, imperial thoroughfares of central Moscow). I sniff the expensive perfume of women and the aftershave lotion of men hurrying to their jobs; for me, this aroma embodies the special energy of New York. It's such a beautiful day that I hardly notice the defining smell of the other New York: stale urine emanating from subway entrances and doorways, where the homeless congregate around Grand Central Station.

About a block from my office, a familiar figure materializes in front of me. He tries to shove an advertisement for a typing school into my hand. "Need a job?" he importunes. My American friends have tried to teach me the purposeful, eyes-to-the-front walk of a New York woman, determined to avoid eye contact with all strangers. This is hard; I'm still too interested in everything around me in this new country to pull the New York shutter down over my eyes. When someone pushes a piece of paper at me, I usually feel obliged to offer a polite "no, thank you" in return, even though I've lived in the city for six months and know perfectly well that hesitation is an invitation to every variety of panhandler and hustler. The typing school sales-man has already stopped me several times on my way to work; today I decide to confront him. Why does he think I'm here every day, dressed in a business suit? What makes him assume I'm out of work, yearning after a job as a typist? "I'm from Russia," I say, "so maybe I don't understand. Why do you keep pushing these papers at me all the time?"

The man—he's white—is taken aback by my question. He stopped me because I was well-dressed, he explains seriously. I looked so neat that he was sure I was capable of learning how to type. And he was equally sure I must be looking for a job. "But why?" I ask again. "How could I afford business clothes if I didn't have a job already?" The man tries to enlighten me. Being a Russian, he points out, I probably didn't realize how much money black Americans spend on their clothes. Yes, it was absolutely true. A black American on unemployment or welfare will spend every last cent on a fancy outfit. So my being dressed in a businesslike way didn't tell him anything about my employment status. This man wasn't the least bit embarrassed by his explanation; his tone conveyed great satisfaction at being able to educate me, a foreigner, about African-Americans. The earth is round. People need oxygen to breathe. Unemployed blacks spend all of their money on clothes. A black American wouldn't have bothered to ask the question in the first place and wouldn't have been surprised by the answer. I'm coming late into a legacy of the racism my grand-parents wanted to spare their own child.

If racism were the only inheritance I'd found in America, I'd want to turn right around and retrace my grandparents' path across the ocean. But bigotry isn't my only legacy. I've discovered more than one white world and more than one black world in this complex land of my ancestors. This time I am no longer a guest, pampered and protected by people of good will, as I was during my first stay in the United States. I'm not a native either, but I am beginning to feel like a relative, at the very least, what southerners call a kissing cousin.

My mother and grandmother raised me to think of myself as a human being first, last, and always. Black was simply the color of my human package. But as far as many, probably most, Americans are concerned, I am black first, last, and always. I think more about my race here, where there are so many blacks, than I ever did in Russia, where there are so few of us. I understand now what Langston Hughes meant when he wrote: "I am the American heartbreak— Rock on which Freedom/Stumps its toe—. When you're a relative, "heartbreak" is the right word: Your heart can't be broken by something, or someone, you don't love.

Both blacks and whites are always telling me I would understand more if I were born and raised here. Of course they're right: I can understand only what I've experienced in my own, partly foreign skin for the past few years. But if the perspective of a black Russian limits me in some respects, it affords me other insights a native American might miss. Sometimes, I wish I could erase these tapes from my memory.

Scene 1: A cocktail party in Los Angeles   I am introduced to a wealthy white businessman who has many dealings with the Soviet Union. "You don't know much about black Americans," he tells me, and launches into a discourse on the evils of affirmative action. Do I know, he asks, that blacks "have a lot more rights than whites when it comes to getting into college?"

I want to tell this man that many more blacks have been denied opportunities because of their color than have received the "special favors" he denounces. I want to talk about my great-grandfather, about the odds he overcame to educate his children a century ago in the South, about how much harder he must have worked than any white man to achieve what he did. But the words stick in my throat. I still feel timid when I try to argue with Americans, whatever their color. (Who am *I* to tell them about *their* country?)

The man continues his sermon on the evils of black America. "Yelena," he tells me confidentially, putting a hand on my shoulder, "you've spent your whole life in Russia. You're educated. You're not at all like blacks here. Look at the prisons in America. Most of the men inside them are black. Blacks don't study as hard as whites, so that's why they need 'affirmative action' to get into college. Frankly, your soul brothers are lazy. They go around making a lot of noise because they don't want to work the way other people do."

This was not some lonely neo-Nazi in Moscow but a respected businessman who met frequently with Soviet delegations. Since most Russians don't know any blacks personally, this man could determine their image of African-Americans. How could he consider it a compliment to tell me I was "different" from other blacks? At the time, I hadn't found an authoritative voice in English. "You can't generalize about all blacks any more than you can about all whites. . . ." I started to say—before he cut me off.

When I meet whites on a social basis, it's usually in my persona as a black Russian. My search for family roots, my Rockefeller Foundation fellowship, my job as a Russian journalist: All of these create opportunity (and necessity) for many personal contacts with whites, though often in a work-related context. And I've been struck by the rarity of interracial socializing outside professional settings. I've noticed that when a white says she has a black friend (or vice-versa), she's usually talking about an office acquaintance. Blacks and whites may respect each other's work, complain about the same troublesome boss, go out for lunch together, but the friendships usually stop at 5:00 P.M. After business hours, they go home to separate worlds. Most Americans take this separation for granted; I notice it and think about it because I was brought up in a different culture. An unanswered question: If I spend years in America, will I too begin to consider social segregation a part of the natural order of things? Accepting separation can be a form of self-protection for blacks: I know if I moved in an all-black world, I wouldn't see and hear so many things that hurt me.

Scene 2: A trip to Arizona. My host introduced me to a white friend of his, the owner of a chain of discount stores. The "discount king" played tennis; it was the only thing we had in common, so I chattered away about my years as a competitive player in Russia. "You must come to my club and we'll have a game," he said enthusiastically.

When we walked onto the court, everyone stopped playing and stared at me. I immediately understood that this was a club—I'd only read about such places—with no black members. My host said, "Ladies and Gentlemen, I want to introduce you to my new friend. This is Yelena. . . ." He paused for several seconds, which seemed like an hour to me. "And she is . . . a Russian journalist." White men and women in white clothes exhaled audibly. Suddenly the hostile stares changed to welcoming laughter. Oh, fine, she's a black *Russian*. The club members crowded around me, expressing delight at my unexpected presence. "We love Gorbachev, he's just great. Isn't it wonderful that the Cold War is over? We need more economic cooperation between our countries, don't we?" I answer. "Yes. Yes. Yes. Yes. International understanding, it's delightful."

All my life, I'll remember those few seconds and my host. Did he want to play tennis with me at all? I doubt it. He used me as a performing monkey in the circus to play a joke on his friends.

Scene 3: An appearance on a talk show   I'm appearing on television to discuss some cataclysmic event: I can't remember which one; there have been so many in Russia during the past two years. The talk show host listens to me intently and encourages me to continue. "Please, Yelena, tell us more," he says. "You're so articulate." I'm flattered, because I think he's talking about my English. The dictionary tells me what "articulate" means: "Using language easily and fluently; having facility with words, . . . expressed, formulated, or presented with clarity and effectiveness." Great—as far as the dictionary is concerned, this is a compliment.

After the show ends, I'm astonished when Lee Young expresses outrage at the host's comment. He explains that "articulate" is a code word, expressing astonishment that a black person can speak in a sophisticated, educated way. I've been insulted and I don't even know it. I think about all of the other Russian journalists who have been interviewed on American television. No one compliments

Vladimir Pozner or Vitaly Korotich for being articulate. No one is surprised when a white, male English-speaking Russian journalist is capable of expressing himself fluently.

I tell two white colleagues about this experience. One says, "Oh, Yelena, don't be so sensitive. The host probably meant it as a compliment. You can't become like American blacks, who see racial implications in everything." In fact, the host probably *did* mean his remark as a compliment. That's part of the pain, because it reveals the assumptions of many white Americans about black inarticulateness. Thankfully, another white colleague understands what I'm talking about and agrees with me. She suggests that I pay attention to American sports announcers, who are always commenting on the articulateness of certain black athletes. If a white athlete is well-spoken, no special notice is taken.

Am I being too sensitive? I don't think so. Almost by osmosis, I'm beginning to take on the protective coloration of African-Americans. I see, for instance, that many white Americans feel threatened by any approach from a black stranger. This experience was entirely unfamiliar to me in my life as a black Russian. It happened for the first time in a small New England town, where I stopped to ask a white woman for directions to the nearest local drugstore. She flinched and I immediately said, "Excuse me, I'm from out of town and I don't know where to find the nearest pharmacy. I didn't mean to startle you. . . ." In New York, where I still get lost from time to time, I prefer to ask black people for directions. When I have no choice but to ask a white stranger a question, I always begin timidly, with a soft "Excuse me." I can't bear seeing fear in the faces of whites. Someone once explained, "It's nothing personal." That makes it worse.

And I am a woman. Black men must experience this gut-twisting sensation, a combination of shame and anger, much more frequently than I do. A friend points out a newspaper article, written by a middle-class black professional, about his feelings whenever he finds himself at night in a white neighborhood. One evening, on a lonely street, a white woman saw him coming from the opposite direction and immediately moved off the sidewalk into the center of the road. The man called out softly, "Don't be afraid, I'm not going to hurt you. I'm just on my way home." I find this story excruciating. Something terrible happens to the human soul when you constantly feel you have to prove you're not a threat to others.

Another uncomfortable question: If I were raised here, would I detest all whites for making me experience this daily anxiety? I listened to my grandmother's stories but didn't really understand them until now. How did my grandparents, so many years ago, manage to see beyond skin color? I have never been more proud of them than I am today. By comparison with their experience, I've been exposed to a mild strain of racism. Yet it's the same virus.

The more time I spend in America, the less comfortable I am with my "special" status as a black Russian in the eyes of many whites. At one dinner party, where I was, as usual, the only black guest, I noticed a black cook, sitting in an alcove just around the corner from the dining room. To every guest but me, she seemed to be invisible. People commented on the tasty food, but no one thanked the cook for her work.

Part of my reaction was certainly attributable to the differences between Russian and American attitudes toward servants. Russian domestic workers (not many people have them) are treated more like members of the family. No Russian hostess would take credit for a meal she hadn't prepared; the accolades would go to the cook who had done the work. And no Russian would call a grown woman "our girl," as my hosts did that night. Of course, I understand that this locution dates from the time of slavery. What I don't understand is how anyone could use such a phrase in 1991.

When I first arrived in New York, a Latino lawyer told me: "If you're a member of a minority, there are two parts to every business task you take on. At the beginning, you just have to establish your right to be there—you have to prove you're as good as everyone else in the room. Then when they accept you, you can get on to whatever you're trying to accomplish for your firm. If you're white, people start from the assumption that you're equal and you don't have to go through the first part."

I didn't understand what he was talking about then, and it's tough to explain to people who are used to being treated as equals from the moment they walk into a room. It's even hard for the American part of me to explain to the Russian part. It's like this: When American journalists talk about American politics, I start from the assumption that they know their stuff, that they have the knowledge to back up their opinions. I might decide I don't agree with them, but I begin with respect. When I discuss Russian politics with white Americans, I often feel obliged to present my credentials as a journalist before I even express an opinion. I don't assume they will pay attention; I feel I have to earn their respect, prove my "articulateness," before I can begin a substantive discussion of the topic at hand. While it's very difficult to explain this sensation to white men, black men—and women of every color—understand. American women who've managed to succeed in a man's world invariably know what I mean. First you have to show that you're not just another pretty face (or, double whammy, another pretty black face); only then can you get down to business.

My grandparents would recognize the ugly side of white America. But I've also found another white world, a place my grandparents couldn't have imagined. Nor could I imagine this place when I first began to look for my family.

When the Rockefeller Foundation awarded me a fellowship, I was interested only in finding my black roots, in fleshing out the sketchy stories of my grandfather's family. I had no intention of trying to look up any white relatives. They had already rejected my grandmother; I certainly didn't want to give them the chance to reject me too.

Frank Karel, the Rockefeller Foundation's vice-president for communications, told me I just couldn't ignore the white side of the family. My reluctance to track down the Bialeks had as much to do with the habits of pre-*glasnost* Soviet journalism, which I hadn't entirely overcome, as with my family history. In the old days, good little Soviet journalists never pushed. That's why Yegor Yakovlev had to work so hard to instill aggressiveness in reporters at *Moscow News,* why he told us he didn't want to see our asses around the office unless we'd gotten the story. Frank Karel, a southerner who speaks in a gentle, almost courtly fashion was just as insistent, in his own polite way. "But they'll probably just slam the door in my face," I said. His reply was, "Then you'll have something to write about that people ought to hear, don't you think?" He emphasized that I couldn't stop searching for the truth because I feared uncomfortable confrontations with my family's past. "You're here because you need to find out what really happened," he said.

When I told a black friend about my boss's insistence that I track down the white as well as the black side of my family, he cynically replied, "Well, of course. Your boss is white. Naturally he's more interested in your white side."

This comment is a measure of the deep distrust between black and white Americans. Frank wasn't more interested in the white than in the black side of my family. He was simply giving me the advice of any good editor: Get all the facts. Get the whole story. Later on, he would give me the same advice about traveling to Tanzania to find my father's family. For different reasons, I was just as nervous about that trip as I was about looking up relatives in white America. Tanzania was, after all, the country where my father was murdered by his political opponents. "Go anyway," Frank said. "You have a family in Africa too. Find them if you can."

If I hadn't taken Frank's advice, I would never have met Pearl Steinhardt, and that would have been my loss. Because Pearl visited my grandmother in Moscow in the sixties my mother remembered that she lived in Los Angeles. A quick check with L.A. information turned up her phone number, and I soon found myself talking to the only living person in America (I think) who knew my grandparents as young lovers.

When I phoned Pearl for the first time in the fall of 1990, she was a bit irritated with me. "I understand that you have been in this country several times already," she admonished me, "but this is the first time you phoned. Now, your grandmother would have wanted you to call me right away." That Thanksgiving, I redeemed myself by calling to wish Pearl a happy holiday. "Well, darling, it's wonderful to hear from you on Thanksgiving," she greeted me enthusiastically. "Why, my son hasn't even called yet." (I assumed her son would hear about this later in the day.)

Pearl speaks English in a familiar, sing-song Yiddish rhythm that reminds me of my grandmother. Why not? Yiddish was their first language, Polish their second, and they both came to America and learned English at roughly the same age. When Pearl talks, I hear echoes of my grandmother's love.

On my next visit to the Youngs in Los Angeles, I met Pearl in person for the first time. Lee drove me to her home after a frantic day filled with appointments, and she brushed aside my worry that it was too late at night for us to drop in. At 11:00 P.M., she waited for us with tea, a gesture that reminded me of Russian hospitality. We talked for hours. "And so are you married yet?" was her first question.

Under a glass tabletop, Pearl had preserved dozens of postcards Bertha had sent her over the course of their sixty-year friendship. My grandmother dashed off cards to Pearl and Misha from Niagara Falls (where she and my grandfather went on a trip with friends from the Party), from camps in upstate New York, from Tashkent, the Crimea, and Moscow. For some reason, probably because of their innocuous having-a-wonderful-time messages, postcards had a much better chance of making it past the Soviet censors than letters. These cards proved that my grandmother never stopped thinking and caring about the friend of her youth, even though she rarely talked about Pearl to Mama and me.

Pearl seems to be just about the only person in America who wasn't astonished by my grandmother's decision to accompany my grandfather to the Soviet Union. "Well, darling, why not?" she asked. "I married Misha and moved with him to Los Angeles; Bertha married your grandfather and went with him to that place in Russia. When you fell in love with a man back then, you went where he went. What is there to explain? I think Bertha would have been happy anywhere as long as she was with her husband. She wrote me that Lily was the only little black girl in Tashkent and everyone thought she was the most beautiful child they had ever seen. What's so unusual?" Beautiful Pearl! "What's so unusual?" How heartwarming to hear someone say that in a country obsessed by color!

Although I'm not actually related to Pearl by blood, she considers me a relative because her husband Misha was my grandmother's cousin. So I am related to their son, the violinist Arnold Steinhardt.

"Yelena dear, you must meet Arnold," Pearl bubbled. "He travels a lot, but I'll get right on the phone and tell him you're in New York. Are you musical? Of course you must be. Your grandmother told me your mother was very talented musically; it runs in our family. By the way, I hope you're eating proper meals with all of the excitement of looking for your family. And you must remember to wear a scarf so you don't catch a cold."

This was one of the people I feared would slam the door in my face.

Here's a tape I enjoy replaying in my memory: Arnold had invited me to a Guarneri Quartet concert at Carnegie Hall, and I was to be his guest at a reception afterward. I was nervous. I anticipated that most, if not all, of the guests would be white. How would Arnold explain me? He said, matter-of-factly, "I'd like you to meet my niece. We've just discovered her." (Actually, I think I'm his cousin.) Because of the painful family history, Arnold's attitude was important to me. He and his mother are the kind of people who make it impossible for me to generalize, to hate groups rather than individuals. Whites do this, blacks behave like that: We all make these generalizations without thinking about them. Which whites? Which blacks? Which Americans?

For my Bialek cousins, finding out the "family secret" was something of a shock, not because we're black, but because my grandmother's brother, Jack, had deliberately concealed the fact of our existence. When his son Eugene finally heard the whole story from his wife, Sheila, who had heard it from her mother-in-law, Minnie, (who had decided it couldn't be kept a secret any more after I began turning up in the newspapers), he sat his children down and informed them, soberly, that he had something important to tell them. Nancy's first thought—only because she was trying to come up with the most shocking thing she could imagine—was that her happily married parents were getting a divorce. As she recalls, the conversation went something like, "You remember hearing about my aunt, the one who moved back to Russia?" "Yes." "You remember we all thought she had married a Russian?" "Yes, what about it?" "Well, she didn't marry a Russian, she married an American." "So . . ." "And we've just found out he was black." "So . . ." "They had a child, and you have cousins. One of them is around your age, Nancy." "Oh, really, that's exciting." One of Nancy's brothers said, "You mean the big secret is we have a black cousin? So what?"

Nancy lives in New York, and I was still extremely cautious, uncertain of my reception, when I got in touch with her the first time. I left a careful message: "This is Yelena Khanga, a Soviet journalist from the Rockefeller Foundation." She called me back immediately and said, "Yelena, what do you mean, Soviet journalist? We're *cousins.*" So we are. Nancy, with her warm brown eyes, bears a strong resemblance to my grandmother when she was young.

Nancy says there was always something of a mystery surrounding her Aunt Bertha. She had only heard about my grandmother in a vague way, as "the sister who went back to Russia." After Jack and Minnie visited my grandmother in Moscow in the mid-sixties, Nancy's parents wanted to hear all about the trip. They remembered that Jack didn't seem to want to talk about his reunion with Bertha. He would say, "Well, things are just fine with her; her husband died and she's living on a pension." Not a word about my mother or me. Everyone in the family assumed that time and distance had left the once-close brother and sister with little in common.

I can't speak for my Bialek cousins, of course, but I've tried to put myself in their place. How would I feel if I found out, after my grandmother's death, that she had kept something of immense importance from me? What if her situation and Jack's were reversed, if she had married a white Jewish man, one of her own kind, and he had married a black woman? What if I grew up loving my grandmother, thinking of her as a completely compassionate and tolerant person, and then learned she had torn up pictures of my cousins so I would never know her brother had a black wife? I would want desperately for my grandmother to be alive so I could ask her, "Why?"

In an effort to help me find out more about the family, Nancy's mother looked carefully for old pictures and letters in the storage boxes from her mother-in-law's house. The pictures my grandmother sent over the years had indeed been destroyed. Only two objects remained: a small enameled pin my grandmother sent Minnie and a large book, mailed to Jack from Tashkent in 1959. The imposing volume is a history of the Uzbek Academy of Sciences, translated into English by Bertha Bialek. The flyleaf is inscribed, "To my brother Jack with love." This gift touches me. It can't have been my grandmother's idea of a wonderful present, but it was something "safe" to send an American relative from the Soviet Union in the late fifties. No one could criticize a Soviet citizen for sending an officially approved translation of a history book to a brother. And Bertha was proud of her work; it was her first book-length translation from Russian into English.

There is also the embroidered yarmulke my grandmother sent her nephew, Eugene, when his son Steve was born. Embroidered by hand, the yarmulke was intended to be used for a bar mitzvah. My cousin kept the yarmulke as a family memento, though his family is nonobservant.

Should the sins of the parents (or, in this case, of the great-grandparents and grandparents) be visited on the children? Of course not. Most people are creatures of their times; those able to rise above the prejudices of their environment, like my grandparents, are always exceptions to the rule.

I look at the portrait of my Bialek great-grandparents, dressed in their turn-of-the-century best in Warsaw. I want to ask them, "Why couldn't you have tried? Why did you leave my grandmother to grow faint in a Harlem apartment, gasping for breath from the strain of being forced to choose between her family and the man she loved?" Above all, I'd like to say to Jack, her favorite brother, "You were the one she loved the most and you let her down." My mother, who is far more outspoken than I, has told Jack's widow about her feelings. During World War II, when America and the Soviet Union were allies, restrictions on foreign contacts were relaxed and many Americans sent food packages to their relatives in Russia. Nothing ever came from Jack for my mother and grandmother, who were in desperate financial straits in Tashkent. Even though my grandmother never stopped writing to her brother, nothing ever came. But it's pointless to argue with the dead. New Bialek relatives, the descendants of my grandmother's other brothers, Sidney and Marcus, are now turning up in our lives. Like Jack's children and grandchildren, they want only one thing—to get to know their long-lost Russian cousins.

Once again, the Los Angeles *Times* brought us together with our Bialek relations. Last summer, Mama made a lecture trip to the West Coast. In Los Angeles, she visited Pearl and eighty-year-old John W. Jackson, one of Hilliard Golden's many descendants. As a small child, John actually met my grandfather—he recalled the nickname "Uncle Buck"—when he visited his family's home in Arkansas. "You look like Uncle Buck," he told my mother. "You're tall and have broad shoulders like he did. But you speak like one of those Russians." The *Times* ran a photograph of Mama, flanked by Pearl and John.

Doris Goldstein, Sidney's daughter, lives in the Los Angeles area. When she saw the article, she realized that Mama must be her cousin. Unlike Jack's son Eugene—and here's one family mystery—Doris always knew she had an aunt who married a black man and went to Russia. But she never knew what happened after that. She sent a copy of the article to her cousin Irv, who lives in Chicago. Irv, Marcus's son, also knew the story of his Aunt Bertha's marriage to a black American. He passed on a copy of the article to his brother Albert, a New York real-estate developer. The story mentioned that I was a Rockefeller Foundation fellow living in New York, and Al tracked me down through the foundation.

Mama, who was living in Chicago last year, met her cousin Irv around the same time I got to know Al. An irrepressibly cheerful, talkative man with an insatiable interest in his family's history, Al saw the surprising appearance of cousins from Russia as a chance to learn more about the secrets of the older generation. He has no idea why his branch of the family knew about my grandmother's interracial marriage while Jack's branch didn't. "We'll never know," he says resignedly. "Obviously, the brothers in America weren't on good or close terms. They're all dead, so we can't ask them why. Religion, politics, money: Families fall out over all those issues. Whatever happened, they didn't tell us, their children, the reasons."

Like my grandmother, the brothers told their children little about growing up in Poland. They omitted even basic facts, like their ages and the dates of their arrival in America. Al didn't know, for instance, that his father was the oldest of the four children, the son who left Poland in 1915 with his father Isaac (Yitzhak, before being Americanized).

Al and I were trying to make some sense of the confusing chronology when Eugene's wife, Sheila, discovered a vital document in her mother-in-law's safety deposit box in Los Angeles. This previously undiscovered piece of paper—everyone had forgotten about its existence—was a 1921 U.S. certificate of naturalization for Isaac, Bessie (in Poland, Pesa), twenty-one-year-old Jack (formerly Jacob), seventeen-year-old Sidney (formerly Solomon), and fifteen-year-old Bertha (called Bessie in Poland).

At that time, children twenty-one or under became citizens along with their parents. Marcus, who didn't gain his U.S. citizenship until 1937, was already twenty-four when his parents and three younger siblings obtained their naturalization papers.

In 1921, my great-grandfather Isaac had already lived in the Bronx for five years. He and Marcus emigrated together, but Marcus went to Montreal in search of work instead of staying in New York with his father. (He joined the rest of the family in New York in 1920, when his mother arrived with the younger children.)

Irv's son Mark, an attorney with the inspector general's office of the U.S. State Department, was able to track down his grandfather Marcus's papers. The 1937 petition for naturalization shows that Marcus also had a non-Jewish alias—"Mailech Gerszoniak." Al thinks his father may have used this alias when he fled Poland to avoid being conscripted. As Al pointed out to me, many first-generation immigrants were terrified that U.S. government authorities would find out about any "irregularity" in their backgrounds, and that fear might explain why Marcus revealed so little about his experiences before he came to the United States.

Recently, another cousin turned up to put a new twist on the secrets kept by my grandmother's generation. At age forty-eight, Burt Bialek, Sidney's son, is the youngest of my mother's first cousins. A typical American child of the sixties, Burt spent many years traveling throughout the world. He now lives in Osaka, Japan, with his Japanese wife and their four-year-old daughter, and teaches high school English.

When Burt was visiting his New York relatives at the end of 1991, he looked me up and told me an astonishing story. He believes that for many years, his father was an FBI informant inside the U.S. Communist Party. (Actually, Burt's sister told him their father was working within the Socialist Party, but Burt and I have concluded that this is a misapprehension created by a common American confusion between socialism and communism. Throughout Burt's childhood, his father received copies of the newspaper *People's World* in the mail. The *People's World* was the West Coast equivalent of the better-known *Daily Worker,* and both were U.S. Party organs. When Burt asked his father what he was doing with that paper—he found the publication extraordinarily dull—Sidney replied, "Oh, it's just something that interests me." It's unlikely that any socialist, genuine or bogus, would have read *People's World*.)

Like most of the older Bialeks, Sidney didn't tell his son much about his or his family's past. "As I grew up," Burt recalls,

> I heard that there was bad blood between my father and his brother Jack, and I heard a story about a sister who ran off to Russia many years ago. . . . I have images of my mother and father sitting at a kitchen table, my father dictating to my mother, and my mother writing something down with a pencil. Every once in a while I'd ask what they were doing and my mother would say, "Just business." Then the next day I'd see my mother typing up what she'd written down. I never really gave a thought to it; it was just a part of our family's normal, everyday life. My memories of this begin around age five, and they go on throughout my childhood.

In 1968, Burt's mother died after an agonizing bout with cancer, and the texture of normal, everyday life fell apart. After his wife's death, Sidney (according to Burt) grew fearful and paranoid. "One night he came into the living room and said, 'But, I'm exposed, they'll find me out.' I didn't know what he was talking about. I asked him who *they* were. He wouldn't say."

Burt initially dismissed the incident as just another example of his father's disorientation after his wife's death. Eventually, though, his older sister told him their father had long been an FBI informant. Putting bits and pieces of memory and new information together, Burt concluded that the sessions he remembers at the kitchen table must have produced his parents' regular reports to the FBI.

In 1968, Burt says his father took an overdose of sleeping pills and died. According to Burt, the whole story bears an eerie resemblance to the popular American television series of the fifties, "I Led Three Lives," about the career of FBI agent Herbert Philbrick. Sidney, too, had two other lives: as the head of a California personnel agency and as an investor in the stock market.

"I can guess it angered my father that Jack turned Bertha on to communism," Burt says. "I think his agreeing to work for the FBI was a reaction to that." Another possibility—we'll never know with certitude—is that Sidney felt an obligation to prove his patriotism to the U.S. government because two of his siblings had been Communists. Sidney was, after all, a first-generation immigrant, and many immigrants felt insecure about their status in American society and feared running afoul of any government agency.

In 1968, a politically explosive year for the United States as a whole, Burt considered the story of his father's FBI activities "just another freaky thing." But he also believes his father's FBI existence affected their relationship. "How could this not have prevented communication?" he asks. "I always had the sense of a great many things unsaid. And that seems to have been so in the other branches of the family as well."

In very different ways, each member of my grandmother's generation participated in the larger drama of the Cold War. Would any of them have believed that the foundations of this war would crumble by the end of the twentieth century?

White and black Americans react very differently when I tell them about my grandmother and my Bialek relatives. "Isn't that great, you must be so proud," many whites say. Some Jews get very excited, remind me that I'm Jewish according to religious law, even suggesting that I take off for Israel to pursue my "Jewish identity."

When I tell certain blacks about my grandmother, it brings a new kind of pain. Before I visited the United States for the first time, I had no idea there was any anti-Semitism among black Americans. My mother, with her historian's perspective, always told me that blacks and Jews had a history of oppression and discrimination in common. How many of the powerful images of black spirituals come from the Book of Exodus!

Because of my strong, emerging sense of identification with black America, it would be more comfortable for me to avoid the whole issue of black anti-Semitism. But my family background won't allow me to do this. Sometimes when I tell blacks about my grandmother, they laugh. They consider it a good joke, an irony of history that shouldn't mean anything to me as a person. Worse than laughter, though, is an occasional angry reaction. "That's nothing to be proud of," they'll say, the mirror image of whites who think I ought to be extremely proud of "their" side of my family tree.

These kinds of attitudes must be unbearably painful for American children of interracial couples. Wherever they go, they find themselves apologizing to someone for one-half of their heritage. I won't do that. And yet . . . I sometimes have to fight the impulse to censor myself when blacks ask about my family background. In many social situations among African-Americans, it's much more comfortable for me to omit any mention of white relatives. Yet this "comfort" also feels like cowardice.

Both black and white Americans talk a great deal about their "identities." This is an unfamiliar concept to Russians. In Russia, no one says, "I have a black identity" or "I have a female identity." You're black, you're a woman: It's taken for granted.

In my American life, there's no question that black identity comes first. With blacks, whether we're related by blood or not, I take a certain bond for granted; then I move outward toward whatever distinguishes us as individuals. With whites, the process is reversed. I begin with an awareness of our separateness and move toward them (if they're responsive) to find whatever we have in common. My first phone call to my cousin Nancy exemplifies this feeling: If she were black, I would never have left a formal message announcing myself as a "journalist from the Rockefeller Foundation." This example says absolutely nothing about me or my cousin as people; it speaks volumes about my new racial consciousness in America.

In the summer of 1990, after my black relatives had visited Moscow, I traveled to Chicago to see them. As it happens, I was on a professional as well as a personal mission. My editor, in the wake of a fire that gutted the offices of *Moscow News* earlier in the year, dispatched me on a fund-raising tour in the hope that Americans would want to repair the offices of the "flagship of *glasnost.*" I began the trip with high hopes of raising money for my beleaguered newspaper; all of the Americans I met in 1987 had only the most effusive praise for *Moscow News.* But I soon learned that a word of praise does not guarantee an open wallet. Foundations and businesses didn't want to entangle themselves with Soviet politics, and my newspaper was undeniably political. After this instructive lesson in the vagaries of the market economy, I resigned myself to going home to Moscow empty-handed.

Discouraged by my lack of success, I arrived in Chicago to meet a large contingent of my relatives. My cousins Delores Harris and Ollie Morris rounded up seventy or eighty members of the clan for a hastily organized dinner to meet me. (My mother attended a larger family reunion a few weeks earlier, but I was off on my futile fund-raising trip.) After listening to my sad tale, the family made sure I wouldn't go back to Moscow with nothing. Someone found a hat to pass. By the end of the evening, I had a purse filled with bills to take home to my editor. The amount of money was beside the point. These people weren't interested in the political stance of *Moscow News* or in the future of the Soviet Union: I was one of their own and if I needed something, they would try to give it to me.

This kind of solidarity isn't confined to blood relations. At a convention of the National Association of Black Journalists last summer, a woman came up to me and asked, "Are you the reporter from the

Soviet Union?" Sometimes I get tired of answering endless questions about how it feels to be a black Russian—"So, what is your position, as a black Russian on getting out of bed in the morning?" I answered the woman peevishly, saying something like, "So, I'm from Russia. My job is just the same as yours." I wanted to apologize immediately when she gently explained, "We all feel proud whenever any black person builds a fine career, anywhere in the world. Each of us is a demonstration of what other blacks can accomplish."

I love this new feeling of connection, wherever it leads. My own family has a little bit of everything: dentists and preachers and teachers and civil servants. We even have one aging gangster. Late at night after our first reunion in Chicago, my cousin Jacqui whispered to me, "There's one other member of the family you should meet, but he's too old to come here tonight." Jacqui drove me through the dark streets of Chicago until we arrived at a nursing home. She banged on the door and an irritated nurse said visiting hours were over. "But this is my cousin from Russia," Jacqui begged, "and it's the only chance she'll have to meet Sam." The nurse relented and introduced me to Cousin Sam, a very old man not the least bit surprised to learn he had a relative in Moscow. "Well, we have a very interesting family," he told me. "Now in the old days, I was a driver for Al Capone and, yes, I did go to jail for awhile, but it wasn't anything like the crime today. Nobody innocent was killed in those days." Sam went on to speak, with great pride, about his activities during the days of Prohibition. My relatives, by the way, take Sam's bragging with a grain of salt. As far as they know, Al Capone didn't employ black drivers. But there's no question that Sam was involved in illegal activities during Prohibition, that he did go to jail in the thirties—he's now in his nineties—and did live well on money no one could explain. We hope he's exaggerating his exploits, in the manner of an old man inflating the romantic conquests of his youth. As far as I know, Sam is the only Golden family secret. Now that he's old enough for the statute of limitations to have expired, he's an open secret.

I wondered whether I should tell the world that the Golden family has its one, aging gangster. One of the worst consequences of racism, it seems to me, is that its victims feel accountable (because society often holds them accountable) for the transgressions of every individual within their group. Many families, especially those belonging to vulnerable minorities, erase the memory of any members with less-than-respectable histories. I find it endearing that my relatives don't deny this old man, that they still find time to visit him even though he'll never receive an award for outstanding humanitarian achievement.

Being black in America—being *among* blacks in America—has opened up channels of emotional expressiveness that never existed for me in Russia. When I saw the movie *The Color Purple,* some barrier—I hadn't even known it was there—came crashing down inside me. Alice Walker's characters spoke to me about life as a black woman in immediately recognizable images, though far removed from my old Russian self.

When I found my great-grandfather's land in Yazoo, I indulged in a bit of American dreaming. If I ever get rich, I thought, I'll build a monument to all of the black people in Yazoo, the people who worked so hard and whose names are absent from the history books.

Before I left Mississippi, I found a lot of this unpublished history. Yazoo librarian Linda Crawford showed me an astonishing list of black craftsmen, contractors, businessmen, and landowners compiled by Harvey Perry.

Beginning with my great-grandfather, there were sixty-six names on the list of landowners.* Nearly all of those families lost their land

---

*This list, which includes black landowners from 1866 to 1988, is a remarkable tribute to Mr. Perry's memory. However, there may be other owners, unknown to Mr. Perry, whose names have been omitted.

Black Land Owners 1866 to Present

Hilliard Golden, Henry Friley, Cap Andreson, Martin Stricky, Green Hudson, Calvin Jackson, Anthony Carter, Alex Daniel, Joe Banks, Henry Powell, Richard Lindsey, Anderson Miller, Chloe Curry, Huddleston Brothers, Alex after Reconstruction; without Mr. Perry's memory, the names would have disappeared. I wish to restore those names to history, if not on a stone monument then in a section of the local library where children can read about what their great-great-grandparents accomplished against all odds. This dream is what I mean by "black identity," or what my Russian self calls a black soul.

Montgomery, Brookins Brothers, Cary Clark, Horace Clark, Walter Clark, Edmund Hicks, James Metchler, Harry Averhart (?), Wallace Johnson, Silas Purvis, Sam Turner, William Turner, Wesley Beck, Molett Brothers, Richard Weaver, Harry Miller, George Bostick, William Carter, Walter Coleman, Gabriel Miller, Jesse Redden, Isiah Millon, Paul Foster, Fouche Family (present), Dollie Woolfork, Barmour Everett, Samuel Davis, and many more. George Wells, Gregory Wells, Willis Wells, John Green, Henry Green, James Broome, Howard Shelby, Jesse Holmes, Wilson Carter, Frank Bell, Alfred Bonney, William Walker, George Vaugn, Will Scott, Jack-Will Scott (Lamkin), Joe Carter (Lamkins), Eziekiel Stewart (Benton), Burrell Smith, Parker Harper, Luisa Crump, Charles Creswell, Mary Ann Taylor, Peter McCommell, Davis Mosley, Sr., Will Johnson (Tokeba).

CHAPTER THIRTEEN

AFRICAN INTERLUDE

"And what about your African identity?" Americans invariably ask. I hadn't been in the United States very long before I realized that many Americans attached a certain status to my having an African rather than an African-American father. Black or white, nearly everyone here seems to have read, or at least to have seen the movie of, Alex Haley's *Roots*. I didn't have to make an arduous, ten-generation journey to find my ancestors. My flesh-and-blood grandmother, ninety-two-year-old Mashavu Hassan, still lives in the family home in Zanzibar.

Blacks are more curious than whites about my African heritage, but Americans of both races often display more interest in Africa than my Russian friends ever did. (*Roots* hasn't been translated into Russian, even though it's exactly the sort of densely peopled historical novel Russians love.) In Moscow, no one outside the family cared about my African heritage. Even the KGB focused almost exclusively on our American connections. Africa, apart from the old regime's desire to foment Marxist revolutions, remained a Dark Continent to most Russians.

If it weren't for my mother, I'm sure I would have grown up totally ignorant of African culture. Through her work, Mama met most of the interesting African visitors to Moscow, dancers and musicians, historians and politicians alike. Her room was crowded with African masks and statues. She collected old folk melodies, as well as contemporary songs, on tapes and records brought by our foreign guests. In my mother's room, I first heard the glorious voice of Miriam Makeba, who has never given a concert in Russia.

I have no memory of my father. He left Moscow forever when I was a baby. In 1991, by the time I finished tracking down my black and white relatives in the United States, this unknown man was the last missing piece in our family puzzle.

While I was growing up, my father was a completely abstract personage to me. I knew he became the first vice-president of Zanzibar after the revolution of 1964. I knew, too, that he was executed by political opponents not long afterward, when Zanzibar and the former British colony of Tanganyika were unified in the new, independent state of Tanzania.

Until this year, I knew no details of my father's death. (To this day, they are not a matter of public record in Tanzania. I eventually found out how my father died from people who knew him, but many facts—dates, for instance—can't be verified.)

I grew up respecting this shadowy Abdullah Khanga for his role in the history of his country. Mama made sure I knew about his dedication to pan-Africanism and to ending colonialism. Emotionally, though, I defined my father entirely by his absence. Having an African for a father didn't seem especially glamorous to me; an American or a Russian would have done quite nicely, so long as he was there. I suppose that's why my emotions about the father I never knew seem "flat"—I dislike this psychobabble term—to some of my American acquaintances.

This emotional history, along with the knowledge that my father was killed for political reasons, made me hesitate when the Rockefeller Foundation offered to fly me to Tanzania in search of my African relatives. I wasn't sure how my father's family would receive me.

My curiosity overcame these reservations. Armed with a list of friends and relatives supplied by Ibrahim Nur Sharif, a former student of my father's who now teaches Swahili literature at Rutgers University, I flew to Dar es Salaam with the ever-vigilant Frank Karel. (Pleased with the results I'd gotten from the search for my white relatives, he wasn't about to let me avoid knocking on doors in Zanzibar.) The person I most wanted to meet was my ninety-two-year-old grandmother Hanga,★

As luck would have it, the first people I met in Dar were Russians. Exhausted from our flight, Frank and I were having a bite to eat when I overheard Russian being spoken at the next table. I introduced myself and was pleased to learn the Russians had read my articles in *Moscow News*. Then one of the men said, "Well, I think we have a little surprise for you. There's a Russian cultural center in Dar. Let's drop by." We banged on the door and a woman came downstairs to greet us. "Yelena," she screamed happily, "don't you remember me?" I did. She was my first English teacher at School No. 46 in Moscow.

The next morning, I boarded a ferry for Zanzibar, where I would finally meet my father's family. Even here, I couldn't get away from my countrymen. There was something familiar about the captain,

---

★The difference in the spelling of our surnames is explained by the absence of an equivalent for the letter *h* in the Cyrillic alphabet. The closest approximation is a Cyrillic character transliterated into English as *kh*. In Russian, the sound made by this character resembles a throat-clearing. My father was always "Hanga" in English, but I've used the *Kh* spelling for his name as well as mine to avoid confusing the reader.

In most cases, Russians pronounce the English *h* as a *g*. Thus, Henry is "Genri" in Russian. If I'd chosen this route, I would be "Yelena Ganga" in Russia. This would have been ridiculous, since it bears even less resemblance to the correct pronunciation of my father's last name in English (or Swahili).

though I was sure I'd never met him. He turned out to be a Georgian, operating a ferry under a joint Soviet-Tanzanian business agreement. He confided that he was making a small fortune and saving money for the future—wherever in the world that might be.

When the boat docked, I noticed a tall, graceful woman with a striking resemblance to my mother. Clad in a long, gracefully draped white *kanzu-ndefy* (a traditional garment worn by most Tanzanian women), she approached me purposefully. "You must be Yelena," she said, spotting me immediately by my Western dress. "I was your father's wife, and I would be so pleased if you would call me Mama Hanga."★ Mama Hanga married my father after he returned to Zanazibar in 1964. She always knew about my mother and me. "Your father expressed the greatest respect for your mother," she assured me, "and whatever personal problems they had didn't affect that. He told me your mother was an admirable woman, of strong convictions and character."

That description applies to Mama Hanga as well. An elementary school teacher, she led a hard, lonely life after my father's death, only a year or two after they married. For many years, no one would hire her to teach; she was shunned by those who feared any association with the wife of a murdered political leader.

Listening to Mama Hanga's story, I understood that her fate—or worse—would have been my mother's lot if she had accompanied my father to Zanzibar. I thought of countless women, in countries throughout the world, forced to live half-lives because their fate was tied to men who wound up on the wrong side of a political battle.

The facts of my father's death, insofar as they are known, do not make a pretty story. I say "insofar as they are known," because the Tanzanian archives that might contain information about his death, and many other executions during that period, are sealed. What I know, I've learned mainly from Tanzanians, those living abroad as well as those in the country itself.

★Her real name is Bimkubwa Hanga.

A quarter of a century later, my father's execution is still a sensitive subject. At my hotel in Dar, I received many anonymous, late-night phone calls from people who wanted only to tell me they had known my father. Tanzania is a small country, of only 26 million people and 365,000 square miles. Word of my presence traveled fast. "Yelena Khanga," one man whispered, "I want to welcome you on behalf of everyone who admired your father. We're so glad you're here." Then he hung up. On the street in Zanzibar, strangers stopped me and offered hasty descriptions of Abdullah: "A real leader," "a believer in social justice," "a dedicated teacher, though I didn't agree with his Communist politics." None of these people would give their names. Tribal, family-centered cultures have long memories. Some politicians from the era of my father's murder (and more of their descendants) still play important roles in Tanzanian public life. No one wants to risk stirring up old ghosts or old hatreds.

In 1964, after my father returned from Moscow, Zanzibar gained its independence in a revolution that overthrew the ruling sultan. My father became the first vice-president of the independent island republic, but Zanzibar's statehood didn't last long. The island's first president, Abeid Karume, soon agreed to join Tanganyika in the new state of Tanzania, under the presidency of Julius Nyerere. (Karume stayed on as second vice-president of Tanzania and president of the island, subordinated to the union government.)

Karume—on this point everyone agrees—was a dictator who dealt with political challenges in his fiefdom by jailing or executing his opponents. (In 1972, Karume himself was assassinated by an army officer out to avenge the death of his father.)

Abdullah Khanga had expected to play an important role not only in the government of Zanzibar but in the newly unified Tanzanian state. "Your father was a very forceful personality," one man told me in another nocturnal call. "That's why people still remember him and why they come up to you on the street. Also, it certainly didn't help him that he'd spent so much time in Moscow. To be seen as Moscow's man wasn't an advantage, with Karume or with Nyerere's government."

At any rate, my father was arrested, taken from his home, and never seen again by friends or family. An eyewitness (probably one of the executioners) reported the manner of his death to his friends: He was stuffed into a canvas sack while he was still alive, weighted him down with stones, and drowned in the Indian Ocean. What can I add? I believe this account absolutely, not only because it is known to so many people, but also because it must have originated with someone who actually saw what happened. "I didn't know whether I should even tell this to you," one man said with tears in his eyes. "This is a terrible thing for a man's daughter to hear. But I think the world should hear this, so that such unlawful, barbaric things will never happen again."

In Moscow, Mama and I always knew my father was killed for political reasons; in Russia, I heard a great many stories of those who perished during the Stalin era. But I never imagined I would one day find out that my own father had died such a horrible death.

In Zanzibar, many of my father's old student's stopped to offer more pleasant memories. They told me what an outstanding teacher he was, how much they respected him. "He encouraged kids to ask questions," one man said, "and that was very unusual for his generation. [My father was born in 1932.] And he was a terrific soccer coach."

One night, a woman about my own age—she worked as a maid in my hotel—knocked on the door. "Khanga. Open," she said in a harsh, abrupt voice that frightened me. Then I realized she spoke only Swahili and was trying to communicate with me in her few words of English. She gestured toward my dirty laundry, pantomimed scrubbing and said, "I wash . . . for you." I reached for my wallet and she shook her head, "No . . . no pay." She managed to explain why she wouldn't take money. Pointing to me, she said, "You . . . your . . . father." Then she pointed to herself and said, " . . . teach . . . my . . . mother." She made a scribbling gesture for writing and pointed to a newspaper. I finally understood. My father had taught her mother to read and write, and she was repaying an old debt by offering to do my laundry.

This incident brought out the emotion I hadn't felt—or allowed myself to feel—about my father. He was more than a doctrinaire

Marxist. He was a man who wanted, passionately, for his people to read and write, he was a teacher revered, nearly four decades later, by the child of one of his students.

And I finally met my grandmother, a slight, fragile-looking woman who swept me into her arms and rocked me on her lap like a baby. For many years, she said, ever since my father told her she had a granddaughter in Moscow, I had come to her in her dreams at night. She didn't know how old I would be or how I would find her, but she dreamed of showering gold coins on my head. Speaking in Swahili, with different members of the family translating (all of my younger relatives speak English), she described the custom of showering coins on a child as a way to ensure happiness. She led me into the street in front of her house and tossed the gold pieces on my head. Neighborhood children gathered around to pick up the coins as they fell. That, too, is part of the custom. You'll only be happy if others benefit from your good fortune.

Just before I left to return to the United States, my grandmother pulled an old key out of her pocket and showed me a locked cupboard in a tiny, hidden room at the back of the house. "This hasn't been opened in twenty-five years," she said, "but now it's time. Your father told me never to show these to anyone, never to tell anyone about them . . . but so many years have gone by. I know he would want you to have them."

What could be inside the cupboard? I wondered. Gold? Jewels? Money? I even thought I might find guns, sticks of dynamite, or documents identifying my father's executioners.

My grandmother turned the key in the rusty lock, which yielded after a few minutes of effort. I peered into the cobwebbed recesses of the teak cupboard and saw something familiar: volumes upon volumes of the collected works of V. I. Lenin. I assumed these books had belonged to my father, but later Mama told me she had shipped them to Zanzibar during the early period of their marriage, when she planned on joining him in Africa. It seems my grandparents brought some of these books with them in 1931 on the *Deutschland*. I fought back tears. Some were for my African grandmother, who didn't know what the books said but kept them because they were precious to her dead son. Some were for Bertha and Oliver, who had so much faith in those words of Lenin. Some were for Mama; the very fact that she had shipped the books to Zanzibar attested to a time when she and my father were still deeply attached to each other.

Some were for my father alone. He obviously considered these books dangerous in the Tanzanian political climate of the mid-sixties. Even so, they were important enough to him that he asked his mother to save them. I admire this stubbornness, this fidelity to principle.

And yet . . . Lenin espoused a political philosophy that encouraged censorship and intolerance. I wonder: How would my father have felt about the banning of anti-Leninist books? A Tanzanian who knew the young Abdullah says he cried upon hearing the news of Stalin's death in 1953. Well, that's not unusual! Many Russians had the same experience and now regard their tears as symptoms of a long-lasting, collective delusion. Would my father have awakened from this delusion? I wish I could ask him now.

I can't claim to have experienced any special revelation about my African "roots" during this journey. Walking along the streets of Dar, I kept waiting for a click, the sense of recognition and identification I've felt so many times among black Americans.

It seems to me that some blacks, especially intellectuals, romanticize Africa. To them, the continent represents a black Eden, the paradise before our people were sold into slavery. But Africa isn't Eden; it's a vast, complicated continent, with a great many peoples struggling to find a place in the modern world. When Americans ask me, "So what did you think of Africa?" I tell them I can't claim to have seen Africa. I've seen only a corner of Tanzania, a country strongly influenced by Islam. Tanzania is as different from Ghana, Nigeria, Ethiopia, and Zimbabwe as Lithuania (rest in peace, former Soviet Union) is from Uzbekistan or Armenia.

The restrictions that Islamic tradition places on women certainly played an important role in my response to Zanzibari culture. Salmin Amour, the current president of Zanzibar, could not have been more gracious; he invited me to dinner in his official residence and treated me as an honored guest. Yet I could easily understand the humiliation my mother felt, so many years ago, when my father allowed her to serve at dinner but not to speak. Mama Hanga accompanied me to the private dinner with President Amour. He impressed me as a man of the future rather than the past, an African leader for the twenty-first century. Our conversation ranged over topics from the precarious position of Gorbachev (my trip took place not long before last year's coup) to the need for black American investment in Africa. President Amour and I talked, but Mama Hanga sat by silently, following Zanzibar's Muslim tradition. As a European woman, considered a kind of honorary man, I alone was permitted to speak.

Beginning with Mama Hanga, I had met a great many fascinating, well-educated Zanzibari women. Their conversation—on every subject from Tanzanian politics to divorce laws—flashed with wit and intelligence. And the talk never stopped, so long as there were no men in the room. But as soon as a man entered, silence fell. I was honored to speak with President Amour, but I also felt a deep sorrow at the silence of my sister. Yes, here was a click, but not the click most Americans expect me to hear.

My grandfather on my father's side, who died many years ago, was a Muslim *imam*. Although my father was an atheist, much of his behavior, especially the attitude toward women that created so much conflict with my mother, was rooted in his cultural and religious traditions. Their marriage was a cultural mismatch. My visit to Zanzibar helped me understand the force of that tradition in a way that was impossible for me as a child.

My father was a man who did not bend on matters of principle; everyone who knew him mentioned this quality of his character. He might be alive today if he had been less forceful, more capable of compromise. For such a man, compromise in personal relationships might be equally difficult. Accommodation isn't my mother's strong suit either; their marriage was certainly a case of *nashla kosa na kamen* (literally, "a scythe going into stone") or, as Americans say, an irresistible force meeting an immovable object.

My brief, firsthand look at the culture of Zanzibar—even though my soul doesn't respond to that culture as it does to black American and Russian culture, enabled me to make a kind of peace with the father I never knew. I can take pride in what he was without blaming him for what he wasn't. I like to think he would be proud of me—even though I could never be the silent woman at the table—if he were alive today. I'm sure we would have shared one thing: a realization of how difficult it can be to live in more than one world.

CHAPTER FOURTEEN

GRAY ZONES

I have been invited to a party at the home of a black friend in Washington, and I casually ask a white colleague if he'd like to come along with me. As soon as my hostess opens the door, I sense from her frozen expression that I have committed a social error: My companion is the only white person in the room. It hadn't occurred to me that this would be the case or that his presence might pose a problem.

Later, my hostess tells me I must never bring a white person to a black home without asking permission in advance. "All day at the office, I have to behave to suit white people," she explains in stern tones. "I speak white, I dress white, I do my hair in a way that pleases whites. Nothing too bushy or too out-and-out black, you know. At home I want to be myself, to speak my own language. I don't want to pretend to be something I'm not, I don't want to worry about what the boss man thinks of me. Maybe you're right, maybe this particular guy is okay. But his great-grandfather might have been my great-grandfather's slavemaster. He might have been yours. I can't forget it, and I don't want to deal with it in my own home."

I am silent. I've only been living on my own in America for a few weeks, and I realize I don't know the rules for interracial socializing any more than I know the rules about everything from handling money to office etiquette. I feel I'm always making mistakes, bringing my Russian assumptions into American settings.

There are too many cultural differences, like attitudes toward money, for me to assimilate them all this quickly. I'm still smarting from the horrified reaction of one new American acquaintance when I asked how much his house cost. In Moscow, this is a perfectly polite question; in America, it's more acceptable to ask about someone's sex life. "You've got to understand, Yelena," my host explained, "that you can't come right out and ask what someone's home cost. And you don't go around telling other people what you paid for something either. That talk is for stores, not for a visit to someone's home."

A question of prices is just a difference in standards of etiquette, but everything connected with race cuts much deeper. My stomach lurched when my hostess attacked me for bringing along a white friend. Were those her personal rules or did most black Americans share her feelings? Because she was black—my sister—this woman had the power to wound me in places no white racist could possibly reach. The realization hit me hard: I couldn't have brought my grandmother to this house without first asking permission.

"You don't understand, Yelena," many black friends tell me. "Blacks cannot be racist in this society, because blacks don't have power." I understand what they mean and I agree, so long as racism is defined as a *system* of oppression and discrimination. For the most part, black Americans don't have the power to hire and fire whites, to deny whites access to housing, to turn away whites who need to borrow money. Systematic racism involves a combination of prejudice and power, and in that sense, African-Americans can't be racists. But prejudice itself is quite another matter; bigoted feelings flourish among the powerless too. When a virus is raging—and that's how I think of racism—few escape. The illness just takes different forms in different people.

When I first arrived in America in 1987, I was always asking, "What do blacks think of this?" or "How do blacks behave in that situation?" It took time for me to understand that blacks are as complex, as divided, as various in their social behavior as any other large group of people. As Lee Young introduced me to friends representing a broad spectrum of political and social views, I began to grasp some of the divisions and distinctions among African-Americans.

Walking the streets of any city, it was easy to see the obvious economic division between the black middle class and the poor. Less obvious, but equally important to me, was the distinction between middle-class blacks who care deeply about their poorer brothers and sisters and "wannabes" who care only about distancing themselves from blacks who haven't made it. Through some of my own encounters with white racism, I'd already decided it was dangerous for any black to think of himself—or herself—as someone who had made it.

My Russian-made image of African-Americans—all for one and one for all—didn't prepare me for another phenomenon: discrimination by skin tone within the black community. I can understand—though I don't agree with—the kind of person who despises all whites because they might have a slavemaster in their family tree. But I can't begin to understand black Americans who reject one another because they are "too dark."

Soon after arriving in Boston in 1987, I lost my way on a tram and asked a handsome young black man for directions to the *Monitor*. He noticed my accent and asked where I was from. He wanted to hear more about Russia, so he offered to walk me to my office. I was a little bit excited by the encounter. I'd met a good-looking black guy just by asking for directions! Who knew, maybe Prince Charming would turn out to be a black American.

As he began explaining his version of black America, I realized he was only interested in the Russian part of me. He talked about his own circle of successful black friends and told me all of them had light skin. "You, for instance," he remarked, almost casually, "would be too dark for me. My friends would be surprised if I turned up with a girl who looked like you." I was amazed. He might have been describing the customs of some forgotten tribe on a South Sea island. Was it possible that I—coppery me, right in the middle of the black-

American color spectrum—would be considered too dark by a black man? What sort of looking glass had I fallen through?

Shortly after this encounter, I saw Spike Lee's *School Daze*, a fascinating movie examining class-caste-color distinctions at a black college. The movie antagonized some blacks, who felt the young director shouldn't be telling "our" dirty secrets in public. As an outsider trying to understand the new world in which I'd landed, I loved the film. It enlightened me and made sense of the bizarre conversation with my light-skinned escort from the tram. (I, by the way, hadn't even noticed the shade of his skin until he mentioned mine. The distinction between dark, darker, darkest made no sense to me, the woman from Mars.) Coming from a country where social criticism was banned for so many decades, I think movies like *School Daze* have a healthy effect, even if they make some of us uncomfortable. A little *glasnost* is good for everyone.

I still think about that conversation in Boston and wonder why the man chose to talk about the subject with me. I think the whole issue must have troubled him greatly, in spite of his matter-of-fact tone, and he chose to unburden himself to me like a drunk confessing his marital infidelities to a stranger in a bar. As a foreigner, I was a safe audience; he talked to me in a way he wouldn't have talked to another black American, especially a woman. If he said the same thing to me today, he wouldn't find a passive listener. *I'm too dark for you? What makes you think I'd want a man who thinks one shade of brown is better than another? As for your friends, why would I want to meet them?*

I now understand that these invidious distinctions date from the time of slavery, when whites preferred light-skinned house slaves and sent darker-skinned men and women to work in the fields. But the heritage of slavery is only an explanation; it's not an excuse for inflicting the same wounds on one another today. There's a famous quote from Chekhov, whose father was a serf. The great writer describes himself as "a young man . . . raised on respect for rank, kissing the priests' hands, worshipping the ideas of others, . . . who squeezes the slave out of himself, drop by drop, and who, one fine morning, finds that the blood coursing through his veins is no longer the blood of a slave but that of a real human being."

As Russians of my generation have ample reason to know, it's never a simple process to rid oneself of the residue of any kind of slavery. Still, I wish that quote from Chekhov had sprung to my mind when I was talking with the man who told me I was too dark for him. I could have said, "Try to make the effort to become a real human being. It's worth it." (As my circle of black friends expanded, I was equally astonished to discover that some African-Americans encounter hostility within their own community because their skin is too *light*. As if anyone, of any race, has any choice about whatever ancestral mix produces a particular skin color.)

In Russia, I had no choices to make about dressing "white" or "black," about wearing my hair in a "white" or "black" way. Being one of a kind, in a society with few consumer choices, simplifies matters. Here there are choices to be made every day.

When I began experimenting with new hairstyles in America (will I ever be free of this hair preoccupation on any continent?), several black women advised me against wearing braids to work. (I tried them and liked the way they looked but found they hurt my head.) "The more white you look," one woman advised me, "the better white people like it. When you need a job in their world, it helps to look like them."

I found this idea extremely distasteful (again, this notion had never occurred to me in Russia). Looking around me, though, I can't deny the truth of the observation. Most (not all, but most) of the successful blacks in white American companies have, if not light skins, Caucasion-looking features. Small wonder that blacks find this a painful subject. It's shameful to know that you may have an advantage over another black because, through a genetic accident, you have thinner lips or a narrower nose or less nappy hair. I want to think of myself as a proud black woman—not as a black with a nose of a certain width, lips of a certain thickness. In Russia, as far as everyone else was concerned, I was just plain black.

The whole question of color distinction seems to wound black women even more deeply than men. I notice, for example, that most

African-American models, in both black and white women's magazines, are quite light-skinned. I love every manifestation of black beauty in this country, from the dark, full-hipped women who resemble statues of African goddesses to the small-boned results, in every imaginable skin tone, of intermingling among blacks, whites, Latinos, Asians—who knows? They're all lovely. But I know that African lips and noses aren't considered any more beautiful by most Americans than they are by Russians. My mother, whose skin is much lighter than mine, receives compliment after compliment from other blacks on the "good" color of her skin. How is she supposed to react to this praise, when she knows it's based on the assumption that lighter is better?

No one praises me for my complexion, but black men sometimes compliment me at the expense of black American women. They'll tell me, confidentially, that black women here are too pushy, that they're not "soft" enough, that they're more interested in what a man can buy for them than in giving and receiving love. This kind of comment strikes two familiar, disturbing chords. I'm naturally reminded of the white businessman who put his hand on my shoulder and said, "You're not like all the blacks here." Once again, I'm hearing something I'd rather not hear—this time from a black man instead of a white man—because I'm a black Russian instead of a black American. Whatever else I am, I'm a black woman, and it hurts me to hear my sisters put down by a man of our own race.

Here's the other familiar chord in this conversation: A great many Russian men say the same kinds of things about Russian women. Russian women are too aggressive, they boss men around, while foreign women are softer, more feminine, nicer. (The situation isn't precisely analogous, of course. Most Russian men don't have the chance to date, much less marry, foreign women, while middle-class black American men can choose women outside their race.)

I think Russian and black American women have something important in common: They've both been the workhorses, often unappreciated, in cultures where life is hard for everyone. It's natural that foreign women seem nicer and softer to Russian men. They haven't been standing in line all day to buy a few potatoes and a scraggly chicken (or, all to often, to reach the front of a line and find there's no scraggly chicken left). At the end of the work day in New York, I have much more energy left to be nice to a man than I did in Moscow. If I have a headache, in New York, I take an aspirin. If I find a run in my pantyhose, I run into a store and come out with a new pair in five minutes. If I'm hungry, I stop in at a restaurant and eat a sandwich. All of these commonplace acts—basic errands for an American consumer—are utterly impossible in Moscow. Of course Russian women are tired at the end of the day; they bear the burden of making a home in a society where the simplest domestic tasks are a constant drain on their energy.

Black American women bear a different burden: They're expected to provide the emotional strength to enable their families to survive in a racist culture, but sometimes their men criticize them for being too strong. Several young black men, all of them successful professionals, have explained to me that they're under intense pressure in their white work environments. "When I come home at the end of the day, I don't want to face arguments at home too. I want to be supported," one man told me: a very natural wish. But black women face the same pressures in the outside world. They want to be supported too. Speaking as a black Russian, I don't think black American women get enough appreciation from men of their own race. It makes me giggle to think that these men somehow think of me as exotic, different from all of those "pushy" black women they grew up with. Is there no end to stereotyping?

I'm the last person in the world to say that we should "stick to our own kind"; I would like to live in a society in which people feel free to love and marry whomever they choose. But I want those choices, including my own, to be based on individual qualities, not on racial or ethnic caricatures dictated by ignorance. At thirty, I naturally think about the whole question of love and marriage more seriously than I did when I was younger.

One difference between America and Russia—a pleasurable difference—is that no one considers a woman of my age an old maid. In Russia, most women regard marriage as a lost cause if they haven't found a man by their early twenties. By the time I was twenty-five, some people began calling me an egoist—it's the same word in Russian and English—because I hadn't married and produced at least one child. In America, both black and white America, an unmarried woman of thirty is a perfectly normal phenomenon. Russians say mournfully, "You've already missed the boat, Yelena." American say—perhaps this is just congenital American optimism—"You're sure to find just the right person." But people don't act as though not having a husband is a failure or a personal tragedy for a woman.

I would like to have children, though, and I want to raise them with a father. My own mother was the best single parent a child could have, but I know how hard it was for her to manage even with my grandmother's help.

Will this theoretical husband be black or white? It wasn't even a question when I assumed I would spend my whole life in Russia, with no possibility of moving back and forth. He would be white, like nearly everyone around me.

In America, for the first time in my life, I've had the chance to date men of both races. My friends—Russian and American, black and white—are always asking me what I see as the most significant differences between black and white men. The subject of interracial romance also comes up on talk shows, which fascinated me when I first came to America. (I don't think Russians would ever agree to discuss intimate aspects of their lives before an audience of millions.) On these shows, I've heard people make generalizations about white men being more considerate and black men being sexier. I always want to ask these talk show guests, "But how many black men have you dated? How many white men have you dated? How can you speak with such authority?"

A truly subversive thought occurred to me after some of my first social adventures in America: White or black, Russian or American, men use the same words when they want to say no to a woman. "I'm under a lot of pressure at work right now." "We're having some trouble communicating." "We're moving too fast." An American friend introduced me to a delightful term for these ways men have of saying "I've met someone else"—"Manspeak." Isn't this an international, interracial language?

One thing is certain: In America, it's more comfortable socially to date a man of my own race. If I'm dating a black man, I know everyone will approve of us as a couple. If I'm with a white man, everyone will have an opinion. It may only be our first date, but people will take it upon themselves to ask, "And what about the children?"

This question also arose in my relationships with Russian men, but I never felt personally threatened in the way I sometimes do here. I know one interracial couple, together for many years, who can't walk down the street since the release of the Spike Lee movie without hearing bypassers scream "jungle fever" at them.

I often make a point of telling people that my grandfather had a black wife who died before he met and married my grandmother. I don't want anyone to think he was the kind of black man who had a "neurotic" (unlike Russians, Americans love to paste psychological labels on every human experience) need to possess a white woman. The truth, as my late cousin Mamie put it, was that Oliver Golden was a man who loved women and was loved by them, without regard to race, creed, or color. "There can be no real love between black and white in this country," a black acquaintance says. Is it any wonder I feel defensive?

On a downtown Washington street, I was exposed for the first time to the hatred some blacks direct toward interracial couples. I was walking side-by-side with a white man, a newspaper colleague I was dating. There wasn't any reason for anyone to see us as a couple though. As far as the black shoppers around us knew, we were just two people, walking and talking. We were headed for a special store, offering a particularly good selection of black hair-care products, where I planned to stock up on magic potions to continue my never-ending experiments on my crowning glory. White Washingtonians don't do much shopping downtown, so nearly everyone else on the street was black. Still, I hadn't given a moment's thought to the race of my companion; it simply didn't occur to me that anyone would take offense at the sight of two people—one black, one white—walking along the street at one o'clock in the afternoon in the shopping district of the capital of the United States.

Suddenly I heard a hiss behind me. "Bitch," a black man called out, using a string of epithets I never heard, in public or private, in my life in Moscow. The insults were both racial and sexual, leaving no doubt about what the man thought of any black woman who walked down the street with a white man.*

On the street in Washington, the man backed up his words with action. He started to shove me. My companion turned around, put his hands out in a placating gesture and said, "Please, leave the lady alone. We don't want any trouble." But the man, literally foaming at the mouth, reached out and scratched my face. At that point my friend said, "Run, get into the store, don't look back."

As I ran and slammed the door shut behind me, I saw the man was getting ready to beat up my friend. The most shocking aspect of the whole situation to me was that no one, seeing this unprovoked assault, offered to help either of us. As they continued to struggle outside the plate glass window, one of the black saleswomen said, "We

---

*I should explain to the American reader that the casual use of obscenities is another major difference between Russian and American culture. My street assailant was no cultivated gentleman, but well-educated Americans also use obscenities with much greater frequency than similarly educated Russians. When I first arrived in the United States, I was personally insulted when Americans would say "fuck" in ordinary conversation. Now, I know it's nothing personal, but I can't, and don't want to, talk or write this way myself. In Russia, the constant use of obscenity marks a person as *nekulturnyy* (uncultured). It's not that we don't tell dirty jokes; there's a whole category of humor, which translates roughly as "your mother," involving sex or the combination of sex and politics. These jokes lose so much in translation that they're not worth repeating. When I try to tell dirty jokes to Americans in English, they invariably fall flat. Russians roar with laughter at the same *anekdoty*. Political jokes, interestingly, seem to travel more easily than sexual jokes from one culture, and language, to another. And of course we all use obscene words, on occasion, for emphasis. But we use these words only when they're intended to convey genuine anger and disgust, not just because we have a headache or the building superintendent hasn't shown up to fix a dripping faucet.

really ought to call the police." The other told her, "Mind your own business. She shouldn't have been walking with that white guy anyway." Finally, we did manage to sprint away and escape the thug in the street.

I was truly shaken by this experience. I mentioned the incident to several friends, black and white. One black woman said, "But you've got to understand where the man on the street was coming from. You're in America now, and blacks don't like it when they see a black woman with a white man. It's a betrayal, because of what happened to black women during slavery. Black women were raped by whites, and their men couldn't do anything to protect them."

This kind of rationalization just doesn't sit well with me. I know perfectly well what happened to black women, before and after slavery. Around the turn of the century, one of my grandfather's sisters was raped by a white man in Mississippi. But how can the cruelties of the past be used as an excuse for assaults on human dignity in the present? After the Bolshevik Revolution, millions of people were imprisoned or sent to die of hunger in Siberian exile because their ancestors were the wrong class of people—nobles, bourgeois merchants, or small farmers, kulaks. (Stalin would have considered my great-grandfather a kulak.) How can I accept the logic of someone who tells me I shouldn't walk down the street with a white man in 1990 because my great-aunt was raped by a white man nearly a century ago?

A final irony: The next day, the same man and I were insulted by whites in the pastoral town of Stockbridge, Massachusetts. We were so upset by the incident in Washington that we decided to get away from it all and drive north to New England to see the fall foliage. With its dignified white clapboard houses, antique shops, and eighteenth-century churches, Stockbridge looks like a picture postcard, my romantic image of old-fashioned, small-town America. My companion and I, this time hand-in-hand, were walking toward an antiques fair when a carful of white tourists, checking out of the charming Red Lion Inn, drove by. "Can you believe *that?*" one man said in a contemptuous tone. "Fifty years ago, you'd never have seen anything like that in a town like this."

It doesn't make me feel better to know that such things happen on both sides of the color line. After the Washington incident, an older black friend, someone I respect very much, told me I was, in a sense, responsible for the attack because I hadn't thought out the implications of walking through a black neighborhood with a white man. He wasn't blaming the victim of making a negative judgment about interracial dating; he was simply telling me I needed to be cautious to protect myself. In Moscow, I could always go wherever I wanted, with whomever I wanted, without considering the possibility of racial violence. (I should acknowledge that this isn't true everywhere in what was the Soviet Union. In smaller cities, especially in Azerbaijan and the Ukraine, there was a good deal of violence directed toward African students who dated Russian women.) Regardless of where I am in America, I always have to give some thought to the responses of others—strangers or friends—if I am paired with someone whose skin is another color. But caution can't keep you safe from racism; it's impossible to anticipate the unexpected. Several of my friends were astonished to hear about both the Washington and Stockbridge incidents; they said they wouldn't have expected trouble in either place.

Interracial couples, though their numbers are increasing, are almost invisible in American society. I was surprised when I read that the percentage of interracial married couples has more than doubled during the past twenty years, in spite of the disapproval these unions engender in so many quarters. According to the U.S. Census Bureau, there were approximately 211,000 interracial married couples in 1990, or four out of every 1,000 marriages in comparison with 1.5 out of every 1,000 couples in 1970. These hundreds of thousands of people are generally viewed through a "jungle fever" prism. I've noticed that television commercials, a barometer of lowest-common-denominator acceptability, portray black couples and white couples but never a mixed-race family. I assume this means advertisers think black and white customers would be turned off by the idea that toothpaste, headache remedies, and laxatives might be used by people of different races within the walls of the same home.

Still, the increase in interracial couples—and recent opinion polls—show that disapproval of mixed marriages is far less prevalent than it used to be. Blacks, according to these polls, are more tolerant of mixed couples than whites. This finding runs counter to my personal experience, but it does show that the negative attitudes I've encountered are far from universal among blacks or whites. (Of course, it's always possible that people are lying to the pollsters about their level of tolerance.)

Still, while interracial romance is hardly the most important issue facing Americans today, I do think attitudes toward interracial sex play a fundamental role in both the mythology and reality of America's racial division. People of different races don't have to love each other or sleep with each other in order to respect each other, but perhaps they do have to find the capacity within themselves to acknowledge the possibility of a love that can transcend bigotry.

And there's a positive side to America's race-consciousness. Americans are more honest than Russians about prejudice at least with people of their own color and ethnicity. In the pre-*glasnost* Soviet Union, the fact that some nationalities were more equal than others was papered over by official rhetoric about harmony and brotherhood among all peoples. The explosion of ethnic hatred since the Soviet empire began to break up shows how thin the amicable layer was; the collection of angry minorities was held together not by genuine understanding but by fear of the army and the secret police.

Intelligent, well-educated people always knew this Soviet brotherhood was a fiction, but the public silence kept many of us from examining our personal convictions too closely. If you had asked me, when I first arrived in the United States, whether I held any prejudices toward anyone in my own society, I would have answered with a fierce, unequivocal "no." Didn't I hate it, and speak up, when anyone in Moscow denigrated "our" minorities, whether they were Jews, Armenians, Georgians, or Asians? In Moscow, when Russians refer to *cherniye* (the blacks), they aren't normally talking about black Russians, Africans, or Americans. *Chyornyy* is a generic term for anyone with a darker complexion than the standard Slavic shade. *"Vsyo cherniye"* ("they're all blacks"), a Russian will say, referring to all darker-skinned people from Asia or the Caucasus. I, Yelena, would never talk that way.

Then a black American friend asked me a hard question. He wanted to know, as almost every American does, who I dated in Russia, when there were so few blacks available. "I understand there weren't very many Russian blacks," he said, "but tell me who you did see. You talk about Russian boyfriends. Did you ever go out with anyone else—Asians, for instance?"

I had never asked myself this question before, and the answer is no. I never dated anyone but Russians. I had many Jewish friends, but I never went out with them. At the university I knew Georgians, Armenians, students from the central Asian republics, but I never went out with them either. I told my American friend, "But it's not just a matter of who you go out with: It's who wants to go out with you." But that sounded like a lame excuse, even to me. I began to realize that I—exactly like a great many black and white Americans—had made all sorts of unconscious decisions about who was and wasn't suitable for me as a serious partner. If I'd started going out with an Uzbek from Tashkent, for instance, my girlfriends in Moscow would certainly have made fun of him and of me. This wasn't just a matter of ethnic superiority. In Russia, people from Moscow and St. Petersburg look down on everyone else. There's no real equivalent of this city chauvinism in the United States; it's impossible to imagine a native New Yorker ruling out a San Franciscan as a potential mate. But that doesn't explain why I never dated, say, an ethnic Armenian who grew up in Moscow. No, I obviously possessed certain emotions and insecurities that I would never have held up to the light, so long as I stayed within my native culture.

My mother used to harp on the fact that all of my serious boyfriends were Russian. In my early twenties, I dismissed her observations as the intrusion of a busybody Russian mama. Now, after spending time in America and seeing the ways in which Americans automatically rule out whole groups of people as mates, I'm being forced to reexamine my own behavior. I don't think my preference for Russians was rooted in any attraction to the forbidden, but I do think I felt more secure in the company of men whose Slavic good looks resembled the classical heroes of Russian novels, the insiders of my culture. As an outsider, being paired with a Russian insider made me feel more like an insider myself. My friends, sometimes even strangers on the street, used to tell me what gorgeous children Misha and I, or Yura and I, would have. Looking back, I know I wouldn't have received these compliments, or heard predictions about beautiful children, if I'd chosen another outsider as a partner. When Yura phoned me for the first time at *Moscow News,* my supervisor picked up the phone. After I hung up, she inquired, "So, you have a new friend?" Then, for no apparent reason, she asked, "And is he Jewish?" When I said no, he was Russian, she nodded approvingly and said, "That's great." I had completely forgotten, or suppressed, this incident until my American friend asked me to think about the ethnic composition of my male friends in Moscow. Why on earth did my supervisor ask me whether a strange man on the phone was a Jew? Perhaps the thought flashed through her mind that I, a black, could only attract a member of another minority?

Maybe I, in some deep, unexamined crevice of my soul, felt better about myself for being able to attract the love of a *chisty russkiy.* (This translates literally as "pure Russian" but doesn't mean "pure-blooded." A better translation might be "classic Russian type." "WASP" is probably the closest American equivalent.) In her memoirs, Svetlana Alliluyeva described my mother as a strange hybrid. By pairing off with a member of the Russian majority instead of with a man from another minority, I made myself feel like less of a hybrid. My black American friend was right: My choice of Russians as partners was not a matter of pure romantic accident. I too was driven by insecurities.

The debate over affirmative action in the United States has made me look at my privileged life as a black Russian in a different, more critical light. I detest the mentality of certain successful black Americans who say to those at the bottom, "I made it on my own, so you should make it without any help too." I now recall, with a good deal of shame, having had something of the same reaction toward a young woman, the daughter of a Russian mother and African father, who came to me for help at *Moscow News.* Her mother called, after I had appeared on Soviet television, to talk to me about the serious problems her daughter encountered at her university after she married a white Russian. "You're successful," the mother said. "You've figured out how to live as a black person in this society. Maybe you can give her some help and advice that I can't." The next day, the daughter turned up at my office. She told me about the hostility of her professors and other students—toward her and her husband—and about her difficulties in finding a job. She blamed her situation on Russian racism. On one hand I was sympathetic, but on the other I was contemptuous of her for bringing her problems to me, a stranger, for talking to me just because I *happened* to be black. I thought, "If I had problems like this, I'd solve them myself. I wouldn't bring them to anyone else complaining about racism." I wanted to think I had accomplished everything on my own; I didn't want to acknowledge the advantages I enjoyed not only because I had a very strong mother but because I was the granddaughter of Americans—not the child of a frowned-on union between a white Russian and an African. This woman, less fortunate than I in her parents' educational and social background, was a challenge to my no-excuses ethic. Years later, having met a few black Americans with the same attitude, I feel a belated sense of shame. No one makes it entirely on his or her own. No one in a bigoted society—whatever form the bigotry takes—is safe.

When you inhabit more than one culture, you start thinking about behavior you've always taken for granted. You give up your cozy, self-congratulatory image of yourself. Uncomfortable as these feelings are, I'm grateful to America for forcing me to examine myself more rigorously.

CHAPTER FIFTEEN

BELONGING

November 28, 1991—Crystal sparkles, candles gleam, and a huge turkey is ready for carving in the dining room of my cousin Al's home in Sagaponack, New York. On this Thanksgiving Day, everyone at the table is talking at once. For the first time, Mama and I have taken our places at the table of our gregarious Bialek family. We are celebrating the holiday with newly discovered relatives from Chicago, Washington, and New York City.

Irv Bialek (he and Al are Marcus's sons) raises his glass in a toast: "To Lily and Yelena, who've added beauty, spice, and new color to our family." Irv, his friend Melody Wechsler, and her son David, have flown in from Chicago for the occasion. Al and his wife, Sheila Hoffman, are putting everyone up in their weekend home on the east end of Long Island, just a five-minute walk from the ocean. Irv's son, Mark, has driven up from Washington, D.C., with his wife, Cindy, and their baby daughter, Cara Michelle. I'm meeting Mark for the first time, but I know he's already spent hours of his own time tracing family immigration documents. Only a few years ago, I would have been appalled to find out that I had a cousin who worked for the U.S. State Department. My instant reaction would have been, "They [the Soviet authorities] will never let me travel now. They'll think I'm a security risk." Whenever I filled out an official form asking about my family background, I always replied that I had "no relatives abroad." That was the safe and, as far as I knew then, true answer. "A cousin in the American State Department!" my mother laughingly exclaimed when she first heard about Mark. "Who would believe it outside of a bad movie, the Russian daughter of an American Communist with such a relative?"

When Al Bialek tracked me down last fall, I didn't know what to make of him, any more than I knew how to feel when I met Jack's son, Eugene, in Los Angeles. Intellectually, I knew these were my relatives—as closely related to me by blood as my black American cousins—but I didn't feel any genuine emotional connection.

Do I belong at this family table, or am I just a guest. Do I even want to be more than a guest? My mother fits right in. (Since Mama has been staying in Chicago for some months, she and Irv are already well acquainted. He's also met some of our black Chicago cousins.) At this Thanksgiving dinner, Mama and Al are meeting for the first time.

"You deserve to be the *tamada* [toastmaster]," she tells Al, congratulating him on his performance as the family chef. "You've made this beautiful turkey, you've been busy in the kitchen all day, and now you should be the one to determine the order of speakers. Besides, in this family if someone doesn't keep order, everyone will interrupt everyone." Everyone interrupting everyone: Yes, that's a perfect image of my newly found relatives.

Mama, her voice breaking, makes a long speech about my grandmother. "If only . . . if only she was here at this table tonight. If only she could see that hatred and prejudice do not have to be passed from the one generation down to the next. If only she could see that people's ideas can change. If only she could know that today, she would not be cast out from her family, that people can grow better. . . ." Mama's accent is Russian, but the cadence of her speech reminds me of preachers in black churches. By the time she finishes, there isn't a dry eye at the table. The women cry openly; the men clear their throats as their eyes mist over. Al lifts his own glass: "What can I say after that? We love you. Finding you is one of the biggest thrills of my life, and I've learned more about my family's past in the last few months than I ever knew before. We can't change what happened in the past, in our grandparents' and parents' generation, but we can have a different future."

In her open emotionality, Mama strongly resembles her cousins. I'm much more like my grandmother, who rarely argued or displayed her feelings. Mama, Al, and Irv fight, yell, and make up. As Thanksgiving dinner drew to a close, they fell into a freewheeling, fierce-sounding argument about America. I didn't catch all the details, but Al, who grew up poor in the Bronx—his father owned a candy store—was waxing eloquent on the subject of economic opportunity under American capitalism. Mama countered with an attack on the expense and class inequities of the American healthcare system. Their voices rose. I was mortified. Here Mama is, eating Al's turkey—prepared with his very own hands—and she manages to get into a fight on Thanksgiving! My cousin Mark, the diplomat of the family, advised me to pay no attention to the political quarrels of our elders. A veteran of many such dinners, he whispered, "We'll just leave the table to them. You'll see, they'll stop as soon as they don't have us as an audience."

Mark knew what he was doing. Within a few minutes, Al and Mama quieted down and started laughing, once again the best of friends. How could this be? I don't have much experience with the kind of people who argue furiously one minute and throw their arms around each other the next.

In spite of my reserve—and the whole process is happening more slowly than it did with my black relatives—I'm beginning to feel that the Bialeks really are family. Irv has invited us to spend next Thanksgiving in Chicago, where all of the Bialek and Golden cousins can meet. What an event that should be! Hilliard Golden's and Isaac Bialek's great-grandchildren in the same room! Will they fight? Will someone, black or white, take offense at something said by a family member of the opposite race?

Wait a minute, Yelena. Maybe they'll have a great time. Why

shouldn't they like one another, anyway? "Oh, forget it," one friend advises. "At least you won't be bored to death at family dinners. And they'll all eat turkey."

Last winter, I rented a pair of skates and skimmed across the Rockefeller Center rink in the heart of Manhattan. At Christmas time, with the glorious tree rising behind the statue of Prometheus, the setting was magic. I gazed upward with as much rapture as the small children crowding the promenade above the rink. Long ago in Moscow, I'd seen pictures of this site, which symbolized American capitalism to me. Rockefeller Center is so famous that news of its 1989 sale to a Japanese firm made the front pages of Russian newspapers.

Suddenly, my mind flashed back to a winter afternoon nearly twenty-five years ago in Moscow's Gorky Park. Mama took me by the hand, found me a teacher, and insisted on skating lessons as soon as my ankles were sturdy enough not to flop over on the ice. This was one more step in her long-term plan to give me everything she never had. In warm Tashkent, with temperatures that almost never dropped below freezing in winter, Mama naturally grew up without learning how to skate. As a university student, she stood on the sidelines while her friends organized skating parties on park ponds and the frozen Moskva River. Mama felt like an outsider on these occasions, which looked like scenes out of nineteenth-century Russian novels. For some reason, Mama didn't think she could learn to skate at the advanced age of twenty.

But I learned, well enough, at least, to skate backwards and forwards and try an occasional spin without falling down. I can still see my small self, a twirling black speck in a sea of Russian winter white, on the ice in the center of the park. There I was surrounded not by skyscrapers and a brightly lit Christmas tree but by silence, by unadorned firs and *beryozy* (birch trees) symbolizing everything pure in the Russian landscape. Once I belonged there, only there.

When I started to trace my family's history in the United States, I thought of myself as the investigator in a detective story. I would fill in the missing pieces of my family's past, put the whole story down on paper in honor of my ancestors, and return home—home to Moscow—to pick up my Russian life as it had always been.

But I didn't know how my sense of myself, my possibilities and responsibilities, would be changed by this journey into the past. I grew up a Soviet citizen, which makes me a citizen of the new, independent Russia. But citizenship is a label, a number on a passport, not something out of which a person can construct a meaningful identity.

A large part of me is, and always will be, Russian.

I never realized that more clearly than I did during last year's coup attempt, when I sat helplessly in front of my television set in New York while the fate of Russia's fragile democracy hung in the balance. How exultant, how proud I felt when I saw people my own age—my friends, my schoolmates—taking to the streets to prevent evil men from turning the clock back in our country.

Our country, my country, Russia.

Yet America is becoming a second home, dear to me in spite of her failure to live up to her own highest ideals. For me, the best part of America is not her material well-being, though that never fails to impress me in spite of the current recession and chronic, severe inequities in the distribution of this society's abundance. (Marx wasn't wrong about everything.) What really moves me, though, is the determination of so many Americans to obtain recognition and dignity on their own terms, not those of the majority. On my first trip to this country, for instance, I was astonished to see demonstrations by AIDS sufferers and the disabled. In Russia, such people hide themselves from the indifferent or hostile majority. But in a humane and truly democratic political culture, no one is ashamed to stand up and say, "I'm a human being. I count too. See me as I am."

In spite of—no, because of—my new sense of identification with America, the country's racial divisions now have the power to wound me in ways that were impossible when I felt myself to be entirely Russian. In May, after a California jury acquitted white police officers in the beating of Rodney King, I experienced a profound sense of shock, disappointment, and anger—and thought of how my grandfather was beaten, more than sixty years ago, by a New York policeman. I sat glued to the television news, just as I had been mesmerized by broadcasts from Moscow during the Russian coup attempt. The violence and hatred in the streets of Los Angeles dealt a second shock to my system. America, I reflected, has no reason to look smugly upon the struggles of democracy in the new Russia.

Yet there was another side to those days of rage. I was living in Cambridge, Massachusetts, having received a fellowship from the Institute of Politics at Harvard University's John F. Kennedy School of Government. The day after the verdict, large numbers of blacks and whites—many of them young people—marched through the streets of Boston in a peaceful demonstration to protest the acquittal. This protest moved me as deeply as the demonstrations that defeated the right-wing coup in Moscow. I believe in the nonviolent struggle against all forms of racism and injustice. The black, American, and Russian parts of my soul are equally at home in this battle—wherever it takes place.

After a year's absence, I returned to Moscow for the first time last fall as an interpreter and all-purpose troubleshooter for Albert Binger, head of global environment projects for the Rockefeller Foundation, for a series of meetings with top Russian scientists.

We stayed at the Marco Polo Hotel, a hard-currency establishment where nearly all of the guests are foreign tourists or businessmen. In a small way, this hotel, which used to be reserved for Party members, embodies the obstacles to genuine transformation of the old Soviet economic system. I often passed the building on my reportorial rounds—it's located near the main Moscow office of TASS—but never knew its function because the premises were discreetly un-marked.

Now the Marco Polo is supposed to be a real business, but it has the same old staff. And no one cares about providing the kind of service expected by tourists everywhere else in the world. Mr. Binger's busy schedule—and the shortage of food everywhere in Moscow—made it tough for us to eat during the day. One night, I checked to ensure that the staff would serve us dinner if we returned from the theater before nine-thirty. We turned up, tired and hungry, at nine-fifteen. And indifferent maitre d' (that's what he called himself) acted as if he'd never seen me. "There aren't any tables," he barked, although only two tables in the large room were occupied. At the end of my patience, I broke into a stream of invective in Russian. "Now look," I told him. "The Rockefeller Foundation—you've heard the name of Rockefeller?—is paying good money so that this man can meet with representatives of the Academy of Sciences. Do you think it's going to look good for you if he goes back and says that he couldn't even have a crust of bread because you're too lazy to get it."

Finally, grudgingly, the man showed us to a table. He simply didn't care whether we ate or not. He knew we'd already paid in advance for our rooms: Why should he knock himself out? This attitude— why do a job well when you get paid just as much to do it badly?—is the product of a system under which nothing could be gained by working hard. It will take more than changing a name from the "Soviet Union" to the "Commonwealth of Independent States" to transform this way of doing business—or of not doing business.

Meanwhile, ordinary Muscovites suffer. My friends spend most of their time scrounging for food. Living in New York for only a year, I'd almost forgotten what it was like to wake up and know you must waste three or four hours of your day wandering from one empty store to another. And living conditions had worsened dramatically since I left Moscow a year earlier, in the fall of 1990.

I went to dinner at the home of my old friend, Katya Chertanova, a professor of English at Moscow State University. She and her husband Sergei, a physicist, have two children. I launched a political discussion. Was Yeltsin really competent to govern? How would the newly independent republics treat ethnic minorities? What were the chances of yet another coup? Katya interrupted me. "You know, I have great news. I managed to buy a dozen eggs today." I didn't pay much attention to her comment and went on blabbing about Gorbachev, Yeltsin, Gavril Popov (the mayor of Moscow), and Anatoly Sobchak (the mayor of St. Petersburg). Again, Katya changed the subject and turned to her husband. "Did I remember to tell you that I found a dozen eggs earlier today?" Irritated, I said, "Excuse me, that's the second time you've mentioned eggs." Katya quietly answered, "I'm sorry, Yelena, but finding eggs is very important to me. My children like eggs; their bodies need protein. They haven't had an egg for three weeks."

My cheeks grew hot. How ashamed I was, that a year in America made me lose sight of how hard life was for my old friends. It always annoys me when Americans talk about the tough transition to a new Russia in purely abstract, political terms. But I made the same mistake: I forgot about individuals while contemplating the big picture.

The flip side of living in more than one world is you sometimes feel like an outsider in both. Is it possible to move among different worlds and do justice to all of them?

Question: Am I a black who happens to have been born in Russia, or a Russian who happens to have been born black?

Answer: Neither. Both.

Not long ago, I took a cab to Kennedy Airport to meet an acquaintance, a Russian political commentator I'd always liked and respected. In Moscow, we'd been on the same side of political issues. Like me, he'd opposed *Pamyat,* a right-wing organization dedicated to the notion of "pure" Slavic culture, free of corrupting minority influences.

On the way back from the airport, the first question my friend asked was, "Is it true that crime is even worse here in New York than in Moscow?" I said yes, it was true, and mentioned a good friend who was raped last year.

His immediate response: "Was it a nigger who did it?" He used the Russian word *chernomaz*—a combination of the words for "black" and "mace." It didn't occur to him that I, his fellow Russian, might be insulted by a racial epithet applied to a black American. I asked why the rapist's race was the first subject that came to mind. He told me Russian newspapers had published many convincing articles on black crime in the United States. "So that's all," I replied. "When you think about blacks in America, you just think about crime and drugs." Sadly, most Russians still don't know anything about the kind of black American family founded by my great-grandfather.

All of us—black and white, Russian and American—know little about the places where we feel like outsiders. I long to speak the language of belonging and connection. I think of my week in Yazoo's once-segregated library, where my grandfather never could have read a book, or even set foot, when the institution opened in 1902. But in 1990, a black and a white librarian, working together, gave days of their time so I could finally learn the truth about my family's past.

We need a language through which we can respect differences while embracing common humanity, a language to speak *dusha v dushu,* soul to soul. That was my grandparents' real dream, and I have shared it since the day I first heard Martin Luther King's voice on a scratchy tape in a Moscow elementary school—a black, Russian, American, human dream.

—New York, 1991

Epilogue

At the end of this long journey into my family's past, one more surprise awaited me: I discovered that my mother is, and always has been, an American citizen. This extraordinary fact was confirmed on February 3, 1992, when Mama received her American passport—No. 024152187—from Nyle Churchwell, adjudication chief of the Chicago-based regional passport agency of the U.S. State Department.

Two of our proud Chicago cousins, Delores Harris and Irv Bialek, accompanied Mama to the passport office for a small ceremony with Gretchen Schuster, regional director of the agency. My mother took special joy, as I know my grandmother would have, in the fact that both the Golden and Bialek sides of the family were represented on the day she reclaimed her American heritage. Passport agency officials had done everything possible to help Mama verify her claim to American citizenship. That in itself demonstrates the vast changes in relations between America and Russia during the past seven years. In Moscow, I was raised on horror stories of McCarthy-era U.S. passport officials, who did everything possible to obstruct international travel by progressive Americans like Paul Robeson.

American friends began telling Mama she was a U.S. citizen when she explained that she was born in Tashkent before her parents became Soviet citizens. Under American law, the child of a U.S. citizen, even though born on foreign soil, is automatically a citizen. Parents may renounce their own citizenship but cannot give up the citizenship of a minor child.

Sheila Bialek—the daughter-in-law of my grandmother's favorite brother, Jack—found the family's 1921 naturalization certificate, giving us incontrovertible proof that my grandmother, along with her parents and two of her brothers, had become a naturalized U.S. citizen. We didn't need to establish my grandfather's citizenship; his old Army record book offered ample proof of his status as a native son.

The only remaining piece of he puzzle was evidence that my grandparents were still American citizens at the time of my mother's birth. The American Freedom of Information Act—a wonderful law of the kind Russia badly needs to protect the rights of her citizens—enabled me to find that proof. In the process, I learned something more about the difficulty of my grandmother's life as a former American in Stalin's fear-ridden Soviet Union.

(I wasn't sure whether the Freedom of Information Act would permit me, a citizen of another country, to receive documents concerning my grandparents. It does.)

On November 29, 1947, my grandmother signed an affidavit, certifying that she became a Soviet citizen in 1936. She sent this affidavit from her home in Tashkent to the American Embassy in Moscow and formally requested that the embassy acknowledge her renunciation of U.S. citizenship.

On August 5, 1948, the American Embassy in Moscow forwarded a formal report of expatriation to the State Department in Washington. The report, released to me on January 31, 1992, reads in part:

> According to her statement, Bertha Bialek, a naturalized citizen of the United States, married Oliver John Golden, a native born citizen of the United States, in 1928 and came with him to the Soviet Union in 1931, where he and fifteen other negro [sic] cotton specialists were invited through Amtorg to work in the Soviet Union. Settling in Uzbekistan, he remained under contract until 1935 when

he became seriously ill with a kidney disease. Deciding to remain in the Soviet Union, he became naturalized as a Soviet citizen upon his own application and persuaded his wife to do the same. It seems probable that the date of his naturalization was the same as his wife; i.e., Aug. 3, 1936.

In one of her letters, Mrs. Golden mentions the fact that a daughter was born to her and her husband in 1934. The embassy is endeavoring to ascertain the whereabouts of this daughter and will invite her to apply for registration so that her claim to American citizenship may be a matter of record.

This document clearly shows that while the embassy acknowledged my grandparents' renunciation of U.S. citizenship, my mother fell into an entirely different category. American diplomats never had any contact with my mother, but that was hardly surprising in view of the deepening Cold War as well as the repressive climate within the Soviet Union. Furthermore, my grandmother never told Mama about her contact with the embassy concerning expatriation.

Why did my grandmother make a point of formally requesting the U.S. government to acknowledge her expatriation, when she had already been a Soviet citizen for eleven years? The period of these communications—late 1947 and 1948—reveals everything about her motivation. Stalin's intense, relentless campaign against "rootless cosmopolitans" was in full swing at the time. In 1948, my grandmother was forced out of her university job in Tashkent. Afraid for herself and for my mother, she must have felt the need to take extra steps to demonstrate the severing of any connections with America.

"There's absolutely no question in my mind that her only motivation was to protect herself and me," Mama says. "She didn't want anyone to be able to claim that she hadn't done everything possible to put distance between her and her American past. As for why she never told me about this, I'm sure she thought it would just scare me. She was protecting me, trying to shield me from painful realities she bore alone."

What irony! My grandmother's effort to show her loyalty to the

Soviet state, to sever our American connection, provided an essential piece of proof that Mama has always been an American citizen.

To receive her passport, my mother did not have to renounce her status as a citizen of the new Russia. Mama feels entirely at ease as a woman with two countries. "There are emigrés here who don't have a good word to say about Russia," she says, "but I don't understand them. You can hate the terrible politics of the past, but that doesn't make me hate Russia herself. My language, my culture, a huge part of my thoughts are Russian. But I feel at ease in America, too—this is my heritage from my parents. It's a good thing to be at home in both places."

I am a Russian citizen but, like my mother, I also expect to belong in both worlds for the rest of my life.

Index